Tom Zass 75

THE
AMERICAN
CHARACTER

D. W. Brogan

THE
AMERICAN
CHARACTER

TIME *Reading Program* RTP *Special Edition*

TIME INCORPORATED/NEW YORK

TIME INC. BOOK DIVISION

EDITOR *Norman P. Ross*
COPY DIRECTOR *William Jay Gold*
ART DIRECTOR *Edward A. Hamilton*
CHIEF OF RESEARCH *Beatrice T. Dobie*
EDITOR, TIME READING PROGRAM *Max Gissen*
DESIGNER *Nina Rittenberg*
RESEARCHER *Olga Skow*

PUBLISHER *Jerome S. Hardy*
GENERAL MANAGER *John A. Watters*

TIME MAGAZINE

EDITOR *Roy Alexander*
MANAGING EDITOR *Otto Fuerbringer*
PUBLISHER *Bernhard M. Auer*

EDITORS' PREFACE

UP TO ONLY a quarter century ago, it would never have occurred to most U.S. citizens that the good or bad opinion of the rest of the world was anything to dwell on, much less worry about. By whatever standards, this was the land of the free and the home of the brave. Only a fool would claim that everything was dandy, but only a misanthrope could deny that any people in history had been given so clear a chance to determine their earthly fate or that any nation had done so much with its opportunity. The U.S. was bursting at the seams and supremely confident.

Now, when we are midway into the 20th Century, something seems to be gnawing away at that confidence. Never have Americans looked at themselves so hard, never have they been so bewildered by foreign sniping. In a day when millions of U.S. tourists have seen the sickening scrawl, "Yankee Go Home," an examination of what we are and how others see us is not only inevitable but salutary. By all odds the most interesting and meaningful starting point is *The American Character,* by D. W. Brogan.

Denis Brogan is a fine antidote to the malicious foreign criticism Americans have come to accept as routine. Perhaps no foreigner in this century has understood the U.S. as well as he. A ruddy, stocky Irishman born in Glasgow in 1900, Brogan has spent a total of at least seven years in the U.S. spread out over more than 35 visits. The son of a tailor, he was educated at the universities of Glasgow, Oxford and Harvard. His first interest in the U.S. came from reading U.S. magazines his father used to subscribe to. (The elder Brogan once lived in California for two years.)

As Professor of Political Science at Cambridge University, he brings to his interpretation of the U.S. and its history an unchallenged academic reputation. Professors who have done the necessary spadework in library stacks are as plentiful as their operative clichés. What distinguishes Mr. Brogan from his fellows is an insatiable curiosity about the U.S., the energy to move throughout its wide open spaces (he has visited more than 40 states), the eye to discern its variety, the ear to record its regional idiosyncrasies. This is certainly more than any other academic foreign critic of this country brings to his job. Mr. Brogan also has a genuine liking for and a creative understanding of Americans and their country that would seem almost to disqualify him as a critic were it not for the bite and snap that he summons when some stupidity or folly raises his Irish.

Mr. Brogan's pro-Americanism does not go unchallenged in Britain, where he is regarded with a cold eye by "Left-Wing students who see America as a threat to world freedom and by old-fashioned English patriots who resent America's rise during the dissolution of the Empire." As Mr. Brogan admits, "I am regarded by some as an American stooge." Whatever some of his countrymen think of him, Mr. Brogan is a thoroughgoing Briton who admires the U.S. but wouldn't think of living here even though he feels "England can learn a lot from America."

Mr. Brogan repeatedly reminds his reader of the importantly obvious, of the central truths of U.S. history that are so easy to forget because the country has come so far so fast: "America had to be made before it could be lived in, and that making took centuries, took extraordinary energies and bred an attitude to life that is peculiarly American. It bred the temper of the pioneer, the temper of the gambler, the temper of the booster, the temper of the discounter of the future who is to some extent bound to be a disparager of the past. It took optimism to cross the Atlantic, optimism or despair and anger at the old world from which the reluctant pioneer had come."

As Henry Steele Commager, the distinguished American historian and writer, notes in the introduction he has provided for this special edition, Brogan's book was written not for Americans but for British readers. His announced intention was "to make more intelligible to the British public certain American principles and attitudes." The book was a critical success in Britain. Even more impressive was the book's reception in the U.S. With rare exceptions its reviewers saw in it the keenest, best informed interpretation of the country by any contemporary observer. One critic wrote that it was "as brilliant a study of the United States as has ever appeared." He proposed that the book be made "requisite reading for every GI when he comes home." Although that never came about, *The American Character* did uncommonly well here. Since its first publication in the U.S. it has had seven reprintings, during the course of which it has been kept up to date by the author.

—THE EDITORS OF TIME

⟨R‖P⟩ *INTRODUCTION*

FOR TWO HUNDRED YEARS America has fascinated Europe. It was a curiosity, a challenge, an object lesson, and an inspiration. It was something Europe had to understand, as a parent has to understand a child; it was something Europe had to come to terms with, as a parent comes to terms with the child who has grown up. Clearly America was an extension of the Old World; just as clearly it was something more. Not only did millions of Europeans flood over to the New World; in some ways more important, New World ideas and practices and expectations washed back onto the Old—ideas and practices about equality, about self government, about education, about change and progress, all working like a ferment in the older societies. Well might Tocqueville say, "In America I saw more than America; I sought the image of democracy itself, with its inclinations, its prejudices, and its passions, in order to learn what we have to fear or to hope from its progress." With most Europeans the fears predominated over the hopes, yet most of them might have said—as Lincoln Steffens said of a very different order—"I have seen the future, and it works."

Of all the thousands of Europeans who have interpreted America, four stand out, conveniently separated by half a century each. The "American Farmer," Crèvecoeur, was the first to ask What is this new man, this American, and to

xi

answer, and no one has ever described more tellingly the processes whereby the European becomes an American. In the eighteen-thirties came Tocqueville, magisterial and profound; he seized on the master idea of equality and applied it with relentless insistence to every aspect of American life and thought. James Bryce, who wrote *The American Commonwealth* in the eighteen-eighties, was perhaps the first of the major interpreters to be interested in the United States for its own sake, the first to base his conclusions on an adequate body of evidence; the chief value of appraising the institutions of the United States, he wrote, "lies in what may be called the laws of political biology, which it reveals, in the new illustrations it supplies of general truths in social and political science."

Professor Brogan, the fourth of the sovereign interpreters, combines the freshness of a Crèvecoeur, the insights of a Tocqueville, and the encyclopaedic knowledge of a Bryce, and adds something all his own—a kind of sophistication, a special liveliness, an irreverence, that bespeaks such intimacy as few other foreigners have ever achieved. Unlike his great predecessors he speaks our language—and likes it; he understands our idiosyncrasies; he enjoys our humor; he even shares some of our prejudices. On the surface—and below too—he knows us better than we know ourselves. He knows Main Street and Zenith City, and Yoknapatawpha County too; he understands the United States Constitution—and the party conventions, and ward politics; he is familiar with the groves of Academe—how many after all he has graced!—and not unfamiliar with her basketball courts and football fields. He is interested in all of these places and activities for themselves and as reflections of the American character, but he never forgets that France has her Main Streets; that party conventions make more sense than black shirts; that the playing fields of American public schools have had a larger influence than the famed playing fields of

Eton. He manages to combine familiarity with affection and intimacy with perspective.

Professor Brogan knows the minutiae of American life, but is not distracted by them; his interest is not really in the particular but in the general. How, he asks, did America manage to create a nation, and to preserve it? Why did unity triumph over particularism? How did Americans manage to turn such things as size, heterogeneity, and religious diversity into assets instead of debits? How did a people who—in the "almost lurid" indictment of Henry James—had none of the ingredients of culture, manage nevertheless to provide themselves with a distinctive culture? Is there an American character—and what are its lineaments?

In America, Mr. Brogan submits, the environment triumphed over the inheritance; what is most American about America is a product of climate and soil, size and resources, isolation and New World experience. Thus the Irishman and the Pole in America, for all their differences, are more like each other than they are like their brothers back home in the old country. How has this come about—how has it come about for the past two hundred years? It was in part the physical environment which transformed them; in part the schools, which turned their children into Americanization agents; in part the voluntary associations like churches and granges and labor unions which assured them a new place and a new role; in part the political system which did not discriminate against them. It was in part, too, that America was promises, and that it was intolerable to think that the promises had not been fulfilled. Happily, for most of the newcomers—or for their children—the promises were fulfilled.

Mr. Brogan examines with special care three features of the making of the American character: the political, the educational, and the military. He has always been a student

of politics—his Cambridge chair is that of Political Science—
and has written a notable book on the *American Political
System*; what he gives us here is not analysis but com-
mentary and interpretation. He knows the Constitution and
the Supreme Court but appreciates—none better—the homely
and practical character of American politics: the job that
politics has to do and the techniques which politicians have
devised to do it. Thus he sees the necessity of the representation of local interests—even where those interests are selfish
or absurd; he understands why Presidents cannot always appoint the best men to important posts, but must recognize
races, faiths, groups, interests, and regions: "For a Pole or
a Slovak to see one of his own kin as a judge or alderman
or congressman is to be ready to believe that American
democracy has some meaning." He argues that the failings
of the American political system are insignificant compared
to its successes, and reminds us that "to have created a free
government over a continental area without making a sacrifice of adequate efficiency or of liberty is a unique achievement in world history."

Mr. Brogan is equally sympathetic with the irrelevancies
and shortcomings of our educational system. For he sees
what almost all other European observers miss, that in the
United States schools were called on to do much more than
to educate. They were called on to teach the language itself;
to inculcate a sense of unity and of nationalism—and without
chauvinism; to bind together a vast country and a miscel-
laneous population. He sees that for long periods of time,
therefore, the intellectual functions of the school had to be
subordinated to their social functions. Nor is he unduly
apologetic about their intellectual functions and attainments.
For he sees that if the demands of mass education made it
difficult to maintain high intellectual standards in the high
schools, the colleges and universities more than held their
own; that higher education in America has turned out to

be quite as high as it is anywhere else; and that "the level of academic learning is perhaps the only branch of American life where the promise of rapid progress upward has been consistently kept."

Mr. Brogan's final chapter on "The American Way in War and Peace" has been completely re-written in this new edition, and has the great advantage of experience with the Second World War and the Korean War, and with the long trial of the Cold War. In all previous wars Americans could count on isolation, on the immensity of their country, on the intelligence and resoluteness of their people, on their productive capacity, and on a Providence which seemed benevolent. But in the last two decades most of these advantages became somewhat irrelevant, and Americans have had to summon up resources for a different kind of warfare—a warfare where neither isolation nor size provided security, where technology made capacity less important than continuous achievement, and where Providence was not always to be counted on. Mr. Brogan is full of admiration for the U. S. achievements of World War II, and for the response to the challenge of Korea, but sees clearly where many of our old assumptions and illusions have vexed our policy and threatened our effectiveness in recent years.

In Britain, where this book was first published, it was called *The American Problem*; that problem, wrote Mr. Brogan, was "to make intelligible to the American people the nature of the changes in the modern world which they can lead or which they can resist, but which they can't ignore." Now in his preface to this edition—written in 1956—he takes some satisfaction in noting that Americans have neither ignored nor resisted the convulsive changes that have swept over the world, but have taken the lead in trying to control them. Somehow the fears of the 'forties— the fear that the United States might revert to isolationism, or that it would plunge into militarism, or that it would succumb to reaction, or that it would be paralyzed by depression—all of these have been confounded. New fears, to be sure, have taken their place, as new and unforeseen problems have started up to glare at us from all quarters of the globe. But what is reassuring is that Americans have somehow managed to shoulder responsibilities, if not cheerfully at least resolutely. "Great wonder," as Mr. Brogan writes, "that, with all the natural grounds for resentment of the human situation, the American has *not* revolted against prudence or duty, that he has accepted leadership every time that it has been offered, has, in such different activities as the Marshall Plan and the Korean War, given the world a lead and an example, has risen to his duty." All that speaks well for the American Character.

—HENRY STEELE COMMAGER
Professor of American History and American Studies
Amherst College

To Nell Burnett

CONTENTS

INTRODUCTION TO
THE VINTAGE EDITION, 1956

THIS BOOK was written during the Second World War under a double preoccupation that, at first sight, seems irrelevant today. It was designed to answer two questions: whether the United States could wage war and whether she could make peace. The first has been answered beyond all dubiety. The world has no doubt of American power or of the resolution of the American people. Nor has it any serious doubt of American willingness to participate in the organization of world order. Indeed, the fears and doubts seem to be reversed. The world often seems to be not afraid that American power will not be used, but that it will, less afraid that America will withdraw from world affairs than that America will impose her way of life on a reluctant planet. American "imperialism," not American "isolationism," is the target for critics of the United States, and if the chief image that the propagandists of Nazi Germany took pains to spread was that of an impotent, ill-armed, vainglorious, but, in the last analysis, contemptible power, the image spread by the Communists, successors of the Nazis, is that of a power, potent, indeed, for destruction, but reckless, "trigger-happy," manipulated by the ruthless capitalist overlords of Communist demonology.

What these pictures have in common is a misunderstanding of America based on an ignorance of America, a

contempt or fear of America based, in turn, on a conviction that the United States is easily comprehensible in European terms, that it can be fitted into a European pattern,
its way of life explained by European analogies, its balance
sheet added up according to the formulas of a European
political arithmetic.

It is the main thesis of this book, and it is the thesis
of this introduction, that the society, climate, geography,
history, political institutions have produced a "new man,
this American," out of a very mixed racial stock. It is a secondary thesis, that American institutions, habits of life and
thought had better be studied, at first, as things in themselves, that we should note what marks the American off
from the European rather than what unites the two kindred
stocks. It would be absurd to carry this practice to an ex-
treme. The Americans are, after all, human. They speak a
language of European origin; most of their institutions have
European roots, more specifically English roots; they are
part of the total Western machine culture that the rest of
the world envies, hates, imitates. It would be possible to
paint a picture of "Western man" and to fit the American
(and the Russian) into it. But that is a task for others. My
aim was more limited; it is more limited. It is the explanation, in American terms, of the American.

I attempted, twelve years ago, to give an explanation
and I still think that the explanation I gave then still ex-
plains a good deal. It was never intended to explain everything. But in rereading and, to some degree, rewriting a
book produced under very different circumstances, I have
been forced to wonder whether my explanation is much less
adequate than it was, whether the great changes that have
come about since 1943-4 have not, among other things,
deeply changed the American. He may still be a "new man,"
differing from Europeans, from other human beings, in

many important ways, but also differing from the American whose special character I attempted to outline.

What are the changes and what are their effects on the Americans? There is, first of all, the atom bomb. I have no doubt that, in the long run, perhaps in the not very long run, the possibility of planetary suicide will transform the American (and the English) attitude to many things—to politics, to business, to religion, to what we call "culture." A great deal, for example, of the noisy patriotism of the American Legion, a great deal of the belief that nothing really happens outside the United States or that, if it does, it is only important because it affects the United States, will wither and die. The old confident basis of isolationism, "You can't do that to me," is eaten steadily away with each drift of atomic dust across American as well as Asian skies. A great deal of the old belief that God looks after "children, drunkards, and the United States" will die and the old, brash confidence with it. But these are long-term results, and it is more surprising to note, as I think one can note, the survival of the old habits of mind than it is to note the first cracks in the armor that the American thought he wore with effortless superiority. Pandora's box is open; it is not safe to say more than that yet.

But the long-term impacts of the discovery of atomic fission (including what may become a renewed American sense of guilt at having pried open the deadly box) are not so important, in 1956, as some changes in the American way and the American view of life. There are material changes of which the most striking is the "nationalization" of American life. There are patches of America still outside modern life, in habits of mind if not in material equipment. The Ozarks of Li'l Abner, the dark places of the earth in Mississippi that recall the Congo of Conrad's *Heart of Darkness,* these exist. But over all the forty-eight states a new urbanized, highly mechanized, materially sophisticated culture has spread. New York and Gopher Prairie are closer to each other than either is to the New York of 1900 or the Gopher Prairie of 1920. The motor car, the truck, the plane, all have diminished distance, flattened out regional differences. The film, the radio, television have provided examples of a life to be envied, aimed at, attained. Advertising has made universally coveted a material way of life that modern industrial technology has made easy of access to all. The old rural folkways have largely been eaten away and replaced by those of the new, burgeoning suburban society of "Levittown," the supermarket, the community high school, the anonymous new society to which all or nearly all Americans are welcome. The urban and the rural slum are not gone, but they are things of a historically condemned past. Here a new American is being made.

What is this new man, the new American? Here we move into deep waters of sociological theory in which I can hardly keep afloat, much less swim. Is the new American society producing a new American or a new myth about the new American? Maybe a new American; but some of the reasons advanced are not totally convincing. The new American may be conformist, but was the old often nonconformist? I wrote in the first edition of this book that "any well-established village in New England or the northern Middle West could afford a town drunkard, a town atheist and a few Democrats." It can now afford more than one town drunkard (called "alcoholics," of course), being a Democrat is less bold today than it was; some of the nicest people are Democrats; but a town atheist? "There are no atheists in the foxholes," and America is now in a foxhole that she may have to inhabit for a generation. The consequence of this predicament is that refusal to give lip service, at least, to the American religion is a kind of treason and is punished as it was in the America of a century ago.

It is not the social coercion of the real dissenter, the man who by his action or inaction condemns the faith of his neighbors, that is the new thing. (All that need be said on democratic conformity was said by Tocqueville.) What is new is the increasing condemnation of the man who conforms *too* vigorously, who pursues happiness in indisputably American terms, but pursues it with too little regard for his neighbor's comfort. Of course he *is* in competition with them, but he mustn't rub that fact in or rejoice too much in victory. He must win without showing it and, to be able to win, he must not antagonize the other runners, who will gang up on him if he does. The race is still to the swift but mere swiftness is not enough if its too ostentatious display leads to some other competitor's bumping or spiking, with the approval of the other competitors—and the spectators. So far this new-found consideration may be only skin deep; it may be only a tactic, but it is interesting that it is a tactic.[1]

It is, on the surface, a long way from the traditional pioneer; it may be more than a change of methods; it may be a change of spirit. And yet, and yet! By European standards, what is still notable about American life is that competition, even by the new, softer, more formally amiable methods, is the accepted way of life. So is the lavishness of the prizes; so is the acceptance of the fact that not everybody can answer the $64,000 question—and the absence of

---

[1] How far the new spirit has gone is illustrated by the innocent remark of an Irish-American contractor, specializing in pulling down buildings and excavating foundations, traditionally tough trades. Mr. Howard Collins notes the change. "'When I started in this business, everybody was a roughneck. Talked dirty, dressed dirty, lived dirty. Now the men come to work in nice clothes, drive nice cars, live in nice houses, have nice families. Funny thing that's happened in this country—nobody *has* to be tough any more.'" *The New Yorker,* December 31, 1955.

jealousy of the winners. This absence of jealousy, this conviction that the game is worth playing and the results not cooked, is one of the chief sources of American wealth, well-being, and political stability. No one (hardly anyone, Negroes excepted) feels automatically excluded from the pursuit of happiness. Even the Negroes feel less excluded than they did. There is consequently a universal acceptance of the legitimacy of the political authority of "We, the People of the United States," that startles and impresses European visitors like Père Bruckberger. In this very important sense, a more perfect union has been attained than is known in any country in Europe and which pleases or angers European visitors in accordance with their personal temperaments and doctrines.

There is, of course, a danger or a promise that the formal good manners of the American acquisitive society will in fact weaken the acquisitive motive and habit. Not only can no one be rich on the old scale (taxes see to that), but achievement in the field of production is not admired as it was in the older, simpler, cruder American society. No great business magnate will ever know the free command of wealth that Rockefeller and Carnegie knew; the admiration, just short of worship, that Edison and Henry Ford I knew. Whether the lessened rewards will begin to eat into the will to "succeed" of the young American we do not yet know. The old battle of the strong had the attractions of battle. The modern business career is more like the peace-time career of the professional soldier than the bloody campaigns that brought the Robber Barons to the top. It is not insignificant that the services of the Robber Barons are now better appreciated when (outside Texas) they are, as a breed, almost extinct.

In discussing this question we are all at school to Mr. David Riesman, and if the "inner directed" are indeed in retreat, are becoming un-American, the United States may be moving nearer the Soviet Union than it realizes, for Communism, too, professes to create a new man as unlike the conscience-driven heroes of Dostoievsky as the modern dweller in the executive suite, in gray flannel, is unlike such flamboyant pirates as Jim Fisk. If it is no longer a matter of "keeping up with the Joneses," but of everybody keeping up with everybody else, it is possible that the American people will end up going round, in happy harmony, a mulberry bush that isn't there. And against such a danger a great deal of modern American religiosity is less than no safeguard.

It is not only a matter of adjusting to the great, anonymous, self-governing, mass-owned corporations to whose service and promises so many young Americans gladly give themselves. It is a matter of adjusting to a world in which mass organizations are the normal centers of life for more and more millions of human beings. It can be asserted that the United States must adjust or perish. And one aspect of that adjustment is the immense growth of the armed forces and of the economic units serving them. Millions of Americans in 1939 had little or nothing to do with the government of the United States. Millions of Americans in 1944 looked forward to a near and victorious future in which they would have nothing to do with that government. They were disillusioned. From that disillusion has come much of what has most disturbed the outside world in contemporary America, McCarthyism, "sounding-off" by cabinet officers, senators, generals, columnists, threats of atomic war, brisk denunciation of allies and the like. The Americans are forced to live not only in a world they have not made, but in a world that they definitely thought they had killed in its cradle. No wonder the average American is uneasy, ready to believe that the cause of all his discontents is treason or folly in his rulers, unwilling to accept the fact that the world was not made exclusively by or for Americans.

Great wonder that, with all these natural grounds for resentment of the human situation, he has *not* revolted against prudence or duty, that he has accepted leadership every time that it has been offered, has, in such different activities as the Marshall Plan and the Korean War, given the world a lead and an example, has, with a readiness totally unforeseen in 1939 and only barely hoped for in 1944, risen to his duty. Those who expected much from the American people have not been disappointed.

There are other ways in which they have not been disappointed. Despite setbacks like the revival of lynching in Mississippi, the frenzies provoked by the threat of desegregation in southern schools, the revival of the most farcical and odious doctrines of race supremacy, in no field of human relations has the United States made more progress than in its dealing with Negro Americans. The churches, laggard enough in 1939, have in many cases been pioneers —above all, the Catholic Church, where bishops have shown that there is something to be said for a church in which authority does not come from the grass roots; grass roots are sometimes poisoned.

American trade unions are not led by or composed of angels. But they have proved a great stabilizing force and if the American economic system, called, a little naïvely, the "free-enterprise system," has secured such universal acceptance, it is in part due to the integration of the American worker in American industrial society by the trade unions.

In the same way, the social services, so bitterly opposed, open as some are to grave and increasing abuse, have made the government of the United States something less remote, less merely demanding than it was. The woes of the farmer may be real, but it is significant that he turns, simply and candidly, to the government to keep him in the state to which he thinks he is entitled. This is a change from the days of "root, hog, or die," but it represents less a change

in attitude than an acceptance of the fact that the urbanization of the American society makes certain proud old agricultural attitudes very expensive. The American farmer, in
his rugged way, would rather have money without control,
and he may get it. But he is not yet ready to join a kolkhoz
to get a living.

There are other changes whose consequences no one,
at any rate not I, can foresee. What is to become of the
equality between the sexes in an economy that both imposes
the draft and pours the horn of plenty of veterans' benefits
solely on the male part of the population? What is to become of the school system when its task ceases to be that
of adjusting the young to a new society to giving them
intellectual tools to run it? What is to become of a society
that can afford leisure on an unprecedented scale and may
have to find uses for free men and citizens, deprived of
their social utility by automation? No one knows and, final
blessing, no one in America really thinks that he knows.
Free from ideological baggage, the hopeful American
plunges rather than strides forward. After all, said Cromwell, no man goes as far as the man who does not know
where he is going. The American may be going to hell in
a wheelbarrow or in a flying saucer. If he is, we'll all go
with him. But I suspect that, humanly speaking, heaven's
his destination. He won't quite get there, but he'll go far
and fare better than if he doubted the general wisdom of his
course. When ex-President Jackson was being buried, a
visitor asked one of his slaves if he thought that General
Jackson (like many soldier Presidents, a belated convert
to formal Christianity) would go to heaven. "He will if he
wants to." General Jackson was and is a symbol of the
American.

Jackson Day 1956

—D. W. Brogan

PREFACE TO
THE FIRST EDITION

THIS BOOK is ambitious in design but modest in its actual detail. It is designed to make more intelligible to the British public certain American principles and attitudes. But it makes no pretense to either profundity or elaborate learning. A great many important aspects of American life have been ignored or treated very sketchily, sometimes because they were irrelevant to my immediate object, sometimes because I thought myself incompetent to handle them.

I have been writing on American topics for fifteen years. Inevitably I have sometimes repeated myself. I have not tried to find novel ways of saying the same thing. "The American Way in War" appeared in part in *Harper's Magazine*.

As readers will soon discover, this is a personal book. I have made assertions because I thought them to be true and relevant, not because they had a weight of independent authority behind them. There may result from this plan of work an air of impertinence and casualness. But nothing could be further from my intentions or attitude than to treat any serious American topic frivolously. My object has been to make what I think is the most interesting country in the world interesting and intelligible to others. Above all, I have tried to make plain that there is no parallel in history to the experiment of free government on this scale. The scale accounts for a great deal, including the apparent justification at some periods and in some departments of American life for pessimism about the present or the future of America. In the past, the pessimists have always been wrong. I think they are still wrong.

—D. W. BROGAN

London, March 24, 1944

INTRODUCTION TO
THE FIRST EDITION

*"The American is a new man
who acts on new principles;
he must therefore entertain new ideas
and form new opinions."*

—J. HECTOR ST. JOHN DE CREVECOEUR

IN THE LATE SUMMER of 1936, I arrived in Kansas City (Missouri). When I tried to buy a ticket for St. Louis at the Union Station, I was interrogated in a friendly, American fashion by the ticket clerk. "You from Europe?" "Yes." "Well, don't go back—it's going to hell." I was more than half convinced that he was right—although I was going back. A month or so before, I had lain on the shore in Somerset on a Sunday evening and had been aroused from daydreaming by a noise in the air and a swirl of excitement around me. Above, magnificent, serene, and ominous was a Zeppelin, moving east. It was low and clearly seen; a day before, it had been in New York; by tomorrow's dawn it would be in Frankfurt. The swastika was plainly visible as it moved on, over Glastonbury, where, the legend runs, Joseph of Arimathea had brought the Holy Thorn and built the first Christian church in Britain. A shadow was crossing England: women on the beach looked at their children—

with a faint and how inadequate perception of what was soon to befall Bristol, where they came from. How remote it all seemed in the hot sun of western Missouri, how remote it was even from me, and how much more remote from the people of Midwest America, with fifteen hundred miles each way between them and the oceans, with the huge war memorial outside the station to remind the citizens of Kansas City of their first adventure overseas and to confirm their resolution that it would be the last!

I went a day or two later to see a friend of mine who lives in a small town in Illinois. We went together to the corner drugstore to get ice cream for supper. It was a scene familiar enough to me and familiar to all moviegoers—the Main Street of a small American town on a Saturday night in late summer. The boys and girls were there in their white summer clothes; there were endless cars; it was possible that here, as in other American towns like this, it was thought more important to have a car, which is a public asset, than a bathroom, which is private. There was over the street and over the town that indefinable American air of happiness and ease, at least for the young. There was that general friendliness and candor. Here, as much as in the Bowery of which he was the Boss, men and women were acting on the principle laid down by Big Tim Sullivan: "God and the People hate a chesty man."

People called each other by their "given names"; there were friendly inquiries and a few introductions of the visitor. It was a world in which the ominous word "stranger" had been given a friendly flavor. "Howdy, Stranger" is not a hostile greeting, and it was invented in America. Looking at the people, at the boys and girls milling round the drugstores, disappearing in cars that shot off into the warm, welcoming darkness, it was hard to remember the tension of English life, the worse tension of French life. Life, it is true, was not altogether easy and agreeable for these people. Those who had definitely put youth behind them showed signs of fatigue and worry. They had reason. This was a farm town and the farmers had had a bad time. Some, not very far away, were still having a bad time. Across the Missouri it was a drought year. In Emporia, Kansas, it was still doubtful, so William Allen White had told me, whether they could reopen the local normal college that fall. There might not be enough water. All that region had been badly hit by very bad times, by crop failures, by bank failures. But there was still an impression of hope, of recovery. There was an air of confident adaptation to their way of life in the dress, the speech, the manners of the young. This, if a world they had not made, was yet a world that seemed to have been made for them.

In the drugstore there was the usual stock of gadgets, of remedies for all ills. There were soft drinks, no hard liquor; but there was—most impressive sight of all—a book and magazine section. There were the books of the films; there was the book of the year or decade (it was the first year of *Gone with the Wind*). If you wanted to know about dressmaking, about cosmetics, about domestic management, about love, about astrology, about business success, about child-training, about how to be happy on a small income (the answer being usually a way to make it large), the printed oracles were there. And the spoken oracles, too, for radios blasted the soft summer night and the heat did not empty the movie house.

And it was all American—even the guiding stars. The advertisements, the gadgets, the radio programs, the movies, the patent medicines, the patent solutions to human woes—all were American, or almost all. There might be in the advertising sections some sales talk for English biscuits or French perfume or Scotch whisky. There might be in the movie house a travelogue by Fitzpatrick; there might be in the St. Louis *Post-Dispatch* a cartoon by a greater Fitzpatrick; bringing home the bitter truth about the outer world. No doubt some residents in the town had traveled (my host had). Perhaps the librarian or the English-teacher had told the women's club of a tour in England or the "colorful Caribbean." Some veterans had memories of France.

The regional press was already doing a first-class job, a better job than was being done by most English papers, to awaken the people to the truth of the new iron age that we were all living in, to the significance of Manchukuo, to the menace of international war in Spain. Perhaps, the parent-teacher association had asked for more instruction in civics and in current affairs. Certainly, appeals for charity, for Chinese, or for Spaniards had been or would be answered as soon as made.

But in the warmth and ease of that summer night, the inevitable, the right, the human character of American natural isolationism was brought home to me. The road from Jerusalem to Jericho did not pass close to southern Illinois, as it did southern England, and there was no visible good Samaritan in Illinois—or in England—to shame Priest or Levite.

Their great highway was the Mississippi; for its control a long and bloody war had been fought and won. From that state had come the leader of the victorious party, but Lincoln was long dead and deified in his tomb a hundred or so miles to the north in Springfield. The whole region had once been a great international prize, but it was a century and a half since George Rogers Clark had seized the little French settlements of Kaskaskia and the rest from the English. It was over a century, too, since his brother William and Meriwether Lewis had marched west at the orders of President Jefferson, making for the Pacific, preparing the road maps of "manifest destiny." It was a generation since Henry Adams had brought his sophistication and his bile to the St. Louis Exposition and thought out again the problem of what makes and moves and unites societies, what was alike and unlike in Chartres in 1200 and in St. Louis in 1904—"the Virgin and the Dynamo." But in 1936 it was the calm, dead center of a tornado whose outer boundaries were too far away for comprehension or apprehension.

There was no way in which the inevitable, deplorable, maddening impact of the outside world on Illinois and on the whole Mississippi Valley could be brought home to the dwellers therein. If men and women in England in 1938 could profess to believe in "peace in our time," why should not these happy Americans believe with far more plausibility in peace in their time—for them? Yet in less than six years German submarines were sinking American ships in the mouth of that Mississippi, secured for the infant United States through the energetic disregard of constitutional proprieties by President Jefferson. And all the considerable cities of the Valley were preparing to defend themselves against air raids, against desperate, forlorn hopes in which the Nazis would strike, whatever the cost, at the most typical, representative, important city of the Midwest —which naturally was Zenith or whatever city was yours.

As the shadow over Europe grew longer and darker, as the darkness was made more terrifying by the whistling with which our leaders tried to keep up their courage and ours, as the chances of peace in Europe became more and more dependent on the temptations of easy victory for Germany, and those temptations more and more controlled by the possible reaction of the American people, the problem of the American temper became more urgent. It was largely a question of time: if the American people had been prepared in 1931 to do what they were prepared to do in 1939, if they had been as ready in 1939 as they were in 1941 for the dangers of the time! But it is an endless sequence of ifs that it is not very profitable to follow out. What is more profitable is to try to make plain how natural, how justifiable, how given by historical conditions was the tempo of American awakening, the slow acceptance of the fact that the shadow cast over Somerset was also cast over Illinois. It took the actual shadow, repeated again and again, to awaken Somerset; Illinois had to awaken with far less help from the eye and ear.

But it was not only Illinois. All over the United States there was the same life, conditioned by the same history, by an experience in which the outside world grew more and more remote, backward, barbarous, and—so it was thought—relatively weak. On the new concrete roads, new-model cars made American nomadism the expression of American civilization. "God's Country"—as the song put it —was the country of the Lincoln Highway. Into the great inland nodal points the trains poured: Illinois Central; New York Central; Union Pacific; Chicago, Milwaukee & St. Paul; Père Marquette; Atchison, Topeka & Santa Fe. But only a few Canadian trains in the north, only a few Mexican trains in the south, to recall the outside world, and doing it not much more effectually than an occasional Rolls-Royce or Duesenberg or Hispano-Suiza lost among the Lincolns, Packards, Buicks, Chevrolets, Fords. The air was getting fuller of passenger planes; the airports more numerous and more splendid. And it was as natural, though as wrong, to think of the new technique as an American invention and practically an American monopoly as to think of Colonel Lindbergh as the first man to fly the Atlantic.

What could it mean to the remote villages of the South, to the people who worshipped in those little wooden churches with their odd, pathetic, and fantastically ugly imitations of stained glass? Did it matter to them that the French had put an aerodrome beside Chartres Cathedral, and that the latest addition to the inscriptions at that place was an appeal for volunteers to join the organization that would move the Chartres stained glass to a safe place when the inevitable war (that no one would admit or deny was coming) yet came? This region had had its war, its record of destruction; and its wounds, material and spiritual, were still bleeding.

Yet that region, in five years' time, was beginning to send its volunteers, via Canada, to fight in defense of that Wells Cathedral over which the Zeppelin had serenely passed.

What could it matter to the *Canadiens* of New England? What did it matter to them that the country that had expelled the *Acadiens* and conquered the Canadiens was in danger and, with it, the ancestral land that had abandoned the good ways of old France and no longer had enough sons to guard her fields? In less than six years' time the New England coast was beleaguered by submarines, and their kinsmen from across the border were dying first at Dieppe and then in a heroic assault outside Ortona.

What did it matter to the less energetic fugitives from a New York winter I saw a few months later, who, resisting any temptation to take a ski train up to the White Mountains, took a train bound for Florida? Yet inside five years the submarines of the enemy were cruising in impudent immunity within rifle-shot of the pleasure cities where the tourists lay on the sand, or profited and lost in Colonel Bradley's hospitable gambling houses.

I remembered, too, the long controversy over bridging San Francisco Bay, the doubts of the War and Navy Departments about the wisdom of building such vulnerable structures across the entrance to a great naval base. Such fears had seemed purely fantastic, purely pedantic. Yet within three years of the celebration of the completion of the bridges, the dead and wounded from Pearl Harbor were being brought ashore in San Francisco. And a few months later I stood in the living-room of a friend's house looking straight into the Golden Gate and wondering, like other people, how the great naval battle of the Coral Sea was going and whether the Japanese would risk putting a carrier or two into the permanent summer fog belt and bomb San Francisco as they had bombed Pearl Harbor. I remembered, too, how I had first seen Seattle, taken over by invading Lions or Elks or Moose or Eagles, and how I had next seen it, with a solitary barrage balloon (from London) floating over the airport, curiously homely and comforting to a passenger who had just seen the great ice fields and glaciers of Mount Rainier below him and had need of something to restore a human sense of scale.

Our fate, the fate of civilization in Europe, the fate of constitutional freedom in America were bound up with the defeat of a self-confident, energetic, efficient, and ruthless political and military system that denied our premises and disliked and despised our aims. This was true in 1936; it was true in 1944. It was the meaning of the shadow cast over England. But that shadow was not cast in such dramatic form over America.

What could this growing shadow mean to the people of Utah? It was nearly a century since the members of the Church of Jesus Christ of Latter-Day Saints had crossed the prairies and the plains to the great empty basin of the Great Salt Lake. Nearly a century had passed since they had made their Exodus, since they had been saved from the crickets by the seagulls sent by God to preserve His chosen people. I had seen the monument to the seagull; I had seen the irrigated fields and fertile valleys redeemed from the wilderness; I had heard the hymn of the new Israel, the Mormon version of the Hundred and Fifth Psalm: "Unto thee will I give the land of Canaan, the lot of your inheritance." The old bloody feuds, the murder of the Prophet, the vengence of the Destroying Angels, were half forgotten by the people who sang "Come, come, ye Saints." Isolated in the great, empty basin, shut in by mountains on all sides, living in the land they had made; with their own, exclusive version of world history to cut them off from the fears and hopes of the outside world, what could Hitler mean to them? Yet in a few years' time, not merely were their sons sent to all corners of the world, but the needs of war economy were transforming Deseret as it had not been transformed since the railroads brought in Gentiles to the kingdom of Brigham Young.

What, I more than once reflected, could all this mean to the shepherds of New Mexico who elected Dennis Chavez of Los Chavez ("Chavez of that ilk," as they would say in Scotland) to the United States Senate? "The blood of the conquerors," to use Harvey Fergusson's phrase, no doubt ran in their veins; so did the blood of the conquered. But that last outpost of New Spain had been for long so peaceful! The Comanches had been tamed, and the bloody memory of the seventeenth-century Indian rising that had for twelve years turned the little capital of Santa Fe into a heathen town was faint, today. The austere and bare mountains of the Sangre de Cristo above the stripling Rio Grande del Norte were as strange as ever to European eyes, as strange as they must have been to Miss Willa Cather's hero when the future Archbishop came to them a century ago, from the strange but not arid, not empty mountains of Auvergne. Peace had at last come to Santa Fe and to Taos. But in less than six years from that summer, there fell on the little cities and villages of New Mexico the catastrophe, the heroic disaster of Bataan. For the local National Guard had been mobilized and sent off to the Philippines, and boys who had known nothing of the outer world died in gallant defense of another relic of the Christian empire of Philip II and Philip III—the Commonwealth of the Philippines, reunited with New Mexico in a common destiny by the power of the United States.

And that power was so easy to underestimate, and each such underestimation made war more likely. It was easy for the Japanese to underestimate it; for, as Mr. Justice Black had pointed out, the Japanese, like the Americans, believed that they had never lost a war. It had been easy to surprise the somnolent Tsarist Russians at Port Arthur in 1904; it would be easy to surprise the complacent, ill-informed, and unsuspecting Americans at Pearl Harbor in 1941—to "catch them with their pants down," in the expressive American phrase; and one of the Japanese diplomats negotiating in Washington while the trap was being got ready prided himself on his command of American idiom.

It was easy for the Germans to despise the people whom Herr von Papen in 1916 had described as "those idiotic Yankees." True, the idiotic Yankees had been too much for Herr von Papen and his employers, but that was in the bad old days. I remembered a discussion in Paris in 1939 with a very eminent White Russian diplomat, a Baltic baron by origin, who told me that his friends in the German Embassy were not in the least interested in the power of the United States. "Whatever they do will be done too late. And if that warmonger Roosevelt does try to impede the policy of the Reich, there will be a revolution against him and his Jewish advisers." So spoke the experts of the Third Reich. I said that I did not believe this; that I knew America well, that to awaken the national pride and anger of the American people would be the most fatal mistake of the gamblers in charge of the destiny of Germany and the peace of Europe. I even told the revealing story of what had happened to John Quincy Adams in 1797 when he was sent by his father, President John Adams, as Minister to Berlin. "When the American Minister to Prussia, the son of the President, arrived at the capital of Prussia, he was examined by a dapper young officer of the guard, who unblushingly admitted that he had never even heard of the United States of America."[1] A century and a quarter later, a successor of John Adams and John Quincy Adams in the White House deposed the Hohenzollerns, and another quarter of a century after that, another successor was commander-in-chief of an army which put more men in the air over Berlin than Washington had Americans under him at Valley Forge or at Yorktown.

I remembered, too, that when the British troops under General O'Hara marched out at Yorktown in 1781 to surrender to Washington and Rochambeau, their bands played *The World Turned Upside Down*. And as in the darkening months and years, I heard the apologists for the new Danegeld preach the policy of buying Hitler off—even, if absolutely necessary, with British property—I wondered whether they, with their subservience to the new enemy of all American political religion, really cared nothing for American goodwill or whether, like the Germans, they thought that it was a mere matter of sentiment, that there was time enough before the American giant awoke to see that he should awake, like Gulliver in Lilliput, bound hand and foot.

But many of them, English and German, did not even think that he was a giant, that the world had really been turned upside down at Yorktown, that it was time for even the smuggest Prussian expert or English politician to learn what it meant that the United States had grown to its present stature and to its present unity.

The whole world learned between 1939 and 1945 what formidable power was in the hands of the Americans, the power of improvisation, of beating plowshares into swords

---

[1] Bennett Champ Clark: *John Quincy Adams*, p. 61.

on an unprecedented scale, the power of threatening the "great globe itself." Leyte and Okinawa, Bastogne and Remagen and, finally and terribly, Hiroshima and Nagasaki taught us all the lesson of American power, but the American problem remains.

It is a double problem. It is the problem of making intelligible to the American people the nature of the changes in the modern world which they can lead, or which they can resist, but which they can't ignore. That is a problem for Americans. There is the second problem: the problem of making intelligible the normal American's view of the world, of his own history and destiny. Full success in the solution of such a problem is impossible; there must always remain an element of the unconscious and unintelligible in the national life of any people. But a little can be done to encourage sympathetic understanding of the Americanism of America.

The problem of modern America is almost literally one of orientation. A century ago Henry Thoreau described how, when he went out of doors uncertain where to go, his instinct always decided for him. "I turn round and round irresolute sometimes for a quarter of an hour, until I decide, for the thousandth time, that I will walk into the southwest or west. Eastward I go only by force; but westward I go free. Thither no business leads me. It is hard for me to believe that I shall find fair landscapes or sufficient wildness and freedom behind the eastern horizon. I am not excited by the prospect of a walk thither; but I believe that the forest which I see in the western horizon stretches uninterruptedly toward the setting sun, and there are no towns or cities in it of enough consequence to disturb me. Let me live where I will, on this side is the city, on that the wilderness, and ever I am leaving the city more and more and withdrawing into the wilderness. I should not lay so much stress on this fact

xliv

if I did not believe that something like this is the prevailing tendency of my countrymen. I must walk toward Oregon and not toward Europe."[2]

All American experience, down to very recent times, was on the side of Thoreau. Oregon was no longer the wilderness; the Columbia River no longer rolled hearing "no sound save its own dashings," but was tamed by the greatest dams in the world and—toward the ocean, at least —rimmed with cities. But the westward drive was still potent; Americans rejoiced still in "the inward eye which is the bliss of solitude." It is only in this century that they have begun to learn, slowly, inadequately, humanly, that the world is really round, that to walk toward Oregon is to walk toward Europe. It has been a shock to their optimism, a shock to their view of their destiny. It is now necessary to turn from the lesson of Thoreau—or to apply it in a new world. Honolulu is west of Oregon; China, "the Orient," is west of Honolulu; the Aleutians and Siberia are north and west. A contemporary of Thoreau knew that mere movement in one direction is not a solution.

"Were this world an endless plain, and by sailing eastward we could for ever reach new distances, and discover sights more sweet and strange than any Cyclades or Islands of King Solomon, then there were promise in the voyage. But in pursuit of those far mysteries we dream of, or in tormented chase of that demon phantom that, some time or other, swims before all human hearts; while chasing such over this round globe, they either lead us on in barren mazes or midway leave us whelmed."[3]

The world is round, and so you come to Europe (or Europe comes to you) by the back if not by the front door.

---

[2] Quoted by Bernard De Voto: *The Year of Decision 1846,* "Invocation."

[3] Melville: *Moby Dick,* Chapter lii.

The world runs north and south as well as east and west. Brazil is a neighbor of Africa as well as of the United States; Canada is a neighbor of Siberia as well as of Greenland.

And it is not only a world that has closed in on the United States (or on whose once remote borders the United States now presses with unconscious weight and power). It is a world in which all nations have to make deep adjustments in their mental habits, have to take stock of what is living and what is dead in their traditions. But that adjustment must, all the same, be made in the terms of the living tradition, according to the spirit. "These are the times that try men's souls," wrote Thomas Paine in 1776. These are the times that try men's powers of sympathetic imagination, of mutual understanding, for without these there will be no enduring structure of peace and order built.

THE
AMERICAN
CHARACTER

Part One

AMERICA IS MADE

*"East were the
Dead kings and the remembered sepulchres:
West was the grass."*

—ARCHIBALD MACLEISH

1

IT IS NEARLY four hundred and fifty years since white men began to settle in North America, and three hundred and fifty years since the first unsuccessful settlements of English-speaking people were founded. The settlement of North America, the filling-up of its vast empty spaces, is the most remarkable extension of one society over an ocean barrier of which we have any knowledge. Century after century, tens of millions of Europeans have crossed three thousand miles of ocean, leaving behind them an old, reasonably adapted society in a familiar and, on the whole, friendly physical environment. They have brought with them European ideas, European techniques, European bodies and physical habits. They have brought these to an empty continent, and it has taken them centuries not merely to fill that continent, but to create ways of life adapted to a different climate, to a different set of economic possibilities, and to a society held together at its beginnings by imported political and social habits, and only slowly and with repeated crises creating American political and social habits to replace the European importations that, with each decade, wore thinner and thinner like an old carpet. In this process the modern American has been created; the interplay of geographic, biological, historical forces has made him. And the process has seemed reasonably complete only in our own time. Only in this century has the continental territory of the United States been formally organized into uniform political units; only in this century has the centuries-old ambition of the extension of the area of settlement westward and farther westward turned from a possibility to a nostalgic dream; only in this generation has the practical cessation of large-scale immigration ensured that nearly all the young people of the United States should be American-born, instead of being diluted by a million new Europeans arriving every year to be adjusted, often very inadequately, to the necessary conditions of American life.

The historical process that has in this century produced so American an American society was long, difficult, and novel. The first settlers in what is now the United States were confronted with forest all along the line from Maine to Florida. Before them lay over a million square miles of "the forest primeval, the murmuring pines and the hemlocks," forest on a scale that Europe had not known for two thousand years. Scattered over that forest were a few hundred thousand natives, Indians. They were limited in their possibilities of adaptation by the comparative poverty of their natural environment and by their incapacity to alter that environment. They had no horses, no cattle; they had to be hunters and planters, and it was impossible to build a populous and progressive society in the forest on these terms. It was not a matter of native incapacity. The Indian took to the horse and the gun with great speed; some of the European techniques he accepted quickly, and others he might have accepted if the invaders had given him time to do so. But the adjustment of the Indian to his environment, often admirable though it was, was not an adjustment that the white man wanted to make or could make. Before an American society could be created by the settlers, America had to be transformed. The forest had to give way to the fields, the plow, the draft ox, the mule, the sheep, the goat, the wheel, gunpowder, steel had to make possible a new life in which tens of millions could live abundantly where a few hundred thousand savages had been living precarious and poverty-stricken lives. America had to be made before it could be lived in, and that making took centuries, took extraordinary energies and bred

3

an attitude to life that is peculiarly American. It bred the temper of the pioneer, the temper of the gambler, the temper of the booster, the temper of the discounter of the future who is to some extent bound to be a disparager of the past. It took optimism to cross the Atlantic, optimism or despair and anger at the old world from which the reluctant pioneer had come. Until this century, there was always tempting the adventurous or the unlucky the dream of a new chance a little farther on. Movement became a virtue, stability a rather contemptible attitude of mind. The frontier in English speech is a defined barrier between two organized states; in American it is a vague, broad, fluctuating region on one side of which is a stable, settled, comparatively old society, and on the other, empty land, a few savages, unknown opportunities, unknown risks. American history has been a matter of eliminating that debatable area between the empty land and the settled land, between the desert and the sown. This elimination has now been completed, but it is too early, yet, for the centuries-old habits to have changed and much too early for the attitude of mind bred by this incessant social process to have lost its power. Bishop Berkeley was a premature prophet when in the eighteenth century he wrote:

Westward the course of empire takes its way,
The first four acts already past.
The fifth shall close the drama with the day,
Time's noblest offspring is the last.

The fifth act is with us, but neither the actors nor the spectators yet know its issue or know whether it will have a tragic or a happy ending.

When the early settlers from crowded Europe saw the more fertile parts of the Atlantic coast, empty, promising, asking for the plow and the herd, it was natural that they should underestimate the difficulties of settlement. It

was natural that speculators in Europe should see themselves, for the expenditure of a little capital, suddenly shot
upwards in the social scale. Land was abundant in America,
scarce in Europe; owning land was socially and finan-
cially the aim of all climbing Europeans in the seventeenth century—and it was a climbing century. The new
western lands seemed to offer promotion for everybody,
for great magnates who wanted even more, for the cadets
of noble houses who in Virginia need not be the victims
of primogeniture, needy younger sons, but could quickly
set up in the New World as equals of their elder brothers.
Even when the dreams of gold and silver were found to
be baseless, there was still the land. And for the first two
centuries of English settlement, it must always be remembered, the astonishing mineral resources of what is now
the United States were unreachable. Gold and silver there
was in abundance—but undiscovered in what was then
Spanish territory. Other metals, iron and copper; other
minerals, soft coal and anthracite; oil and natural gas; the
repeated bonuses Nature paid to the Americans in the
nineteenth century were withheld from the first settlers.
And because this was so, the dream of an easy ascent to
gentility without labor was a dream that never came true.
The role of the mere proprietor, the mere owner of naked
legal titles to land, was never an easy one. To make money
out of land in America, you had to work and watch; a
mere gentry living off rents could not be and never was
created. The American equivalent of the English squire
was never a close equivalent; he had to be a gambler, an
entrepreneur, a capitalist; he had to be vigilant, generation
after generation, to keep his old land from deterioration
and to secure his share of the new land. If he did neither,
he could not keep up with the Joneses who on the frontier
were repeating the pattern of the first settlement. From
the very beginning, American life was competitive from

the top downward. There was no real stability, no real security for anyone. Here and there a family might stay put; here and there mere stability paid well enough. But such cases were few, and fewer still the fortunes, the social and political positions, preserved over centuries without repeated effort, without setbacks and windfalls. There was no high plateau of effortless superiority to be attained, by Byrds in Virginia or by Saltonstalls in Massachusetts. A family or an individual had to have what it took to survive—and it took adaptability, toughness, perhaps a not too sensitive moral or social outlook. The would-be profit-drawers in England simply contributed capital on which no return was or could be made. The would-be gentry unlearned the idle lessons of gentility or sank into poverty or returned to the easier world they had left. From the beginning it was "root, hog, or die." And the American razorback hog that the forest bred, with little meat and much muscle, was a symbol as well as a product of the process of adaptation.

The poor who came to America—the majority of the settlers—had fewer illusions to shed than had the gentry. They took a rationally pessimistic view of the world and did not expect to get anything for nothing. Whether they were solvent enough to pay their way (the mere cost of transportation was relatively very high indeed in these days), or sold themselves as indentured servants to earn, by seven years' serfdom, the passage to America, or were transported, free, by a vigilant government for offenses ranging from taking the wrong side in a rebellion to plain and fancy felonies, the move to America was important and final. They did not expect to go back; if they were religious or political refugees they did not want to. And the new world into which they came had to be made habitable by them.

Adaptation again was the key. How many early settlements—Spanish, English, French—withered away or were swept away by famine and disease! To pick the wrong, malarial, snake-infested, swampy site for the settlement, that was a mistake paid for by the loss of the meager capital resources so painfully accumulated—and often by the forfeit of life as well. To fail to plant the right crops at the right time was a mistake as deadly. The early settlers of New England bore in their memories the duty of gratitude to the Indians who taught them the completely novel technique of planting Indian corn (maize), the making of the little mound like a golf-tee, the use of fish as a fertilizer —ways so new to wheat-growers, to users of plows and breeders of cattle. The timing of your arrival on the American coast (as much a matter of good luck as of good navigation) might mean death for all or most of a party before the first crops could be harvested.

The early settler had to have an eye for the country, he had to be a real-estate dealer, to make a good first choice, to decide whether it was wiser to hold on, whether it was wiser to cut your losses, to file that petition in bankruptcy which moving on constituted, whether it was possible to unload your losses on some more optimistic and more gullible newcomer. Again, there were some exceptions. The Germans who settled in early Pennsylvania have stayed put ever since, and their fertile, well-formed, stable countryside often evokes nostalgia in European breasts. But America was not made by ways of life that evoke European nostalgia or by imitations of European stability, and the "Pennsylvania Dutch" have played a far less important role than those more American-type immigrants, the so-called "Scotch-Irish," the Ulster Presbyterians who took into the Indian country whisky, Calvinism, a high degree of pugnacity, and a taste for acquisition on a big scale.

In the first century, geographical stability was suggested if not imposed by the lie of the land and the balance of power. In harbors and up rivers were the natural centers of settlement. Great mistakes were made; "obvious" sites like New York were for a time neglected, hopeless sites like a score of decayed or abandoned old settlements were chosen. But with the sea behind them and the numerous rivers opening ways inland, the early settlers were distributed, very thinly, all along the coast in a fashion fairly obviously dictated by geography. The sea still bound them to Europe, to an England which was from a transportation point of view easier of access from Charleston (South Carolina) than was Boston (Massachusetts) from the same port. The umbilical cord that bound the new, unadapted settlements to the mother country ran up the great rivers, too. Where ships could go, un-American forces were still holding the settlers to the Old World and to old ways. The West might beckon—the American sees the sun move from the ocean inland; his evening view over the Atlantic is gray and grim, while "to the west the land is bright." But where falls and rapids broke the easy navigation channels, the "Fall Line" of the geographers limited settlement. Beyond that, it was no question of ships out of London or Bristol, but of that admirably functional invention of the Indian, the canoe, and in winter that other Indian invention, the snowshoe. (Only comparatively recently has the American adopted the even more functional Norwegian ski for winter use, for cattle-tending as well as for winter sports.)

Along the coast, clearing the forest was comparatively easy; communication between settlement and settlement, between colony and mother country, comparatively easy too. But away from the coastal plain it was very different. The only easy river way into the heart of America was in French hands, so the masters of the St. Lawrence were exploring the Mississippi and seeing the possibilities of what is now the site of Chicago, while the English settlers were

8

still pinned to the coast. True, there runs inland from New York the admirable natural road of the valleys of the Hudson and the Mohawk. But across this corridor lay the most formidable of Indian warriors, the Five Nations of the Iroquois. They were allies of the English against the French; they co-operated with the first great Irish-American politician, Colonel Thomas Dongan, Governor of New York for James II. But they were a barrier that the feeble colonists could not then force.

And far more feeble tribes than the Iroquois were barriers too. In the early days the Indians were not outnumbered. As they got guns from the quarreling European settlers, they were not hopelessly outclassed in equipment, and the forest, hundreds of thousands of square miles of it, was their home. To it they were adapted; to its climate, its trails, its honey, its cranberries, its game, to its possibilities for the hunter and warrior. The English settler had to learn all this; perhaps no settler really learned the necessary woodcraft—but his sons did. An Indian war in the seventeenth century was no joke. To push too far inland was to risk disaster and the holding up of westward advance for a generation. This was learned on the Connecticut River round Northampton, more recently famous as the home of cautious Cal Coolidge and of one of the most famous of American women's colleges, Smith. Monuments, tradition, a local patriotism that is genuine if carefully cultivated, keep this memory green among the Polish and Italian children of the region today. It was a far more vivid and compelling memory a century ago, and a positive barrier to reckless advance two centuries ago. When the whole frontier flamed up in one of the recurrent wars with France, fortunate and few were those, from Maine to the Carolinas, who lost neither life nor scalps nor cattle nor friends. Eternal vigilance was the price not of liberty only but of life; the early settlers long needed to acquire a craft equaling the craft of the savages and a savagery not much inferior.

It is hard to remember this today in a pleasant village like Farmington, even with the sparsely settled communities of Maine not far north of Boston to remind us how American America was. But it has to be remembered all the same.

If the settlers on the Atlantic coast had to adjust themselves to a new world, how much more the settlers in the late eighteenth century who passed the mountain barrier and entered the Mississippi Valley! On the seaboard the ocean route to England was still open. The planter, the merchant, the minister, the physician could order books and clothes and luxuries from the Old World; he could and did dream of a visit "home," could sigh like Increase Mather after the metropolitan delights of Newington Green, could recall in tranquillity like Franklin the courts he had seen and the king he had dined with. Across the mountains, it was a far newer world. All the Great Valley was veined with creeks and streams and rivers—all finding their way to the Mississippi and the Gulf of Mexico. Once in the Valley, geography conspired to unite all the Valley dwellers one with another and to cut them off from the seaboard and from Europe. Many hundreds of miles away lay the Spanish King's city of New Orleans that one Bourbon monarch had transferred to another just as the English-speaking tide began to lip over the mountains. To that remote trading town the rivers drew the settlers. For them there was no importation of English broadcloth and Spanish wine. They had to fend for themselves, make their own crude tools and their own rough textiles, ship east their one valuable small-bulk product, whisky, and their bulk products, corn and hogs and hides, down the rivers to New

Orleans. Down river was easy enough, but up river was slow, dangerous, and unprofitably laborious. The men and women who went into the West were necessarily stripped to bare necessities by their environment.

The primitive life of those stranded pioneers, belated survivals of the eighteenth century, the mountaineers of Tennessee and the Ozarks, shows what was involved in settling the Great Valley. Men and women came into it with capital laboriously brought from Europe or laboriously accumulated on the seaboard. And that capital was sunk in opening the West. The children of the settlers were more American than their parents, better adjusted to their environment, with less of the luxuries of the Old World about them. They read less—if they could read; they had fewer books, fewer refinements; their equipment of English and Scottish ballads, their Bibles, their *Pilgrim's Progress* and Blackstone's *Commentaries* represented diminishing assets. In the seaboard settlements it had been possible to create, on a basis of tobacco and rice raised by slave labor in the South, of slave trading, of careful commerce in rum and molasses and cod and ships in the North, a reasonably plausible simulacrum of the contemporary civilized society of England. Boston and Philadelphia, Charleston and the great Virginia plantations were not in the least barbarous communities, though their wealth, their culture, and their social structure were more adequate than ample. The Virginia plantation houses were elegant, at any rate when they were first built, but by the standards of English magnates they were small and cheap. Even Westover was far from being a Woburn or a Chatsworth. The little cities were clean and often in parts elegant; Charleston was beautiful. But they were small and provincial compared not only with London, but with the Edinburgh of Principal Robertson, the Glasgow of Professor Adam

Smith, the Birmingham of Joseph Priestley and James Watt. They were outposts of the Old World rather than capitals of the New.

Far more American and far more touching to the historical imagination are the old towns of the Middle West. They are not old by American standards, much less by European; some of them—St. Louis and Cincinnati, for instance—have become great cities like other great American cities. It is not the cities that made the grade which are touching and symbolic, but the little towns that did not. Vincennes, Marietta, Bardstown, Lexington—these were centers of civilization, of learning, of religion, of commerce. Some, like Gallipolis, represent highly unsuccessful enterprises; others had their brief day and now are content to be minor centers, like Cairo. Here was an early college; there an early cathedral. This town had the first steamboat in its region; that one sank all its capital in a now grass-grown canal. And all around these little settlements was the forest or the ominous empty meadows of Kentucky's "dark and bloody ground." All around them were the Indians; the southern kinsmen of the Iroquois; new tribes like the Choctaw and the Cherokee. New names replaced old Indian names. Pontiac and Tecumseh played the roles of Powhatan and King Philip. There were wars and massacres. Chicago remembers the massacre of Fort Dearborn; all the West remembers Tippecanoe and Fallen Timbers; knows who opened Ohio, who Alabama, for whom Jackson and Fort Wayne are named. That typical Middle-Western town of Muncie, Indiana—the city made famous as "Middletown"—gets its name from an Indian tribe whose chief Little Turtle gave his daughter in marriage to the white adventurer who opened up the region as Powhatan had given Pocahontas to John Rolfe. The place names show the intermingling of races and cultures in the vast forest land. Indian names are everywhere: Ohio and Tennessee, the Wabash and the Scioto; Chicago and Sheboygan. There are French names—Vincennes and Jawbone, which was once Narbonne. There are St. Louis named under Louis XV to commemorate Louis IX, and Louisville, which was called after Louis XVI, as Marietta was called after Marie Antoinette. There is Terre Haute in Indiana and its Hellenized version, Akron, in Ohio. There is Lexington, which commemorates the first battle of the Revolution, and Washington and Jefferson, Madison and Franklin, are commemorated over and over again. There are Springfields that recall New England, and "licks" like French Lick that tell us that here the necessary salt was found. There is Memphis as well as Cairo, Salem, and Warsaw. Ypsilanti recalls the Greek War of Independence; there is Toledo and New Madrid; Racine and Oxford. It is a palimpsest with one line hastily written over another as the whites moved in like so many imitators of Adam, naming rivers and lakes, hills and towns in the land they had to conquer and create.

For even more than on the seaboard the forest was here an enemy. So it was attacked as an enemy; devastated like the Palatinate by the French or Munster by the English. It was burned; forest fires were the most natural thing in the world with the newcomers pressing on. The great trees were girdled, their bark cut through till they died; their stumps were left in the ground; the pioneer farmer plowed or planted round them. The rifle and the ax were at least as necessary as the spade or the plow. Many of the first settlers were semi-nomads like Lincoln's father, fonder of hunting and fishing than of the steady toil of the peasant; ready to move on when the deer and the fish, the bears and game birds grew scarcer or the half-stripped land either salable or obviously worthless. These men were illiterate, often drunken, often violent. They had lost a great deal in their adaptation to the Indian world of the forest. They resented, sometimes, the book-learning coveted by boys like the young Lincoln; they would have appreciated better a son like Huckleberry Finn. They might have become as completely assimilated to the Indian way of life as did so many of the French *coureurs de bois* like the great Du Lhut, after whom the great iron port of Duluth is named. But they were saved from that by their numbers and by their women. To live like the Indians meant to live thinly, scattered over the forest, paying respect (except in wartime) to the hunting rights of neighboring tribes, meeting on neutral grounds like Kentucky; a way of life that the world has delighted to read about since Cooper created the Indian legend, but which the modern world has refused to live. The men crossing the mountains from the English settlements were not a handful like the French coming into the Great Lakes from the St. Lawrence; they came in tens of thousands, year after year; they crowded out the Indians; they crowded out their own semi-nomad population. They were farmers, not fur traders or hunters; they were bad, wasteful, unsettled, technically backward farmers, but they were farmers all the same. And they did not come alone—the women came with them.

It was a hard world for the men; it was a far harder world for the women. For all the elements of a woman's life had to be created; the home had to be built, the settled community life had to be created; the possibility of a non-savage life for the children had to be made out of nothing. It was on the women, confined to the cabin, that the worst hardships fell. They died of plagues like the milk-sick; their children died of it. They died in childbed; if modern America seems full of widows, America a century ago was full of widowers. It was the women who suffered from the laxity of the marriage bond, from the footloose husband or lover, from the savage feuds bred in drinking bouts, from the shiftlessness of the man who could and did live much as does an animal, taking little permanent interest in his children or their mother. It was Lincoln's stepmother who encouraged him to read, who gave him his first glimpse of civilization. It was she to whom his gratitude went out; his father he despised and ignored. It was Lincoln's wife, from the comparatively old and well-settled state of Kentucky, who tried to make a tidy, socially ambitious man out of the frontier lawyer; she failed, but the second wife of her old beau and her husband's great rival, Stephen Douglas, was more successful. She made the Little Giant dress better and drink less. When Mark Twain made Tom Sawyer's aunt undertake the civilizing of Huckleberry Finn, he may have had his own experience in mind, the adjustment of the manners of a Mississippi pilot to the social standards of Elmira or Hartford; but, whether he had or not, he created an effective symbol. The Mississippi Valley needed to have its hair combed, it needed to have someone see that its boys washed behind the ears.

It was the women who supported the missionaries who came into the wilderness to preach against drink and fornication, to preach for stable marriage, for the literacy needed to read the Bible, for those bourgeois virtues that the Middle West then needed so badly and is only now rich enough, settled enough, secure enough to begin to think it can despise. Great Methodist circuit riders like Peter Cartwright were makers of the society of the Great Valley. So in a less dramatic way were those less flamboyant pioneers like the "Yale Band" who tried to carry New England orthodoxy into a region that needed stronger meat. The revival meeting, orgiastic, anti-intellectual, often ludicrous, was as necessary to the organization of a stable society in the Middle West as the steamboat that could move upstream from New Orleans to St. Paul. Religion, if sufficiently emotional, simple, and relevant, could move upstream, too, against the permanent temptations to savage anarchy that the frontier pressed on men who had a natural bias toward anarchy, toward adventure, or they would not have crossed the mountains into the untamed land.

And it was not only the preachers and the women who fought anarchy, who fought the temptations of savage life. The politicians did, the lawyers did. They were great figures in the West round 1800. Sometimes, like Andrew Jackson, they were soldiers and planters as well as politicians and judges. But the Western leader who came to the top by his power of speech, of debate, by his energy and courage (he might have no other standard virtues) was a founder of commonwealths. The young Henry Clay, "the mill boy of the slashes," moving from Virginia to Kentucky and leading the "War Hawks" of 1812 who wanted war to punish the English—and weaken the Indians—was a maker as well as a product of the West. And his power was the power of speech, the power of law. So it was with less brilliant, less well-remembered figures like Thomas Hart Benton, Jackson's leader in the Senate. So it was with that extraordinary figure, Sam Houston, adventurer, politician, soldier, who actually passed years living among the Cherokees with an Indian wife, ready for that unknown destiny that was to make him the hero of Texas—relying as he did, in old Roman fashion, on the favorable omen of an eagle. Clay, Benton, Houston, all had in common a devotion to the Union, to the political system that had made their careers possible, that had in two generations filled the Mississippi Valley from the Canadian border to the Gulf of Mexico with free commonwealths, linked together by the most sacred bond, the Constitution of the United States. That Constitution-worship which sometimes seems so odd today was not odd to them. It was the moral far more than the physical authority of the federal government that had held the infant Union together in the critical years before President Jefferson bought Louisiana—that is, the western bank of the Mississippi and the essential gate to the outer world, New Orleans—from Napoleon. It was Jefferson who had broken the conspiracy of Aaron Burr. It was Jackson who had given the toast: "Our federal union, it must be preserved." It should be remembered that it was quite easy for the settler in the Middle West to have no dealings at all with the government of the United States. He paid no direct taxes; he very often wrote no letters and received none, for the good reason that he and his friends could not write. Yet the only ubiquitous federal officials and federal service were the Postmasters and the Post Office. There were no soldiers except in the Indian country; there were federal courts doing comparatively little business. True, the new Union had built the National Road, down which creaked the Conestoga wagons with their cargo of immigrants' chattels. It fought the Indians from time to time and it had at its disposal vast areas of public lands to be sold on easy terms and finally given away to settlers. But no government that had any claim to be a government at all has had less direct power over the people it ruled. Politics was bound, in these conditions, to be rhetorical, moralizing, emotionally diverting, either a form of sport or a form of religion. The political barbecue, the joint debates between great political leaders were secular equivalents of the camp meeting and the hell-fire sermon.

In the hard and often drab life of the slowly consolidating Western society, politics, for the men at any rate, was a welcome diversion. Torchlight processions, debates that sometimes ended in fights, violent press campaigns that sometimes ended in duels—these were welcome in the days before organized sport had undertaken to provide vicarious excitement for millions. But the role of politics was not always so divorced from drab economic reality.

17

It was a fact of great importance that the West was developed with hardly any interference from the outside, that the necessary minimum of political organization was provided locally and spontaneously, that the West got as much law and order as it thought it needed—and its needs were not exorbitant. There was no organized police force; the local sheriff, totally dependent on local opinion for his posse, for his power of effective action, was no very good match for such organizations as the Murrell gang before the Civil War or the James Boys after it. But when disorder became intolerable, there was a new sheriff, or a lynching, or what in the Far West came to be called a Vigilante organization. As settlement grew closer, simple murder and banditry became more difficult and less tolerable. But the idea of the imposition of order from the outside, of an absolutely inflexible system of law enforced with cold impartiality, was not a Western idea. A lawyer there needed to have more than his wits about him; he needed personal prestige—a reputation for honesty, courage, presence of mind, or accurate marksmanship, or for all of these qualities—before he could be a success as a defending counsel, not to speak of a district attorney or a judge. Effective law was an aspect of the character of some man or men.

Yet if there was a good deal of lawlessness, there was real respect for law. There was a general acceptance of the authority of the State and the Union. There was no equivalent of Spanish-American revolutions, no encouragement given to mere *pronunciamientos,* though a man like Andrew Jackson in a Spanish environment would have had all the talents and temperament and temptations of a dictator. But Jackson and his followers and enemies gave to the Constitution of the United States the reverence due to "the supreme law of the land." The federal government was forced to make adjustments in its too rigid land laws, to recognize the effective rights of squatters on the public lands. Locally, it was polite not to ask too many questions of a man arriving from another state, with or without a lady companion. But no society could have grown so fast if the minimum basis of law had not been provided by the free choice of the people, the only effective authority. On the Western frontier, the general will, like the political equality of all (white) men, was no fiction of a political philosopher but an observable reality.

The system was tested very severely indeed in California, where for the first time the Americans had to deal with the problems of a society suddenly made rich by gold, not slowly made rich by work, a society in which there were few women, a society in which cities sprang into existence overnight without the long discipline of exploration, settlement, urban growth. Any human society might have been baffled by the problem of San Francisco in 1850 —and some societies would have found better remedies for disorder than highly respectable organized lynch law. A few years later, British authority preserved legality and order far more effectively in Australia and in British Columbia than American authority did in California. But then among the things with which California had to contend was an invasion of "Sydney ducks" and other hard cases from the convict settlements of infant Australia and no Californian looking at the results—Australia and California—will doubt which method bore the more delicious, superior, and colossal fruit. Yet even in California, the civilizing influences were soon at work as the story of the mother of the philosopher Josiah Royce shows. The first, masculine, anarchical barbarism was soon being assailed by women, by teachers, by politicians. California settled down—at any rate, as much as it was reasonable to expect of that favored land and exuberant population.

Few things, on consideration, prove less surprising

than the evaporation of federal authority over the South once secession was adopted. Almost the only federal institution that meant anything to the common man was the Post Office—and by a statesmanlike turning of the blind eye, the new Southern Confederacy continued to allow the federal government to deliver the mail even after the seceding states had formally broken with the Union. What is surprising is not the disappearance of federal authority from Washington south to the Mexican border and west to Arizona, but the fact that, at a cost of half a million lives, it *was* restored in a four-year war that imposed on the North as great an ordeal as any victorious nation has undergone until our times, and on the South a defeat whose penalties in loss of life, wealth, and security were proportionately far greater than those imposed on Germany by the loss of the war of 1914–18.

The impact of the Civil War on American life and American memory can hardly be exaggerated. It is still "the war"; its heroes on both sides gave their names to forts and training camps (Sheridan, Thomas); from its leaders, on both sides, tanks took their names (Grant, Sherman, Stuart). From 1868 (the first postwar election) to 1900 inclusive, every man elected President of the United States had with one exception been an officer in the Union army; all but one were ex-generals. Round it legend of all kinds clustered; it is still a sure-fire subject for fiction and the movies. Its battlefields and war cemeteries are sacred in a special way. Chancellorsville, Fredericksburg, Vicksburg, Stone River, Chickamauga, Lookout Mountain, Atlanta, Petersburg—these are still fighting names. The tactics, the strategy of the war are fought over again in magazines, in reviews, in books. South of the Potomac it is still a near-fighting word to call this conflict anything but "the War between the States." There are still unreconstructed rebels in Georgia and men who still think treason odious in Vermont—and northern Tennessee. The Civil War is not the only genuine American war (as apart from wars waged by the United States). There is the War of the Revolution, there are Bunker Hill and Brandywine. There is the War of 1812 with its memories of victories on sea to offset defeat on land—and the memory, too, of that crowning victory of New Orleans, won after peace had been made, a victory cherished for its very pointlessness—and for giving in Jackson Day (January 8) a national festival to the Democratic Party. There are Indian wars, too; in Minnesota, perhaps the Sioux War of 1862 is as important as the share of the new state in the Civil War. And in Texas, the war against Mexico is the center of state and world history. But all of these wars are American wars, fought on American soil about issues local to America, relevant to the great theme of the conquest and use of the American soil. In the first European war more American lives were lost than in any domestic war except that of 1861–5; but it was not merely an undertaker's ramp when the bodies of the American dead were brought back to America. There was no American equivalent of Rupert Brooke's conviction that his body would make "some corner of a foreign field . . . forever England," no monument in the Argonne or at Cantigny or perhaps even the flag hoisted on Iwo Jima in a later and greater war that has anything like the hold on American hearts and memories that Vimy Ridge has for Canadians or the beaches of Gallipoli for Australians and New Zealanders. No war fought outside the present boundaries of the United States has so far been taken to the hearts and memories of the American people. The Marines may commemorate "the halls of Montezuma" and "the shores of Tripoli," but for the average American, the really sacred sites are places like Concord, where the first shots of the Revolution were fired against the British, or Gettysburg, where Lee's army,

> *broken, reeled*
> *From a stubborn Meade and a barren field.*

And Concord and Gettysburg have this other claim to memory that their ideological meaning was made plain by two utterances that have become American classics. At Concord, said Emerson:

> *By the rude bridge that arched the flood,*
> *Their flag to April's breeze unfurled,*
> *Here once the embattled farmers stood*
> *And fired the shot heard round the world.*

And that shot echoed eighty-eight years later in Lincoln's declaration that "We here highly resolve that these dead shall not have died in vain—that this nation, under God, shall have a new birth of freedom—and that government of the people, by the people, for the people, shall not perish from the earth."

It has long been fashionable to reduce the ideological content of the War of the Revolution and the Civil War to, at most, a trace. But even if the "glittering generalities" of the Declaration of Independence, like their echo in the Gettysburg speech, will not stand strict semantic or historical examination (which is not yet proved), the fact that the American people believe that their two great ordeals by battle, in one of which the new nation was born and in the other saved, had their origin in different views of the political good life is a fact of great practical importance. It puts a limit to the possibilities of mere *Realpolitik* as a possible American policy. To ignore this is not to be realist but to be romantic.

Nevertheless, the emotional interest evoked by the

Civil War has other roots, too. For what was at issue was not solely the moral character of slavery (though that was at issue), nor the rights and duties of minorities (though that was at issue), nor the nature of the federal union (though that was at issue). It was the unity, the future of the great interior valley in which alone the character of a new American people could be given to the immigrants, from Europe and from the Atlantic seaboard alike. The decisive event of those years was the entry of the railroad into the Mississippi Valley, an event even more decisive than Nicholas Roosevelt's first Mississippi steamboat. For the steamboat only made it easier to exploit the river system; the railroad made it possible to defy it. No longer must traffic run north and south, with such successful though not decisive modifications as the Erie Canal that joined the Great Lakes to the mouth of the Hudson and made New York the unquestioned metropolis, or such failures at modification as that Potomac Canal in which George Washington saw the solution of the old problem of joining Virginia to the West. The railroads defied the map. They went west across the mountains or, when New York got round to it and found its canal monopoly threatened, by the flat road Nature had provided up the Hudson and across by the Mohawk. They linked the Mississippi Valley to the seaboard as it had never yet been linked. The Union was made real by the new iron bonds that each year got farther west—to Albany, to Pittsburgh, to Wheeling, to Columbus, to St. Louis, to Chattanooga, to Atlanta, to Chicago, to St. Joseph. But these bonds were bonds binding the West to the North. Only Chattanooga and Atlanta were southern versions of the great American novelty, the town whose basic position was created by the railroad, such as Chicago and Kansas City and Omaha. No longer did the rivers tie up the Great Valley to New Orleans; the railroads tied it up to New York and Philadelphia and Baltimore. The battle for the control of the new West, economically, politically, socially, was won by the side that had the most railroads; the war in a double sense was a railroad war; it was fought to upset an old economic and political balance of power, and the war that arose from this attempt was won by the side that the railroads fought for. It was symbolic and more than merely symbolic that the only really important case in which Lincoln was ever briefed was a railroad case; that his rival, Stephen Douglas, was a great railroad lawyer and spokesman; that President Jefferson Davis of the Southern Confederacy had, as federal Secretary of War, tried to secure that the transcontinental railroad, when it came, should take the southern route.

Within ten years of the end of the war, the great representative river port, St. Louis, at the junction of the Missouri and Mississippi, had built its magnificent Eads bridge over the levees at which the river steamers were beginning to be tied up to rot. And it was no accident that within five years of the ending of the war, the English-speaking tide that had slowly crept from the Atlantic to the Missouri in two hundred and fifty years had rushed over the fifteen-hundred-mile gap to California.

With the coming of the railroad, some victories over the American land were made possible that no energy, courage, or ingenuity could have won before. The settlers, habituated to the great forest, had reluctantly and with much trepidation ventured forth on to the lone prairie. Indeed, it was English settlers, more used to open country, who in Illinois had dared to leave the well-watered and wooded river bottoms for the great sea of grass. On the open prairie there was no timber for housing to build the log cabins of the pioneers, to provide timber for the rails that Lincoln, like so many more, had split to make fences, no timber for fuel, and little water that had not to be dug for. But with the coming of the railroad came corrugated iron and wire fencing and commercial timber for houses, and young trees to make windbreaks, and traveling salesmen from whom the farmer could order newfangled gadgets like windmills and reapers, and his wife could order newfangled gadgets like sewing-machines. The railway that brought could take away; the once practically self-supporting farmer was now forced to sell his grain at world prices, fixed in Liverpool and relayed (with modifications) through the Chicago Board of Trade, the "Pit." He had always been a gambler; now he was more of a gambler than ever, a gambler with little knowledge but with great courage. But the land was fertile. Europe was growing richer and more greedy. To the west lay the High Plains where the buffalo roamed in millions till the railroad cut the great herd in two, till the Winchesters of tourists and buffalo-hide hunters and cattlemen eager for grazing lands reduced the bison to a few thousand guarded specimens on reservations where the Indians, deprived of their whole economic basis, had preceded him. It was no wonder that to the outside world the typical Western hero of this generation should be called "Buffalo Bill."

For a few years, the open range reproduced the life of the nomad Indian with the semi-savage Texas Longhorns and the not very civilized cowboys as representatives of the buffalo and the Indian. Those were the days when the great American legend of the Wild West was created for the delight of the whole white world. Then the great Western bandits and bad men replaced the Gargantuan figures of Mississippi legend like Mike Fink, the giant boatman, or the Finn McCool or Little John of the northern forest, Paul Bunyan. Mike Fink and Paul Bunyan were legends; not so the James brothers or the Dalton brothers or such precocious bad men as Billy the Kid or the most remarkable killer of them all, the boy John Wesley Hardin.

Again, settlement had gone much faster than order. The new frontier was lawless enough. Cheyenne, Dodge City, Tombstone with its Boot Hill cemetery for those deceased residents who had died with their boots on—these were reflections on the American sense of order.

So, too, were the Indian wars which the experience of Canada showed could have been avoided and which produced the apparently ludicrous spectacle of two great soldiers like Sherman and Sheridan, who, a few years before, had commanded armies of scores of thousands, directing the movements of little columns pursuing such masters of American war and politics as Chief Joseph, Geronimo, and Sitting Bull. And there was irony as well as tragedy in the fact that in the year in which the centenary of American independence was celebrated, the Sioux under Rain-in-the-Face destroyed the dramatic and dramatized General Custer and all his men at the Indian Cannæ, the Little Big Horn, where the mounted savages rode round and round the doomed whites like Hannibal's Numidian cavalry and —more fortunate than the Carthaginians—left their own pictographic record of their victory. But no savage generalship could defeat civilization. On the plains of Texas the six-shooter made the white man on a horse more than a match for the mounted Indian with his bow and arrow, who had hitherto been more than a match for a man armed only with a single-shot rifle. The Winchester repeating rifle did the job farther north, and more and more railroad lines cut across the prairie and the High Plains. Sheepmen came into the cow country and fought for the possession of the strategic water holes without which it was useless to have legal title to tens of thousands of acres. New mining camps like Leadville repeated in Colorado the violent history of California. The open range over which cattle moved a thousand miles from Texas to Canada began to be cut up into ranches, wired off and guarded.

Big cattlemen fought open and concealed wars with little cattlemen, using force when chicane failed. The bitter winter of 1886 ruined big and little alike—and put an end to the easy profits of the Edinburgh land companies which had revived in Scottish breasts the seventeenth-century hopes of easy profits to be drawn across the Atlantic. New state after new state was added; the last free Indians were herded into reservations; vigilant and quick-shooting sheriffs like Bat Masterson provided a reasonable amount of law and order; and by the centenary of the Constitution (1889) the West was no longer, by Western standards, wild. It was served and ruled by the great railroads whose names are as magical to Americans, almost, as the names of the great rivers that the railroads robbed of so much economic importance: Union Pacific, Southern Pacific, Texas Pacific, Northern Pacific, Great Northern, and that line which, in its very title, sums up the history of the American movement into the country of the Indian and the Spaniard—the Atchison, Topeka & Santa Fe.

In 1890, a hundred years after the four million settlers on the Atlantic seaboard were first numbered, the federal census took note that the frontier was closed, and a poet in one deservedly immortal couplet summed it all up:

Across the plains where once there roamed
the Indian and the Scout,
The Swede with alcoholic breath
sets rows of cabbage out.

By that time it was easy to be sentimental about both the Indian and the Scout. Little boys, all over the white world, played in Indian dress and, reckless of historical accuracy, imported into the forest habitat of Seneca or Mohican the magnificent but, in that environment, quite impossible feather headdress of the Sioux or the Nez Percé. Buffalo Bill, from a scout, became a circus turn. While the

27

last veterans of the old circus West were dying, the movies were born to make the American Sherwood Forest part of the world's great legends.

But the seriocomic ending of the great western movement should not blind us to its importance. It was one of the most decisive campaigns in world history, won in nearly three hundred years of ceaseless battle. And the unity of the great central, fertile, and fantastically rich mass of North America had been fought for desperately, successfully. The almost invisible and practically impotent federal government of 1861 had survived one of the most desperate ordeals by battle that modern history has seen. Those political institutions that seemed incapable of minimum order, of minimum efficiency, that political system which seemed a mere amusement answered the question put by Lincoln whether "a nation conceived in liberty and dedicated to the proposition that all men are created equal . . . can long endure." It did endure, and the losers in the great battle, with their bitter sense of defeat and their more bitter sense of exploitation and betrayal by the victors after their defeat, accepted the judgment of arms. It was Jefferson Davis who at the end of his long apologia for his cause and himself put the motto *Esto perpetua*. However bitterly the ex-President of the Confederate States of America may have felt, none of his fellow Southerners have ever again attempted to undo that "more perfect union" promised in 1789 by the Constitution to the struggling and straggling seaboard states when the greatest of European states was entering on that cycle of revolution from which neither France nor Europe has yet emerged. The United States have stayed united; the American people has been made.

2

IN THE COURSE of conquering America and so making Americans, habits were adopted out of urgent necessity which may have survived that necessity. There was, for example, the need for overstatement. To get settlers to move to America it was necessary to paint "America the golden" in very golden colors indeed. Very skilled hands undertook this necessary task: good prose-writers like Richard Hakluyt; good or goodish poets like Michael Drayton; good story-tellers of the "when I was in Transylvania" school like Captain John Smith.

And once the voyage was made, the hazard of new fortunes undertaken, pride, exultation at one's own daring, recurrent optimism as new dreams replaced the old, led to the constant "sale" of America to the Old World. For the genuinely adventurous type, for the man and woman whom nature had made ready for America, the exultation and the pride were genuine. Those who did not share in this pride and exultation were probably ill adapted anyway; they died or returned home or kept quiet. They had better, for from the beginning the settlers had no use for "knockers," for anybody who committed the crime of what was to be described in a later age as "selling America short."

The pioneer American had a real economic as well as emotional interest in growth, in encouraging the booster spirit. If he wanted to stay in the new settlement that he had chosen, he had an interest in other people's staying too. Only so could the profitable rise in values which he counted on be realized. Only so could money be borrowed on the future prosperity of the settlement. If the town refused to grow, if it, in fact, was written off as a failure and abandoned by any serious number of its residents, not only were the anticipated gains lost but real losses were suffered, especially after the Supreme Court put the federal government's power behind the claims of the buyers of municipal and county securities. It mattered little or nothing whether the loans had been prudently or even legally contracted; the Supreme Court, over the protests of that great Iowa jurist, Mr. Justice Miller, insisted on collection from the remaining inhabitants. And while the ingenious borrowers might be enjoying their capital gains in the interesting little town of Los Angeles, the less foresighted inhabitants of a town or county on the prairie were forced to pay or be sold up. They were in the position of a Russian village community under the Tsar from which a number of freed serfs had vanished, refusing to pay their share of the redemption price. Pessimism in such a world was treason. And as long as this boom spirit was flourishing, treason it remained. Thus, in a later age when the Florida land boom was collapsing, many communities made desperate, indeed magical efforts to persuade themselves and the world that values were holding up. And on July 4, 1926, the city of St. Augustine, the oldest settlement in the United States, formally buried as an embodiment of that treasonable pessimism "J. Fuller Gloom," with a funeral ceremony conducted according to the rites of the Chamber of Commerce.

But magic notwithstanding, land booms always burst. There have been few American cities that have not had on their outskirts ambitious "developments" that have not come off at all, or have come off only after a long period of holding on. Sometimes the holding on was no great strain. It may be assumed that the losses incurred during the period when only handsome street lamps and magnificent pavements marked most of the development of the old Rockefeller farm in Shaker Heights on the outskirts of Cleveland were no great strain on the Rockefeller fortune. But for less well-financed speculations, the period of holding on might be fatal. The first speculator has so often taken the rap. How few American railroads, how few New York hotels or even more splendid structures in Texas, have not gone through the wringer! How profitable has been the job of receiver! Indeed, there have been times when the innocent investors have been forced to wonder whether "receiver"—meaning the recipient of stolen goods —was not merely a special case of "receiver" meaning the officer appointed by a complaisant court to take over and administer the bankrupt assets of great and small concerns alike. It would be unkind to say on what American railroad this incident occurred, but when I complimented a friend of mine on the improved service on his local railroad, he replied, with no conscious irony: "Oh, service has been swell since it went into receivership; the management can afford to spend money now that it hasn't got to worry about the stockholders." This was a commuter's view, not a stockholder's, but there has always been among Americans, including the luckless investors themselves, a philosophical acceptance of the fact that somebody must hold the bag for the great economic improvements of modern America.

The American farmer is perhaps rather less philosophical than the urban investor. He thinks he has a right to expect not a good living or a good cash income but a permanent and certain increase in the selling value of his land. It is this expectation that makes him hold on through drought and storm, flood and tornado. On this expectation he borrows money and, as a permanent borrower, he has no fear of inflation; like the small boy in the story, far from being troubled by the thought he simply loves it. He knows, in a general, intellectual way, that somebody will have to be the last buyer, but he hopes and trusts that it won't be he. He will be living off the profits, perhaps invested in new lands, perhaps taken out in mortgages or in a rent that takes full account of the presumed value of the land, future as well as present. And the American absentee owner is not necessarily somebody like the late Lord Clanricarde, celebrated miser, tyrant, and last chief of the elder line of the Burkes, but a mild, modest ex-farmer living in decent comfort in the neighborhood of Los Angeles, raising the moral tone of the neighborhood and swelling the crowds at Iowa picnics. He may be simply a resident in a small Iowa town, able to afford a trip to St. Petersburg to pitch horseshoes in the winter sun of Florida. Or he may be like the Vermont farmer who, when asked by a scornful Midwestern visitor what crops were raised on those stony hills, replied: "The chief crop is those good five per cent Iowa mortgages we hold." Every farmer may not have his Cadillac and his town house in Urbana-Champaign or fly his private plane to the county fair, while his wife has her ranch house and picture window, but he hopes to have them. He may ask the government to guarantee "parity," but he does not mean that the floor should also be a ceiling. The web of speculation, of optimism, of boosting is cast over all the nation.

But, of course, there was a real interest in persuading people to stay. The local banker made his money by backing rising values; he lost if they *all* fell. The local doctor who, like John Hay's father, chose the wrong town to settle in, paid for it in a life of comparative shallows and miseries. Hence the importance of prophetic statistics. "Albuquerque 40,000 by 1930." "Hamlet is a fine town, population 800." I don't think Albuquerque made it by 1930, and I suspect that Hamlet had slightly inflated its figures. But editors of encyclopedias and guide-books have got to accept the necessity of printing not only the federal census figures, but the local estimate—which is always larger; millions of Americans appear to sleep out of town on census day.

One way of anchoring a settler is to get him married and settled down to raising a family. Hence the emphasis on good schools; lavish expenditure on school buildings is not necessarily a totally disinterested tribute to education; it is a bribe to wandering parents. But of course it would not be a bribe to parents who had not the inherited or acquired New England belief in education as a good thing. Even more effective anchorage was investment in a house —or, as the Americans say, a home. And expensive, highly ornamental homes were proof that the settlement was taking root. As Mark Twain put it long ago (in *Life on the Mississippi*): "Every town and village along that vast stretch of double river frontage had a best dwelling, finest dwelling, mansion—the home of its wealthiest and most conspicuous citizen." They still have, although today one would hardly expect to be believed if he asserted what Mark Twain asserted with no apparent fear of contradiction: "Not a bathroom in the house; and no visitor likely to come along who has ever seen one."

These optimistic exhibitions of civic pride have long been a British jest, a jest which sophisticated Americans have more recently joined in. But most Americans are still touchy on the subject of local improvements, as I discovered when I made an innocent joke about the Chicago drainage canal in a London paper. The European visitor lacks the eye of faith. Thus Dickens made Cairo, Illinois, the butt of his angry wit in his picture of "Eden" in *Martin Chuzzlewit;* but twenty years later, Anthony Trollope found that picture too flattering. "I doubt whether that author ever visited Cairo in midwinter, and I am sure he never visited Cairo when Cairo was the seat of an American army. Had he done so, his love of truth would have forbidden him to presume that even Mark Tapley could have enjoyed himself in such an Eden."[1] But only a quarter of a century after Trollope played the sourpuss, Cairo was given a big hand by a local resident. "Three years ago people said all the hateful things they could about Cairo. Now they are lavish in their praises. The paper says we'll monopolize all the trade of the Mississippi, Ohio, Tennessee and Cumberland Rivers. Our new grain elevator is one of the largest in the world, new railroads are constantly striking us. We've the most magnificent hotel (run on the grandest scale) in this part of the country, telephone system, new Opera House, elegant one, going up, street-cars soon to be running, and we are altogether citified."[2] So wrote a very bright, very nice local girl, a girl nicer and certainly much brighter than any Dickens or Trollope heroine I can remember. Cairo did not become a new St. Louis or Chicago, but "Maud" liked it and believed in it, and what was good enough for her should have been good enough for any reasonable body.

This conception of growth as everybody's business, everybody's interest, is deep-rooted in the American national psychology. The bulky real-estate supplements of the Sunday papers are no doubt largely kept going as an advertising revenue-producer, but they would produce no advertising and no revenue if no one read them. The Englishman, hidden behind his hedge or wall, is not interested in his neighbor's house, and the idea of wanting to read about houses bought, sold, or built by total strangers is not even funny; it is merely absurd. The only time real-estate development is news in England is when a temple is found in the foundations. The Cockneys took much more interest in the temple of Mithras than in the Bucklersbury House to be built on the site.

---

[1] Anthony Trollope: *North America*, Vol. II, p. 121.
[2] *Maud*, edited and arranged for publication by Richard Lee Strout (Macmillan), p. 22.

But to an American, it is not only important, it is comforting, it is gratifying to know that other people are improving your home town; even people who have no personal economic stake in the rise of real-estate values feel the same kind of interest that makes a motherly woman smile with genuine amiability on the children of total strangers. The very linguistic difference between "house" and "home" is significant. All Americans who live in houses, not apartments, live in homes; the Englishman lives in *his* home but all his neighbors live in houses or flats.

The interest of the American in community growth is not confined to homes. He is far more aware of the size and importance of public and business buildings than anybody in England is. To the inhabitants of Minneapolis, the Foshay Tower was a symbol of growth, of maturity, that did not lose its value when the too enterprising entrepreneur went to jail. But in London, people do not long notice what new buildings have gone up and, after a month or two, find it hard to remember what stood on the site cleared by a German bomb. The idle, the curious are no more numerous in America than elsewhere, but those gazers on men-at-work on a new building whom the Americans call "sidewalk superintendents" are a more representative class of citizen than their English fellows. When John D. Rockefeller, Jr., built a covered-in observation post for the comfort of these spectators during the winter when Rockefeller Center was being built, he was not only acting with genuine American hospitality, he was recognizing a genuine and generous American interest in building as such. It is not at all unlikely that, among the spectators who watched with approving interest the new buildings which were rising with a speed that, by our standards, is really not very much slower than the speed with which Aladdin built his palace for the Princess, were stockholders in the Empire State Building. And they had nothing but a truly American tradition to encourage them to cheer the progress of a rival monument to the passion for the bigger and better—or, at any rate, bigger.

In pioneering conditions, personal credit—credit for courage, for competence, for industry, for economic promise —was all-important. A pioneering community was composed of people all of whom were extending credit to each other as well as to the locality. When conditions were a little better, a little more settled, credit in the ordinary sense became important, but it was personal, too. The village banker in America was not in the position of the village usurer in Europe. His debtors could walk out on him; they were not anchored to the spot by tradition, by hereditary investment in land and family pride, by the difficulty of finding any place to go—except America. Indeed, in Ireland, classic land of the village usurer, lending money to pay fares to America was one of the chief business opportunities—and risks. So there was a mutual assessment of need and greed. But the village banker, unlike the European village moneylender, was himself living on credit; and when it failed him, he might be the sudden migrant, leaving his debtors legally tied to his creditors, while he sought fresh woods and pastures new. Altogether, moneylending and borrowing were more of a sport in America than in Europe, and banking, in the West at any rate, called for rather different qualities from what it demands from a citizen of London or a financier of Wall Street. Mr. Ogden Nash's gloomy reflections on the parentage of great American bankers are not, as far as I know, borne out by the facts, but they fit the national tradition of classing bankers with the other robber barons—though it must be remembered that these robber barons were highly popular as long as they shared or were believed to be sharing the spoil.

But one result of this necessity for and acceptance of the conditions of credit is that publicity must be accepted.

If you want (as most American women do want) to have a charge account or a series of charge accounts, you must submit your husband's credit rating to professional and competent investigation. It is of little use for the American husband to try to obey the old maxim of folk-wisdom that bids a husband keep secret from his wife the amount of money he has, if she can, in effect, make a pretty good guess by trying to stretch his credit at a department store. The general acceptance of debt, however disguised, as a normal state of existence for many worthy people no doubt leads to ostentatious expenditure, to conspicuous waste, as it leads to non-functional automobile design and other specimens of art for show's sake. But it also leads to a fish-bowl existence in which the English passion for privacy would offend public opinion and constitute a luxury that only a very large independent income could support. What I have been told of life in official circles in India—that the public knowledge of the incomes of all the nice people cut out certain kinds of ostentatious expenditure—applies to many American communities, too. They all try to keep up with the Joneses, but they are local Joneses, with accounts at local banks and stores. The attempt to keep up with remote Joneses, to ape the manners and expenditure of remote social circles, and the refusal to admit that there is in that community anybody with whom it is really possible to associate on terms of equality—this is more common in Streatham than in Bronxville. American life imposes respect for the human interest of the community in your private affairs; a refusal to conform at that level is, in fact, a vote of censure on the community which it has no intention of submitting to. You can defy it, but at the cost of being laughed at, not admired—and possibly at the cost of having the local bank wonder if anybody so high-hat can be a good risk.

It has to be admitted that this national spirit was often hard on dissenters—dissenters, that is, from the religion of economic and political optimism. A pioneer community could afford to house very hard citizens; it often benefited by the energies of persons who, to use modern terms, "cut their ethical corners rather fine." Courage, enterprise, ingenuity—these were qualities from which everybody benefited, or nearly everybody. So, in many ways, the frontier settlement was very tolerant. But it was not tolerant of the man whose arrogance or pride or morbid pessimism made him a nuisance in a society where all had to hang together if they were not to starve or be scalped separately. Pennsylvania could afford some Quakers, but not too many, in a great crisis like the French and Indian War; but the Revolutionary party in 1776 could not afford to be tolerant of too many Tories (i.e., Loyalists), since it was by no means certain how the lukewarm majority would react if given a strong lead by the Tories. So it was necessary to give them a strong lead on the revolutionary side.

Religious dissent was more tolerable—as long as it was not dissent from the social creed of the growing nation, or disbelief in economic prosperity, or objection to military service, or real belief in the imminent end of the world. And dissenters or even "atheists" or "deists" were often very energetic and valuable citizens, promoters, and fighters. Indeed, it is possible that as things settled down, as communities acquired more coherence, the role of the religious or political dissenter got harder, since his other qualities became less necessary. But there remained legitimate grounds of dissent. After the Civil War any well-established village in New England or the northern Middle West could afford a town drunkard, a town atheist, and a few Democrats.

But a habit grew up in which it was necessary to call on some courage and perhaps on some independent economic resources before defying the local folkways. The

very friendliness of American life made the dissenter more
conspicuous. In a country where minding your own business is *de rigueur,* nobody need care what that business is.
But in a country where all life is or should be lived pretty
publicly, there is more intolerance of an individual eccen-
tricity which is being continually thrust under the eyes of
your neighbors. The high degree of social integration of a
small American city (above a certain income level) plays
its part, too. The tragedy of Mr. John O'Hara's *Appointment in Samarra* involves more than the weakness of the
hero; it involves a life made intolerable if the country club
and the local business community are mobilized against
you. The highly individual character is a misfit in a community in any country, whether his weakness is genius or
madness. If he has a private income like Cézanne, he may
pursue his vision unmolested. But what Cézanne called
"les grappins" are more tenaciously extended in America
than elsewhere; they put out their tentacles more determinedly, and a persistent evasion of their embraces is
more offensive than it would be in a French or English
town with no common social life anyway.

And since the common interest of the community
is still assumed to be economic growth, attained by the
"American way," the dissenter from the end, or the means,
is especially open to suspicion. But 1929 wrought a great
change, probably a permanent one. The sponsors of the old
programs have not quite the same confident ring in their
voices; too many things have been tried and have failed;
the "American way" has been found to be a term less pre-
cise than it seemed in the presidential election of 1928, when
the problem of poverty was solved and when the good
citizens should have been busily expanding their garages
to take the second car that was coming along with tomorrow's sunrise. The boom of 1929 was nothing to the
boom of 1956, the prosperity of the age of Coolidge nothing

to the prosperity of the era of Truman and Eisenhower. Yet the memory of the great deception remains. The memory of the yesterdays that lighted fools is still lively; the American public still has its fingers crossed; and, perhaps, has more fear of a depression than of treason, though treason can be talked of and denounced while the dread word "depression" can hardly be murmured.

Nevertheless, the strident tone of American controversy, though not unparalleled in modern British history, is a reminder of a national tradition, pragmatically justified, in which dissent, especially continuous pessimistic crabbing, was near to treason. So the High School of Muncie teaches loyalty to Muncie as well as to the United States, and in less straightforward communities something of the same spirit prevails in more sophisticated forms.

3

IT WAS NOT surprising that the Americans, at the end of their long march from ocean to ocean, should have too hastily assumed that they "had America licked." But it was an error, all the same. The continent remained not so much hostile as capricious; the gorgeous West, pouring out wealth with lavish hand, often had more than a hand inside the glove. The settlers in the South and in the Mississippi Valley had had to deal with diseases that, to northern Europeans, were very hard to manage. There was yellow fever, coming in from the West Indies; there was pellagra; there was hookworm; there was malaria. Some of these diseases became manageable as modern medical technology developed; Gorgas and Manson and Pasteur and Ross not only made the Panama Canal a possibility—they also made an easier and safer life possible in the continental United States. Pellagra is curable mainly through a rise in economic standards, and—so far as that has come about—pellagra has been cured; although in the poverty-stricken and decaying regions of the South it is still a menace to white and black poor alike—and a disease that makes life disagreeable in Umbria has even less to make it tolerable in the derelict regions of Georgia. Malaria needs fighting by cleanliness, and this, too, involves economic factors, for it is far harder for the poor to be clean than for the rich. Hookworm is highly debilitating, but you are much less likely to get it if you wear shoes—and shoes cost money; there is nothing romantic about being a barefoot boy in the hookworm belt. Improved water supply, improved medical services, even the rudiments of organized sanitation were necessary to turn the depressed and despised "mudsills" of the South—once denounced for their quite sensible habit of eating "dirt" (i.e., earth) as a remedy for the deficiencies caused by hookworm—into healthy and energetic citizens. The work of the Rockefeller Foundation and of the state and federal governments did more for this Southern problem than cubic miles of Southern oratory—although some excellent oratory was devoted to getting the South to accept Northern aid. And among the many things which the New Deal set out to do for the South (where so many New Deal votes were cast and some New Dealers even got elected) was to subsidize the building of privies. When the federal government went into the same business as Lemuel Putt of Sangamon County, that was news—and good news.

But the South was especially handicapped, climatically, historically, racially, economically. The problem of making the Middle West habitable was much easier; it required wealth and energy and scientific knowledge, which the region acquired in abundance. It also required a high degree of political efficiency, which was not so abundant. The Chicago drainage canal, though a reasonably adequate solution for Chicago, was less attractive to her downstream neighbors. But other breakdowns only prove that human institutions are human; a local collapse of sanitary efficiency is no more to be wondered at in Chicago than in Croydon.

Even the most favored regions had their drawbacks. The first settlers who moved into the Pacific slope were richly rewarded. Oregon, reasonably warm, well wooded, well watered, was more like Devon than like Illinois. And California, to the pioneers coming over the High Sierra or round the Horn, was a new Canaan. Indeed, as the first Americans began to visit the Californian coast, the great empty land with its scattered Mexican ranches was more like the world of Abraham than like the new machine world that already existed on the other side of the

Atlantic. California cried out for more energetic settlers, and a swarm of Moses appeared to seize the land where, in its last spasm of imperial energy, Spain had created the little missions of San Francisco, Santa Barbara, San Luis Rey, San Luis Obispo, San Diego, and—destined to a highly paradoxical destiny—the village called after "Our Lady, Queen of the Angels." California had many attractions, but one struck home in the Great Valley: it had no malaria; "the shakes" were unknown. But, as the unkind Frenchman said of New Zealand, "There are no snakes, but a great many Scotchmen," and even California had its drawbacks. It had no weather, only the most perfect climate in the world, where season followed season in perfect regularity, with hardly an exceptional day. It seemed to be too good to be true. It was. The most regular feature of San Francisco weather was the summer fog, and in even more favored southern California (as a saboteur from Florida put it in *The New Yorker*), "there is no rain, but the heavy dew sometimes washes away the railroad bridges." All around Los Angeles, the justification for this hit below the belt can be seen; empty river beds lined with concrete, provided with admirable bridges, recalling the Manzanares at Madrid. But the old joke to the effect that the Madrileños ought to sell the bridges and buy a river is pointless in the Californian outpost of New Spain, for when the rains do come, they come down with a speed and exuberance that are worthy of the Golden State; seven inches in two days makes very necessary indeed the bridges and parapets that control the arroyos turned torrents. Nor are floods the only trouble in California. The state has no equivalent of those terrible lightning storms of the Middle West, but it does have earthquakes. Significantly, it is still a little tactless to refer (in San Francisco) to "the earthquake of 1906"—you should say "the Fire," because that result of the natural catastrophe is less painful to recall. Fire is a manageable enemy of man and an old one, but when the foundations of the earth move, the most optimistic Californian is reminded of the untamable nature of the American land.

And at the other side of the continent, the rival paradise of Florida has had its bad shocks: in sudden frosts that kill the citrus crops; in devastating tornadoes that wreck the Miami waterfront as thoroughly as a second-class air raid could, or sweep the sea over such bold works of man as the road across the Atlantic to Key West.

In the other parts of America the savage possibilities of the climate are never forgotten. All Ohio remembers the great flood year of 1913, whose impact on Columbus Mr. Thurber has made familiar to English readers. From that disaster came an elaborate and expensive system of flood-control in Columbus, in Dayton, in all southwestern Ohio. But other river towns in other states have had their own and much more recent disasters. The Wabash does not, alas for the citizens of Indiana, always stay within its banks; and when we get to the Mississippi, we are faced with the greatest engineering problem in the Western World. Only the great rivers of China have so bad a record. The floods starting when the ice and snow melt, fifteen hundred miles away from the subtropical delta, present a problem every year. And the news that is flashed down the river has the urgency of an air-raid alert, for ten feet of extra water at Paducah may mean disaster if something is not done *at once* at Vicksburg. So men and boys, white and black, are called out to pile cotton bales and sandbags on the threatened levees; women and children get ready to flee from the rising wall of water being funneled down the river. And somewhere the sides of the funnel give way and tens of thousands are made homeless, hundreds are drowned, and an economic catastrophe that would ruin a minor European state has to be coped with.

Even in the long-settled East, the water is still restive. The Connecticut River, normally as placid as the Thames at Teddington, sometimes goes on the rampage, reminding the inhabitants of cities like Hartford that life and property are still insecure. Great storms drive the sea over the summer cottages of Block Island. And there was a historical appropriateness in the comment Nature provided for the end of the tercentenary celebration at Harvard, for on the last day the great "storm wind of the equinox" that had been rushing up the coast from Florida struck Cambridge (Massachusetts) with a force unknown to Cambridge (England). It showed that for the sons of the Puritans the God of their fathers was still an angry God of storm and rain like Him who had smitten the army of Sisera and had later toughened the New Englanders. And it was perhaps not misogyny that led the meteorologists to give girls' names to hurricanes, but the same superstitious fear that made the Greeks call the dreaded Black Sea the Euxine. So Carol and Edna, cutting a swath of destruction across New England, would seem less dreadful than if they had been given numbers instead of names.

Even when there are no catastrophes, there are constant climatic problems. The mere range of temperature is a problem. How do you plan your life in a place like Bismarck, North Dakota, where the July temperatures have ranged between 32° F. and 108°, and the January temperatures between 45° below zero and 60° above? What do you do, even in normally kindly New Orleans, where the January temperatures have ranged between 15° and 82° and the July temperatures between 35° and 102°? In Wyoming at the source of the Colorado River, there is frost in every month of the year; over many states there is never any frost at all for decades at a time. *But* no part of the United States—not Texas, not Florida, not California—is free from frost that will, when by a freak it does come, kill lemons and oranges and avocados and break the hearts or strain the consciences of local boosters.

It seems likely that not until this century did the Americans really adjust themselves to the climate—as far as it is humanly possible to do so. Those who were of British origin were especially handicapped, coming as they did from an island where no one had been really comfortable in winter between the departure of the Romans and the coming of the more exigent type of American tourist. It is worth noting that one of the most important inventions of that most representative of Americans, Franklin, was an efficient stove (another was the lightning conductor). But to make houses even reasonably airtight was a problem; the log cabin, whether or not it was of Finnish origin, was a solution better than any that English practice would suggest. The continuous series of farm buildings—house, stables, barn, all in line so that the farmer could pass from the kitchen to the horses and on to the cattle without going into the bitter air—was another necessary adjustment; moreover, it provided a fine range of buildings that could be turned into rumpus rooms, garages, etc., when city folk took over the New England countryside. With primitive central heating, the last lap was entered on. It is possibly no accident, again, that the most modern thermostatic systems of central heating owe their essential equipment to a firm in Minneapolis where the winter cold can kill ten times as often as it can on the milder Atlantic. An Iowa farm, painted in midwinter by Grant Wood, with its red barn and dominating silo is highly functional: devoted to the job of keeping men and stock alive and food and feed usable through the long siege of winter. No American farm-bred boy or girl is likely to think that he or she has America licked. Everywhere nature is tough and dangerous, and it is no accident that a great

American fairy tale, *The Wizard of Oz,* begins with a tornado and a storm cellar.

Nor, indeed, is the town boy, who, as he grows up, will have at least one memory of a great and killing cold spell, even if it does not become so legendary as the great New York freezes of 1837 and 1888. Gardeners will long remember the late winter of 1933-4, which killed so many plants and shrubs on Long Island; and all regions of America, except the South and the Pacific Coast, have their own stories of death by cold, of stalled buggies or sleighs or even cars, of the dangers of bad chains or defective car-heaters, of a winter climate that always bears watching.

And summer demands it even more. For the early settlers were even less acclimated (as Americans put it) to heat than to cold. For one thing, as Professor S. E. Morison has pointed out, they wore far too many and too thick clothes. Even the Andalusians of Columbus' crews wore too many garments for a Caribbean summer. North Europeans did worse. There were economic obstacles, of course; until cotton textiles became cheap and abundant around 1800, linen was expensive and woolens uncomfortable. But there was more in it than that. Long after adequate textiles were abundant and cheap, fashion—not merely style but moral fashion—kept too many clothes on the American man and still more on the American woman. Men might wear "dusters" like Lincoln, or "seersuckers" like the prosperous middle class of the eighties. If they were prepared to be conspicuous, they might wear white linen suits like Mark Twain. But they still wore too much and, for dress occasions, they had to wear "Prince Alberts" (i.e., frock coats), tall hats, broadcloth, and starched collars and shirts. Theodore Roosevelt was regarded as pretty eccentric and reckless of the conventions, yet his typical costume was very formal and very uncomfortable indeed, compared with that of his niece's husband, a later President of the United States. It was still thought worthy of note when William Jennings Bryan took his coat off at Dayton, Tennessee, and defended Genesis in his shirt-sleeves—and that was as recently as 1925. And the uniform of the American army that went to France in 1917–18 included a stiff cloth collar that made the British officer's uniform the envy of his semi-strangled comrades in arms.

As for the women, to look at fashion magazines of 1900, to read in *Middletown* of the clothes worn in Indiana in the summer little more than a generation ago, even to recall the fuss made about the length of bathing-suit skirts and other problems of sartorial morals in the 1920's, is to be as struck with astonishment as were the Greeks who learned from Herodotus that among the Lydians it was thought shameful even for men to be seen naked. No one, least of all a woman, need be overclothed in an American summer today. Indeed, unless she is clever with the needle or can afford custom-made clothes, any American woman who resolved to wear at least half as much as her mother used to would be baffled in any department store however big. The South Sea Islanders, put into "Mother Hubbards" by American missionaries and in consequence suffering discomfort, or even death, have been thoroughly avenged.

It is not only the American house that has at last been adapted to the American climate. American food has, too. Although Americans have always, by European standards, been abundantly fed, they have not until recently been well fed. One early difficulty of adjustment was that of diet; the average pioneer wanted the roast beef of old England or its equivalent, and was not to be put off with such newfangled dishes as turkeys, tomatoes, corn, etc. He did adjust himself fairly quickly, but only in the sense of adding American items to European, not of balancing his diet or making it suit the climate and the work he had to do.

Of course some classes and some regions have been badly fed for economic reasons. "Hog and hominy," the diet of the Confederate army, was bad, but any other diet would have been a novelty to Southern poor whites. Negroes were and often are badly fed from any point of view. But travelers and critical Americans alike long lamented the monotony of American food, the good food ruined in that enemy to the pursuit of happiness, the frying-pan; the saleratus bread which was debited with the American sallow complexion and the melancholy view of life characteristic of many Americans in middle age. Until modern storage methods came in, the severity of both winter and summer made variety in diet difficult. Ice, indeed, was an early American passion; in water, in coffee, in juleps and other alcoholic concoctions. But it was ice cut and stored in a New England winter and shipped to South Carolina—and India —in a highly speculative voyage. For if most of your cargo arrived safe, your fortune was made, while if your ship was becalmed, all you had was extra water ballast of no market value. One of the minor hardships of the Southern gentry in the War between the States was the shortage of ice, no laughing matter in the mint-julep country of tidewater Virginia.

With the coming of artificial ice, the worst was over and ice in summer became almost as necessary as coal in winter. European pioneers made refrigerator cars possible, to the profit of the meat-packers of Chicago and the fruit-growers of California and Florida. But American men still ate too much meat, ate it too often, and did not balance it with sufficient fruit and vegetables. It is only in modern times, very modern times, that the American diet has become varied, light, and suitable for the climate. The electric refrigerator is becoming a necessity; deep freezing promises new culinary resources, and air conditioning promises a new climate—indoors, at any rate. There is no visible prospect of any method of obviating the Turkish-bath sensation that hits the person who goes out from an air-conditioned train or store or movie house on a very hot day. It is still too early to relax. America has always managed to keep her children on their toes; she still manages to do so. But the day is not in sight on which science and business together will be able to guarantee the climate and natural resources of California to the whole Union—or even to California.

4

BY THE END of the nineteenth century, the frontier era was over and the conquest and taming of the wilderness by American men and women entered into its modern phase of making rapid adjustments to a new way of life in which American men and women could take their ease in the Zion they had conquered and made to flow with milk and honey. It was certainly flowing more copiously than it had when the first scouts had reported. Though a long time was required to find it, there *was* gold in those mountains. And there were iron and coal and natural gas and copper and oil. Above all, oil. The United States "struck oil" just under a century ago. From the earth came bursting out the unsuspected black gold, the simplest way known to man of conferring treasure upon a prospector. Wealth poured in on communities and individuals little better prepared than Osage Indians who were taken overnight from a thrifty life whose problem was to save, to a life where rational spending was the problem. It was no wonder that the extravagant spending of "Coal Oil Johnny" became traditional.

Nor was oil the only source of new wealth. There were the gold magnates who exploited California; there were the even more splendiferous silver magnates of the Great Bonanza. It was not only the father of Evalyn Walsh McLean who struck it rich—thousands did; in a sense the whole United States did. There was the Mesabi Range, in which you just scooped the iron out, like cheese. There was the mountain of copper in Butte, Montana, which made the fortunes of Sheridan, Kelly, and Clark and became the basis of the Anaconda. Fantastic mansions on Fifth Avenue and Nob Hill reflected the sudden wealth of prospectors like

Flood and Clark and the more prudent businessmen who sold to and bought from prospectors. It was over the exploitation of oil that the first great modern economic controversy was raised; the Standard Oil was the first trust; the Rockefeller fortune, the first that really passed the dreams of European avarice. To monopolize the sources of such wealth was the key to power—and it meant denying to other would-be exploiters their chance of a share in the loot. Faced with these great corporations, the old common law, the old democratic machinery, seemed not even to belong to a horse-and-buggy age. They were almost pre-wheel.

But with native capital pouring out of the soil, with the paying-off of the European mortgage on American resources, with the parallel growth of industry and new techniques, the American man and, still more, the American woman entered on the more abundant life. Europe began to be outdistanced in wealth, in economic efficiency, in modernity. As late as 1867, when Mark Twain and the other tourists of the Quaker City went to Europe, they were visiting not only a continent full of interesting relics but a continent far more advanced in technique and wealth than the United States. A few years before, young Henry Adams had gazed with rather horrified interest at the English black country, as a train whirled him, far faster and far more comfortably than any American train could, from Liverpool to London. He knew that he was gazing at a sight unique in the world and in the history of the world. The American tourist, like Mark Twain, was overawed by the French railways and railway stations, by the wealth and display of the Paris shops. The Grands Magasins du Louvre were a sight as unparalleled in America as the Musée du Louvre. Effective systems of street lighting, of water supply, moderately clean streets and smooth roads—these were as much a European monopoly as Notre Dame or the Colosseum. Europe as a going concern was deeply impressive. The wealth of European magnates was stupendous. F. Bret Harte made his parody of Disraeli's *Lothair* turn upon the purchase of Chicago by the immensely rich young nobleman Lothaw. There was even, a few years later, an agitation against wealthy Englishmen buying up large sections of the United States. How soon that changed!

The American woman was the chief gainer. No doubt most of the money originally passed through men's hands, but women had the spending of it. The American man was freed from most of the risks and back-breaking physical labors of crude pioneering, but the pioneer tradition of endless industry, of more and more, was unaltered by the change in circumstances. But to the heiress of the pioneer woman, the sewing-machine, an effective system of heating, good oil lamps burning the good cheap oil sold by Mr. Rockefeller's octopus, running water in the cities, then in the towns, the coming of anesthetics and of less deadly childbearing, the appearance of an economic margin to spend on what had been luxuries and of time in which to spend the margin—these were really revolutionary changes. Of course they did not come all at once or universally over the country. In some backward regions they have not come yet. The last great frontier movement, which led to the settlement of the High Plains, inflicted as much hardship on the pioneer Scandinavian settlers, especially on the women, as any previous movement had done. To survive a winter on the plains, in a "sod house" dug out of the soil, called for the qualities of giants in the earth as truly as surviving in a half-faced camp in Kentucky had done. But the revolution spread rapidly. President Folwell of the University of Minnesota died full of energy a month before the bull market broke in 1929. Yet he could well remember that his mother, in upstate New York, had set herself off from many of her neighbors by never using "sluts"—that is, rags floating in fat and burning in a dish. She always used candles which she made herself, till the sperm-oil lamps came into use. The development of the mail-order house with its ready-made clothes lightened women's labor, as the sewing-machine had lightened it earlier. There is less of a jump from ordinary baker's bread to processed bread, wrapped in cellophane and sliced, than there was from the heavy chore of home baking to baker's bread.

The American kitchen was well on the way—the first primitive washing-machines; the first efficient iceboxes; the telephone for public gossip on the party line; the new plumbing; sinks designed to break fewer backs; lighting planned to ruin fewer eyes; gas stoves, then electric ranges, to reduce the strain of cooking. The can-opener became a standard article of equipment and the basis of jokes for hardworked comedians. In time, indeed, an efficient can-opener reduced the last hazards of kitchen work. The day of the Hoover cleaner agent and the Fuller brush man was at hand. So, too, was the day of leisure. The pioneer American feminists had to be Mrs. Jellybys or spinsters. It was impossible both to set the world to rights *and* to keep house with the old equipment. But by 1900 the American woman had been liberated (apart from the great majority, who were farmers' wives or wives of manual workers) from the worst servitudes of her sex. Without any very public campaign urging it, birth-control (or what President Theodore Roosevelt had called "race suicide") was adopted; there were fewer children, and there was far more time to devote care to them. The diet of Junior became a serious preoccupation, and the need to straighten Sister's teeth. So did the public schools, at which both of them might pick up foreign accents or worse. So did the summer camps to which they could thankfully be sent. The change was not sudden until the moderate-priced car came; it merely marked the emergence of the American mother, a Martha solicitous now over only two things: her children (or child) and the world. It was as much as ever the duty of the husband to be a "good provider" and, as real incomes rose, what had been luxuries became necessities—especially if the children needed them.

As long as the American land was not completely settled, the elements of civilized order not yet imposed on the frontier, the permanent American passion for dealing in futures was devoted to prophetic brooding on material expansion and to prodigious efforts to make those prophecies either come true or turn out to have underestimated what could be done. But with the closing of the frontier, the discounting of the future took a more human form: it became the ambition of the American man and woman to provide a world in which life should be easier for the next generation. And as the closing of the frontier meant— psychologically if not materially—a closing-in of the horizons, since it was no longer possible to dismiss the problem of youth's economic future with a brisk "Go west, young man, and grow up with the country," the provision of a world in which young men and women could grow up in a fairly stable country became a national preoccupation. It was reflected in the increasing interest in, belief in, and credulity about education. It was reflected in the sharp fall in the size of the family. If, on the other hand, the old farm and village tradition survived that every boy, no matter how well off his parents, did chores at home and earned a little money outside, it gradually came to be slightly artificial. When the merchant's or the lawyer's son made some extra money by delivering papers or mowing lawns or (most serious chore of all) tending furnace, this was—like fagging in English public schools—a disciplinary ritual rather than a strictly economic function. The boy who was made to earn a dollar or two a week in such ways might be arguing, with tenacity and success, for the right to a car of his own or to a free hand with the family car.

As sons and daughters grew fewer, they were indulged more liberally—a phenomenon not confined to America. The American mother with only one or two sons was more hopeful of making a world fit for them to live in than the mother of six or seven could easily be. The very age limits of childhood shifted upwards. In New England a century ago, men barely out of their teens were commanding clippers on voyages to China. The youthful character of American life struck visitors. Dickens was not exaggerating much when he took for children the young married couple in Martin Chuzzlewit's boarding house. A young man like MacKenzie could leave West Point during the Civil War and end it as a corps commander. But in modern America there is far more reluctance to admit that real maturity has come than there was even forty years ago. The excessive length of American professional education, which prevents a young doctor or lawyer from earning his living, or even beginning to earn it, until he is twenty-eight or older, may have something to answer for. So may the prolongation of youthful habits and ambitions into middle age which justifies the title of "girls" assumed by the plump matrons of Miss Helen Hokinson's art. (But I have been told by an eminent clubwoman in the Bay region that it is hard to get really young matrons to join clubs today. They don't want to run the risk of being figures of fun from *The New Yorker*.) But there has been a real shift in meaning between the days when "the boys in the back room" meant *anybody,* and our modern times in which robust and vigorous young men are called "boys" and treated as boys. Youth has become scarcer and more precious, and the natural and touching desire to shield the young, more uncritical and overpowering. So the Republican platform of 1940 was not ill designed—and probably not devoid of real meaning and feeling—when it recalled that "we are still suffering from the ill effects of the last World War; a war which cost us a twenty-four-billion-dollar increase in our national debt, millions of uncollectable foreign debts, and the complete upset of our economic system, in addition to the loss of human life and *irreparable damage to the health of thousands of our boys.*"

5

THE ADOPTION of the woman's thrifty view of human life, as compared with the extravagant masculine attitude, was only one sign among many that American society was moving from its frontier condition in which, no matter what theories were advocated, life had to be governed by masculine standards. Only a century ago, it is odd to remember, not merely were American women excluded from open politics as they were in England, but the Puritan standards generally accepted in American life denied them that illicit —or, at any rate, unofficial—influence which some English women exercised. I cannot think of any woman who played an important role in American politics before Peggy O'Neale induced President Jackson to champion her premarital chastity and thus forced a quarrel between the President and those members of his cabinet who had wives and so had to support the severest standards of female decorum—all to the profit of that subtle widower, Martin Van Buren, who thus became heir apparent to the presidency. But even society had comparatively little place for women, despite the social graces of the sprightly Dolly Madison. Men preferred to talk to one another and leave the women to themselves—a barbarous custom that shocked Mrs. Trollope, Miss Martineau, and other female visitors from the then more advanced country of England. Mrs. John Adams might complain that all men would tyrannize over their wives if they dared; it was not until the reforming forties that women's rights—with abolitionism, spiritualism, socialism, Mormonism, and transcendentalism —testified to the breaking-up of the orthodox ice that, for two centuries, had restrained the ardent spirits of New

England. And only twenty years or so late, Lincoln could say to the author of *Uncle Tom's Cabin:* "So you are the little woman that caused this great war."

When the tide began to flow, it flowed rapidly. With *Little Women* and *The Battle Hymn of the Republic,* Frances Willard and Lucy Stone, the American woman was no longer silent. Even the business woman began to appear, in the ambiguous form of the Claflin sisters and then in the form of the classic American miser, Hetty Green. And if the religious movements of the pre-Civil War period, like Mormonism and Perfectionism, had found a place for women, it was in the postwar period that the most original development of American religious optimism was announced by Mary Baker Eddy.

The law, which had pressed hard on women for so many generations, now began to press hard on men. Marriage continued to be a lottery, but the law no longer allotted all the blanks to women. Divorce became easier and alimony more abundant. The first effective women's colleges, Vassar and Mount Holyoke, were founded or developed out of schools. State universities began to admit women on equal terms, and some Western states gave them the vote. The woman doctor and the girl "prophet" of *The Bostonians* were both typical products of this age.

And the American woman began to clean up America, to make it less dirty, less sinful, less a boarding house for bachelors and more a home. The towns were taken in hand first; the farmer's wife had, as yet, not enough leisure to reform the countryside.

An example of the conquest of the American town by the American woman was the successful campaign against the toleration of organized prostitution, the tacit or open earmarking of an area of a city as a "red-light district." Novels and films have now given us a kindlier view of this solution of the sexual problem than was generally held when it was in its glory. The *entrepreneuses* of the brothels, the "madams" of the "sporting houses," were all, we now learn, ladies under the skin, their hearts as golden as their hair. This was doubtfully true in some cases; and, even if it was true in a majority of cases, the whole attitude involved in this solution was an affirmation of that exclusion of American women from the whole of life against which they fought. The brothel, like the saloon, was a challenge to the American woman's passion for reducing masculine disorder and moral anarchy to reasonable limits (reasonable by female standards). Men were trying to have it both ways: to demand from "good" women rigorous standards of ignorant decorum, and in addition to have license for themselves. The American woman who had played—and who knew she had played—so great a part in creating American society, and who proposed to play an even greater part in molding it, was not disposed to lie down under this threat, this insult. And, in practice, long before women got the vote, it was politically already very risky to cater too openly to the brothel interests, whatever lesser breaches of political decency like selling traction franchises might be pardoned to the political machine if it were otherwise respectable—i.e., Republican in the North, Democratic in the South.

Campaigns against organized vice were waged over and over again, mixed up with mere campaigns against indecent books and pictures. But the opinion is hazarded here that American women did not really worry much about banning books or pictures; *September Morn* left them cold. The test case was the brothel and its political tie-up, and even more the cynical and (from a feminist point of view) contemptuous arguments with which the existence of such an institution was defended or palliated. When the great department store, Macy's, moved uptown and built its vast new store on the site of some of the most

famous brothels in New York, the early twentieth century
opened with an omen of a new triumph for the American
woman. And few are the cities in which the old system
survives today, even in a disguised form. Few are the cities
in which open streetwalking is as much a national institution as it is in Britain. The "love-nest" is known; the visit
to the local tourist camp for the night is known; little
"dens of iniquity" such as that which housed the hero of
Pal Joey are known. But not merely are these at least formally secret, not merely does vice pay the real homage of
more or less expensive hypocrisy to female and sometimes
to male virtue, but in all these illicit arrangements there
is no element of undisguised official toleration and there
is no double standard of morality. In America, as in England, that old dispute is over, for the time being, anyway.
The war between the sexes is now fought on the level, even
if it is a low level by nineteenth-century standards. But
as the researches of Dr. Kinsey have shown, the contrast
between law and practice is as great as ever. Even petting
is illegal in several states and the battle of *Law* vs. *Libido*
is still fought, the law going down gamely in repeated de-
feats like a British heavyweight.

But the great triumph of the American woman was
prohibition. It is true that many American women had by
1919 become sophisticated enough to like a drink themselves. But there was more wit than statistical truth in the
jest (possibly Mrs. Parker's) that "the American woman
got the vote just too late to save the old-fashioned saloon."
It is true that nowadays very few saloons, however old-
fashioned, dare exclude the ladies, and those that do are
likely to be treated with the scorn which, so I have been
told, American ladies at Pompeii and Naples met Italian
attempts to exclude them from the more curious relics of
the culture of imperial Rome. But whatever may be the
case today, a generation ago, two generations ago, the

American woman declared and waged war on drink. It was the great enemy of her social and economic security. The bottle rather than the blonde was the rival she had to fear for her husband's income and for his otherwise certain devotion to his children. Strong drink was abundant and cheap; mere beer and wine are nineteenth-century importations into the American diet. Whisky, as has been said, was the chief export of the primitive frontier, and whisky was only one of numerous tipples. There were peach brandy and apple jack, white mule, Jersey lightning, Medford rum, and Bourbon and rye whisky. For long they were lightly taxed and fantastically cheap. Social life depended on them; great men like Daniel Webster lived on them, more or less. Even the clergy were not debarred from enjoying them. European drinking habits in the curious combinations of climates known in North America often produced catastrophic results. Hot buttered rum to keep out the winter cold, mint juleps to keep out the summer heat—these were drastic solutions for a serious climatic problem.

Drink was an occasion of sin and a cause of waste. Not only was it customary for newspapermen to go off for a week or two of hard drinking, but even such dignified persons as department-store buyers who went out to lunch with customers often failed to come back. Mr. Saroyan's hero who held up the alcoholic arms of the telegraphist had his analogue in every American town and village and in practically all professions. Whether President Johnson and President Grant were drunkards, or merely had very poor heads for liquor, was the subject of much bitter political controversy. And it is perhaps significant that the first time the White House had to undergo the rigors of a dry regime was when Grant's successor, Rutherford B. Hayes, announced that since neither he nor Mrs. Hayes had approved of serving liquor in Columbus (Ohio), they would not change their habits in Washington, D.C. After that, as Secretary of State Evarts put it, water flowed like champagne in the White House. No subsequent President made such an issue of the liquor question as had President Hayes; but, whatever sophisticated half-foreign dwellers in Washington may have thought, millions of Americans warmly approved of the Hayes gesture—and their number increased.

The first prohibition wave which marked the period of ecstatic reforming before the Civil War ebbed. Only Maine, first to go dry, kept the law on its statute books, and it was perhaps in homage to the ethos of his adopted state that James G. Blaine had a report that he was "suffering from gout" amended to read "suffering from rheumatism." Even in the capital of moral reform, Boston, the dry laws were openly defied. It was, so the story runs, in one of the best Boston hotels that a classical rebuke was administered to a melodramatic pessimist who asked what he could do if a friend, say from St. Louis, wanted a drink. "I should say: *'Fils de Saint Louis, montez au ciel,'*" replied the realist, pointing to the floor above, where there was a well-equipped speak-easy.

This defiance of the law, whether the defiance took the form of tolerating prostitution or tolerating liquor, was resented by the women, who found masculine indiscipline intolerable. It is true that such defiance was often not merely anarchical. There were substantial profits to be reaped by somebody, even by a community as a whole. Some students hold that the economic predominance of Seattle over its rivals on Puget Sound is due to the initial start it got from the popularity of its tolerated and famous brothels among the sailors and lumbermen of the last frontier. One otherwise undistinguished economic center, Moorhead, Minnesota, for long owed a good deal of revenue to its role as a licensed Alsatia in an area of legal Puritanism. St. Paul was frowned on by its neighbor

Minneapolis for its worldly tolerance. The New England moralists of Greeley, Colorado, had no liking for the wide-open character of Denver. And the sins of San Francisco were long a cause of mournful pride to most of California and of a combination of contempt and envy to Los Angeles. But prohibition of liquor, of prostitution, even of cigarettes, was warmly advocated by the most vocal American women. All tobacco-users (i.e., snuffers as well as smokers) were regarded as doubtful characters; and, as for smoking by women, that was a proof either of complete social squalor —as among the female pipe-smokers of the southern Appalachians and Ozarks—or of definitely sinful propensities. It is only within the last twenty-five years or so that ciga-rette-manufacturers have been able to get away from subter-fuges, such as making a pretty girl say "Blow the smoke my way," and to come out and face the fact that most young American women smoke.

The slackness of male enforcement of these taboos led to direct action. Carry Nation broke up the saloons of Kansas, then those of other states, finally carrying her cru-sade as far as Glasgow. And by the Eighteenth Amend-ment and the Volstead Act, the sale of beverage alcohol was made illegal all over the United States, even in sinful cities like New York and Chicago. There is no need to go into the sad history of what Mr. Hoover called "an experi-ment noble in purpose." The limits of mere law were re-vealed. The old frontier habit of shooting it out turned to the East, and the old circus act of holding up the Dead-wood Coach was repeated, not in fun, on hundreds of new concrete highways. The authority of state and federal governments was made ludicrous, and regions and sections of society which in modern times had never really known the open use of alcohol saw the naïve hypocrisy of highly alcoholic remedies for aches and pains replaced by openly sinful bathtub gin and moonshine. As prohibition was mainly a women's triumph, imposed on the reluctant politicians by fear of the women's vote, the failure of the experiment should have been highly educational. It showed that there were limits to the degree to which the old Adam could be expelled by noble purposes; it revealed some of the realities below the façade of mere voting. The laws, voted by women and evangelical zealots, were enforced by policemen and other legal instruments, and few of these had any belief in the desirability of drying America by law—or in any other way. It was the belief of many intelligent supporters of prohibition that a generation of boys and girls would grow up who, not knowing the taste of alcohol, would not want to drink—and perhaps the belief was not entirely foolish. Because no one could hold such a view about sex appetites, moral legislators in that field had always known that they had their work cut out for them. But the prohibition experiment never got a fair chance, since no generation of American adolescents had ever had more real alcoholic temptation put in its way than the generation that grew up during the years when booze was news—daily, dramatic news. Indeed, fears that cigarette-smoking breeds cancer and even more widespread fears that beer-drinking breeds poundage have done more, in recent years, to limit the use of tobacco and beer than the moral precepts of previous generations ever did.

There is a close parallel between the optimism that led to the enactment of prohibition and the optimism which welcomed that international Volstead Act, the Kellogg Pact. In that optimism there was a strong element of the old-time religion, of belief in the old evangelical mass conversion. Hundreds and thousands had renounced the world, the flesh, and the devil in Kentucky or in the "burned-over" district of New York State; why should not the nations renounce mutual murder? And this conversion involved no serious mental stock-taking, involved no more than a firm resolution that the United States would not attack any nation and a belief that no nation would attack any other—especially the United States. That peace requires positive as well as negative action, that works as well as faith are needed, were ideas unwelcome in those golden days when, drink and poverty having been put on the road to extinction, war was scheduled as next to go. General amiability, a Good Neighbor policy that it was hoped would spread—these were to be enough. It was not that the other signatories to the pact were trusted implicitly, but it was obviously such good morals and such good business to renounce war! That there were rulers of peoples, in power or soon to be in power, who took a different view of morals was ignored. So, too, was the fact that it was all very well for President Coolidge to announce that "the business of the United States is business." Other powerful peoples did not agree that their business was exclusively business. What was at most true of American society at one moment in its history was taken as universally true. It was soon not even true of the United States. But for a time these illusions concealed from the American people, especially from the American woman, a truth enunciated by Mr. Dooley at the beginning of this belligerent century. As he pointed out, you can refuse to love a man, you can refuse to play with him, you can refuse to lend him money—but, if he wants a fight, you have got to oblige him.

War, even more than drink, was an absurd relic of man's barbaric and disorderly past. It was destructive; it destroyed what women made: children and homes. It led to waste of national resources on armaments. It was a purely masculine activity, and in every society in which it was a main activity it was inevitable that the position of women (the infallible index of civilization, so nearly every American woman believed and nearly every American man professed to believe) should be inferior.

And those who, like William James, looked for a moral equivalent for war were put off with violent games such as unreformed college football in which the players' armor underlined its adequately "dangerous" character as the American parallel of the bullfight. In campaigns for all kinds of objects military metaphors were freely used, and the American tradition of processions, of demonstrations, of massed emotional meetings, going back to the frontier camp-meeting and the frontier political campaign, provided substitutes for real military parades; so did military uniforms and military nomenclature.

The combination of a profound hatred of war and militarism with an innocent delight in playing soldiers is one of these apparent contradictions of American life that one has to accept. The American state universities for the most part started as land-grant colleges—that is, they were given large areas of federal land to subsidize education in agriculture and the mechanic arts. But, as the grants were made during the Civil War, military training was demanded, too. The American army, once the South was conquered, shrank to a few thousands again; the militia was merely an amateur police force; nevertheless, military training of a kind remained a vague obligation of the state universities. It was not necessarily very functional. I myself have been served in a university restaurant, a few months after Pearl Harbor, by students wearing movie-usher uniforms plus swords; they were going on a parade as soon as the washing-up was done. The possibilities of exhibiting female legs in vigorous action provided by making "majorettes" (high-stepping and high-spirited young women) the chief feature of a college military band have not been neglected, and one of the most eminent American social critics has given us a highly plausible account of military training at Ohio State University during the earlier German war. "We drilled with old Springfield rifles and studied the tactics of the Civil War even though the World War was going on at the time. At 11 o'clock each morning thousands of freshmen used to deploy over the campus, moodily creeping up on the old chemistry building. It was good training for the kind of warfare that was waged at Shiloh, but it had no connection with what was going on in Europe. Some people used to think there was German money behind it, but they didn't dare say so or they would have been thrown in jail as German spies."[1]

An apparently odder example of innocent militarism is provided by the military schools. These are not schools preparing for the army, or with a strong army tradition like Haileybury or Wellington, and are not to be confused with real military academies for training officers like the Virginia Military Institute or the Citadel at Charleston, South Carolina. (The last institution has been pilloried in a novel as being a smarter version of an army prison camp like "the Stockade," but it has probably suffered little thereby.) They are simply boarding schools organized on military lines. They may be described as English public schools organized round the O.T.C. instead of the cricket team. The boys wear uniforms, uniforms a good deal more dashing than those of the American army or even of the Marine Corps. School spirit is translated into military terms; the "Buckle down, Woonsockie, buckle down" type of song is set for bugles. Military methods of command are relied on to discipline the boy who is a handful at home, and a certain amount of elementary military training is provided. To see the Eton O.T.C. learning the manual of arms in what Americans call "cutaways" is to realize how

[1] James Thurber: *My Life and Hard Times* (Harper), p. 123.

much better they do such things at Culver. But there is no real military indoctrination, no militarism, no resemblance to the "leader schools" of the Third Reich, nor even to the slightly fevered atmosphere of the old United Services College as seen by the retrospective Kipling in *Stalky & Co.* I don't know of a Quaker military school, but I really don't see why there shouldn't be one.

There was some pacifist agitation against compulsory military training in colleges. Probably some parents decided against sending their boys to military school because it *was* military. But both college and school military training were so obviously unmilitarist in spirit that only the most morally sensitive really felt strongly about it. To worry about the militarization of young America was about as foolish as to worry about those colonels' commissions that Governor Ruby Laffoon, of Kentucky, was showering on every girl and on most men who got within hailing distance of the capitol at Frankfort. Never did America more determinedly *not* raise its boys to be soldiers than in the years before the coming of the most terrible foreign war in American history.

The American people, it must be repeated, have always been anti-militarist but never anti-military. They have combined a rational and civilized horror of war's waste and inhumanity with a simple and, for peoples of European origin, natural pleasure in the trappings of war. Their view of what constitutes the due "pride, pomp, and circumstance" of warlike parade is not that of the English or the Germans or the Japanese, but it is genuine all the same.

Nevertheless, the survival of this pleasure in the circus side of warlike activity and a great deal of rather naïve patriotic enthusiasm about the past was accompanied, between 1919 and 1939, by an equally vociferous zeal for perpetual peace and a refusal (equaled only in Britain and the British dominions) to see that peace could not be bought by mere resolutions of good behavior—might indeed call for such efforts of self-discipline and self-criticism that war would come to seem almost preferable.

As has been suggested, the growing and deserved power of American women had something to do with this attitude. So had a genuine and very justifiable optimism about America and a natural and in many ways admirable pride in the facts that so much of the world had now come to school to America, and that the prestige of American ways of life was so high. Had not a distinguished Frenchman, M. André Siegfried, said that the world would have to choose between Henry Ford and Gandhi? And few were the Americans who believed that, if the choice were given, any serious number even of the most benighted foreigners would choose Gandhi. And even if they did, the one thing Ford and Gandhi had in common was pacifism.

In the growth of this attitude there was, however, one factor of overwhelming importance: the widespread, almost universal American belief that intervention in the war of 1914-18 had been a luxury, and a foolish luxury at that. No nation likes being "played for a sucker"; no nation likes to think that it has been the victim of a gang of international spiritual comrades of Mr. W. C. Fields, all resolved not to give the American sucker an even break. American slang is rich in terms to describe the fate of the victim of the con man. America, so the American people was soon told, had been robbed by international crooks who had found the job of swindling her appointed guardians no more difficult than "rolling a lush." America was the lush, and the booze that had made her so easy a victim of international pickpockets was propaganda.

For the student of that art, the history of the American campaign of propaganda against propaganda must always rank as a masterpiece. Compared with the agents of Britain whom they denounced, the propagandists against propaganda were real masters commenting on the daubs of well-meaning amateurs. Like their British predecessors of 1914–17, the American artists were often perfectly sincere, not merely bringing more learning, more talent, and more knowledge of the market to the job, but doing all this with a conviction of moral superiority that the most naïve Briton could not have excelled. It is possible that some of the leaders in this campaign were slightly cynical. After all, it was in more than one way not unprofitable to see the world through German spectacles. Others were animated by the natural human reaction, especially natural in the young, against believing all or much of what your pastors and masters have told you. And lastly it was to the interest of the Republican Party to discredit the policy of the Democratic administration. "The war is a failure" was the Democratic Party line invented to discredit Lincoln in 1864. "The war was a fraud" was the slogan of Republican Vallandighams in 1920 and later.

But there was in American resentment a genuine moral element. The world had been made safe for democracy (Chesterton's reminder at the time that it could not be, that making it so was a dangerous trade, had been ignored). In many ways the world got worse while the United States got better, and even when the smash of 1929 proved that the American way of life could go backwards, too, it was natural to blame some exterior force. All the nations that had suffered from the war of 1914–18—victors and vanquished alike—naturally found comfort in blaming outsiders, with a good deal of justice since the outsiders *were* blamable. So a situation was created in America in which candid thought about the late war was made almost as difficult as it was in any of the countries that had suffered far more deeply.

It is the comparatively slight statistical impact of the

First World War on America, set in dramatic contrast to the psychological impact, that makes it hard for the foreigner to be just to the American revulsion from that war and from all wars that seemed like that war. American losses in life were far less, both absolutely and in proportion to the population, than American losses in the Civil War. The American motor car was a far more efficient killer of American youth than the German army had been. Some not very large towns in England and Scotland had suffered more fatal casualties than some American states. Yet the feeling that there had been great waste and *mere* waste was genuine. These American boys need not have been killed at all. A boy killed by a speeding car died a natural death; a boy killed in the Argonne was killed by propaganda, but for which he would have stayed at home.

Again it must constantly be remembered that before this war no nation had ever fought on such a scale so far from home—and in the Second World War it was again the Americans who fought on the greatest scale far from home. True, this was in itself an advantage to America. The people of London learned in 1940 what the French learned in 1914–18, that it is no matter for rejoicing to have a war on your own doorstep. If the real interests of the United States were involved in either of these wars, the American people were to be congratulated on keeping the river of destruction away from their door. But simple people in any country refuse to reason that way. The remoteness of the battlefields, the thought that their sons were going into exile as well as into battle, were painful to American fathers and mothers. The thought of their dying so far from home was more bitter than the thought of their simply dying. The French soldier of Napoleon's army, dying on the retreat from Moscow, whose only complaint was: "It's a long way to Carcassonne," expressed a universal and ancient attitude: *"dulcis moriens reminiscitur Argos."*

Even had the world of 1919 onwards been obviously a great improvement on the world of 1914, the American people might have succumbed to the temptation to do some excessively rigorous political bookkeeping. But as it was, the theory that all this waste and suffering *could* have been avoided was sure to be readily welcomed, and it was. And the simplest form of the mere waste theory was the belief that propaganda had dragged America into a mess she had not made and in whose cleaning up she had no serious interest.

An eminent Victorian rationalist, it is asserted, once refused to "plaster the fair face of truth with that pestilent cosmetic, rhetoric." Something of the same vehement passion for truth in political advertising overcame the enemies of propaganda. In their zeal for calm, objective, disinterested statement of the truth, they were themselves at times betrayed into what was rather like the style of the much abused propagandists. "In the Great Society it is no longer possible to fuse the waywardness of individuals in the furnace of the war dance; a new and subtler instrument must weld thousands and even millions of human beings into one amalgamated mass of hate and will and hope. A new flame must burn out the canker of dissent and temper the steel of bellicose enthusiasm. The name of this new hammer and anvil of social solidarity is propaganda. Talk must take the place of drill; print must supplant the dance. War dances live in literature and at the fringes of the modern earth; war propaganda breathes and fumes in the capitals and provinces of the world."[2] At

[2] Professor Harold D. Lasswell: *Propaganda Technique in the World War*, quoted in James R. Mock and Cedric Larson: *Words That Won the War* (Princeton University Press).

first sight this reads like a description of a jitterbug session, but for all its Corinthian exuberance of style it is an admirable piece of propaganda against propaganda. For it suggests to the impressionable reader that propaganda can work only one way—in the direction of action, *undesirable* action. Whether desirable action can be stimulated, or whether desirable action is above the need of stimulation, or whether inaction (the adoption of a generally skeptically indifferent attitude) is a good thing or a preservative against obviously bad things—these were questions that the average forward-looking writer did not put, questions which, if they were put, he did not stay to answer or hear answered.

The American people had, of course, many other reasons for skepticism. There was a considerable waste of simple faith and trust in the advertising world, not so much because the standard of advertising veracity went down (actually it went up), but because the seriousness with which advertising was treated led to a general customer's attitude: "You've got to show me"—and the customer, bidden to think hard or dangerous or unpleasant thoughts, naturally asked to be excused. All the heart-warming epithets left over and still usable were quickly debased by their excessive employment in football pep talks. The naïve student whose "I'd die for dear old Rutgers" got an easy laugh was replaced by the cynical student whose unwillingness to believe in or act for any cause was taken as a proof of sophistication. The old were afraid to profess and the young too shy to admit any generous sentiments at all. Ill-understood words like "semantics" were bandied about; never was a generation so much under the influence of rhetoric, of mere words, as that American student generation that prided itself on standing, clear-eyed and cold, on a mountaintop from which it could look down on the gullible generations of the near and distant past. Young people make very poor cynics, very poor realists; and the American young were no exception. But since the young hate being out of the fashion of their own age, a determined hardboiledness became the only tolerable wear, a sort of ideological equivalent of crew-cut hair and brogues.

The arguments advanced by the enemies of the policy of the Wilson administration—and accepted by many of its friends—were not merely convenient; they were plausible. American intervention in 1917 had been represented in two lights, neither of them of sufficient candle power to make the whole picture clear. There was the view that promises of good behavior made by the Germans had been broken, that the dignity of the United States had been attacked, that the flag had been fired on, that American men, women, and children had been murdered on the high seas on their lawful occasions. That view was true as far as it went. It was a powerful stimulant to emotional action while the old, simple view of national dignity and honor was still powerful. But just as the firing on Fort Sumter and on the flag was only the occasion of the Civil War, not its cause, so the German submarine campaign was not a real cause. The German government's use of the submarine was not merely meant as a reprisal for the British blockade—it aimed at the destruction of British military power by naval means, by the naval means open to the lesser naval power. The calculation that this was the best and cheapest way to win the war even if it brought the Americans in was deliberately made. Only the Americans' acceptance of whatever this policy involved—and, far more important, their acceptance of whatever consequences the success of this policy involved—would have saved the United States from war.

This was evident to acute American publicists, to students of public policy. Some were willing to take the risk of a German victory, some were not. Some believed that there was no real risk of such a victory anyway; others, that the United States could get along in a world in which sea-power and land-power were united; still others, that unpleasant though such a world would be and expensive though living in it would prove, the cost of averting such disasters by entering the war on the side of Britain and France was excessive. It does not always pay to insure; the premium may be too high.

But the American people, used to the idea of immunity, their eyes turned inward by centuries of historical necessity, ill informed as to the issues of power involved, and skeptical as to the risks for the United States of any shift in the balance of power, could not be moved to action by any such reasoning. "One Yankee could lick any ten foreigners"—and this argument was even advanced about navies—a quarter in which gallantry is no substitute for ships. By 1914, the only naval power in a position to threaten the dominance of the British navy was the German, not the American; despite this fact, it was believed that—as a writer in *Munsey's Magazine* put it—the superior qualities of the officers and men would more than compensate for the inferior number of battleships and the complete absence of battle cruisers.

The American people has to be stirred to action by an emotional cry, and doubtless it was greatly stirred by the insult to the flag when its ships were fired on by German submarines. But it was not stirred quite enough to generate the emotional temper required for stronger action than the mere arming of merchantmen or the convoying of shipping. The "little group of willful men" in the Senate who filibustered against the armed-ship bill were probably as unpopular with the majority of the American people as they were with President Wilson, but they would have been more numerous and less willful if they had been oppos-

ing the sending overseas of an American Expeditionary
Force.

It was not merely the power issue nor even the issue
of national dignity that provided the driving force. It was
the growing American conviction that there was a danger
to the American way of life in the triumph of a government like that of imperial Germany. The American people
had become more and more convinced that there was far
more in common between them and the British and French
than there was between them and the Germans. They were
stirred by the invasion of Belgium, by the devastation of
France, by the public bad manners of the German government (bad manners that long before 1914 had been an expensive luxury for the Germans). It was sometimes said or
was sometimes written that the Germans lost their propaganda battle because the British cut the cables to America
and the Germans could not tell their own story. But even
in 1914 the wireless system existed and it was quite possible
for the Germans to tell their own story, not only directly
to America by air but indirectly through the American cor-
respondents in Germany, through men like Von Wiegand,
and through other visitors to and admirers of the efficiency
of the German army and state like Joe Patterson, then of
the *Chicago Tribune* and later of the New York *Daily News*.
What cramped the style of German propagandists like
George Sylvester Viereck in 1914 and 1939–41 was the awkward fact that the British agents, with all their cunning and
unscrupulousness, were telling the truth—and of course em-
broidering it. What explained the trend of American
opinion was not that there were certain difficulties in making clear why the Germans had to invade Belgium and
sink the *Lusitania*. It was the fact that the Germans had
invaded Belgium and sunk the *Lusitania*. If the German
propaganda offices in Berlin had been able to denounce

the reports of the burning of the Louvain Library and the destruction of Reims Cathedral as lies made up out of whole cloth, that would have been something, just as their stout denial of having sunk the *Athenia* in 1939 was something—at least, for those resolved to believe anything.

It is not impossible that the world would have been better off, that there would have been an effectual exploitation of the victory of 1918 to secure peace for several generations (an aim that would have seemed preposterously impracticable to most of the human race a century ago), if the case for American intervention in 1917 had been represented in less moralistic terms. As it was, the American people saw themselves as giving—giving food and munitions and men to a general cause in which all the other peoples had material ends and the American people, alone, had purely moral ends in view. It was an attitude expressed in the words of a great man who was not sufficiently self-critical or critical of the aims of his own people. "Sometimes people call me an idealist. Well, that is the way I know I am an American. America is the only idealist nation in the world." So spoke Woodrow Wilson. It was not a very helpful attitude to bring to the solution of the problems of a world in which other people were as idealistic as they could afford to be, even if they could afford less idealism than Uncle Sam could. And only a nation giving constant proof of altruistic idealism could possibly have got away with this attitude of high moral superiority. No nation, not even the American nation, can keep at this high level all the time. So Europe was ironical at the expense of America, and America was shocked by the sight of Europe.

It might have been better if the Americans had had less high moral hopes at the beginning and, with a strong admixture of Yankee practicality, had compromised, openly, with the Mammon of Unrighteousness, taking this sinful world and the so-called human race more as they are and less as they should be, noting that men were made a little less than the angels, but did not stay at that high level.

There was a mutual disillusionment. Europe, which had hoped for a new birth of freedom, resented sermons from the United States of Harding and Coolidge. America, which had rightly seen herself as a liberator, was not ready enough to see that a real liberation had taken place and that there were possibilities in the Europe of Versailles if it could be integrated into a world system.

It is unnecessary to go into the long tragicomedy of disillusionment and recrimination. The intellectuals on both sides of the Atlantic had so much to say for Germany and so little to say about Germany and her neighbors that the man-in-the-street was embittered or bored. Being less sentimental and less optimistic than his intellectual betters, the American man-in-the-street saw, from the beginning, that the only way to stop Hitler was to stop him—and the sooner the better. From 1933 on, it was a case for the sheriff or a vigilante committee, not for discussions as to why bandits turn bandits. The feebleness of the western European powers in those years justified any form of American contempt and, indeed, of American resentment. It was true that it was American aid that gave the Allies decisive victory in 1918. Why were the fruits of that victory let go so easily? Why were the Nazis allowed to begin with successful petty crime like stealing apples and confronted only with sermons? If this was all right, what had the last war been about? I have heard a distinguished American ask this question of a very distinguished Englishman who had nothing but the usual nonsense about Versailles, etc., to offer. It was not good enough—as that Englishman learned before his death, when he had to fight an attitude of mind in America that he had helped to justify.

The Americans who asserted that America had been

duped in 1917 did not need to use either German or American arguments; they had only to listen to the speeches, read the writings, and—still more—inspect the conduct of the rulers and leaders of France and Britain. But of course these last had plenty of help from Americans. Scholars, sciolists, charlatans, mercenaries, all combined to darken counsel. Moral optimism about Germany combined with moral pessimism about Britain to induce a more or less contemptuous resignation. Many complicated questions of historical responsibility were settled out-of-hand, and men famous for their vigilance in domestic matters were remarkably credulous outside the ring-fence of American territory. They were optimistic because they greatly underestimated the difficulties and, still more, the cost of keeping that fence in repair; they greatly underestimated the power of the nations that had designs on the fence and on what it enclosed. They extended their own view of the world too easily to other peoples. Beard, the most eminent of all, thought that *All Quiet on the Western Front* was a German film—which not only was unjust to Hollywood, but had the consequence as well that too little attention was paid to the films that UFA and Hugenberg were providing for the German people, and too little attention also to what the German people were reading besides *All Quiet on the Western Front*. And really, if you classify *Carnival in Flanders (La Kermesse héroïque)* as a film showing the unattractiveness of war, your judgment of general human nature has been distorted to the point that limits your usefulness as a publicist. American war films, about the Second World War, about the Korean War, about the preparation for a possible future war, have made armed service seem more worthy of respect than it was taken to be between the two wars. Even the film of *From Here to Eternity,* with its combination of sex and sadism, gave to the old regular army some of the glamour that Kipling had given the old

British regular army. The military way of life is now, reluctantly, accepted as a necessary part of the American way of life, an acceptance inconceivable before 1941, and films and novels about the military mind, ranging upwards from Mr. James Jones to Messrs. Marquand and Cozzens, testify to both the natural curiosity of the American people and its changed temper.

6

MAN DOES NOT live by bread alone, even pre-sliced bread, and the material optimism bred by American experience has not been accompanied by an equally incontestable spiritual self-confidence. Americans are men and women, subject to the strains and ordeals of humanity, and they have, besides, inherited from Europe a cultural tradition that fights against mere naïve confidence in a world that, every day and in every way, gets better and better. Nevertheless, the American tradition is tied to the idea of progress. It has grown during the centuries in which that novel and revolutionary idea took possession of man's mind in the West, and all American experience has seemed to confirm the view that the world is advancing toward something better, to a fuller, richer life for more people, more of the time. What a great English scholar has written of the Dark Ages, out of which modern Europe and modern America have emerged, is almost comically unlike America. "If that age was an age of faith, it was not merely on account of its external religious profession; still less does it mean that the men of that age were more moral or more humane or more just in their social and economic relations than the men of today. It is rather because they had no faith in themselves or in the possibilities of human effort, but put their trust in something more than civilization and something outside history."[1]

The American historical experience has been totally different. It has been the product of profound faith in man's possibilities and of repeated historical justification

[1] Christopher Dawson: *The Making of Europe.*

for that faith. It is true that the religious tradition imported from Europe by the earlier settlers, especially in New England, had its ingredient of Christian humility and pessimism. President Eliot of Harvard, in the confident nineteenth century, was proclaiming an old New England attitude when he altered the inscription over the door of the new philosophy building in Harvard from "Man is the measure of all things," chosen by the philosophers, to "What is man that Thou art mindful of him?" chosen by himself. But even President Eliot was full of American optimism, as was made plain when in the person of George Santayana he encountered a representative of genuine Mediterranean pessimistic clarity. Another Eliot, in a later generation, was to take rather the side of Santayana than that of Charles Eliot, but Mr. T. S. Eliot, in choosing to live in England rather than in St. Louis or Boston, passed judgment not only on the American scene but indeed on his own fitness to adorn it.

Even in early New England, as Professor Perry Miller has shown, optimism about the destiny of man and society was always breaking in. The New England Calvinists of the first generation of Massachusetts and Harvard were, by the rigorous standards of sixteenth-century Calvinism, deplorably lax—not quite Arminian, but not really orthodox either. The American experience fought against the orthodox doctrine of Protestant Europe. When Jonathan Edwards in eighteenth-century Massachusetts tried to turn back the tide, he was defeated not merely because of his tactless investigation into the reading habits and the free conversation of the sons and daughters of the best families of Northampton, but because the campaign had already been lost. It was not even a rear-guard action that he was fighting; it was a return from Elba for the old orthodoxy, a return that ended with a decisive Waterloo.

American religion was committed, more and more,

to an optimistic view of God's purpose in the world and to an identification of that purpose with the purpose of man, especially American man. Religion more and more lost its supernatural and other-world character. God was conceived of as a kind of King of Brobdingnag convinced that "whoever could make two ears of corn, or two blades of grass, to grow upon a spot of ground where only one grew before, would deserve better of mankind, and do more essential service to his country, than the whole race of politicians put together." And not only than politicians but than unproductive saints. The American religious mind was made ready for the acceptance of the optimistic deism of Franklin and Jefferson, and thousands who would have been horrified to admit that they shared the religious views of those great heretics did in fact share more of their views than they suspected and were further removed from the views of old orthodox Christianity than they realized. The evangelical denominations might still insist on faith before works, but faith was expected to show forth its fruits in works, especially in economic works like abstention from extravagant vices like drink and sexual sin; greed or acquisitiveness was not only not condemned but more and more became a virtue.

It is no new opinion that since the Reformation there has been a more open identification of worldly prosperity with virtue than had been preached, whatever the practice may have been. The virtues inculcated by evangelical religion bore fruit in wealth that was accepted as a proof of virtue. So far the American experience does not differ from the English. But the American experience has gone farther. In some popular versions of modern American religion, prosperity is not merely evidence of virtue—it *is* virtue. It is no mere matter of seeking first the Kingdom of God and having wealth added unto you. Wealth, material success, happiness in this world *is* the Kingdom of God. If a reader doubts this let him read the literature issued from Moscow, Idaho, by Dr. Frank B. Robinson,[2] or "The [late] Great I Am," or listen to Father Divine, or con the advertising pages of the press of that great religious center, Los Angeles. What the early Christians promised for the next world, what other great religions have tried to persuade their adherents to despise, is for many Americans (in this possibly just one jump ahead of the English) the aim of religion. And Christian Science, in a less naïve way, represents the same refusal to accept the grim view of life that

[2] See Dr. Robinson's advertisement in *The World Almanac* for 1943:
"'I TALKED WITH GOD'" (Yes I Did—Actually and Literally) and as a result of that little talk with God, a strange Power came into my life. After 42 years of horrible, dismal, sickening failure, everything took on a brighter hue. It's fascinating to talk with God, and it can be done very easily, once you learn the secret. And when you do—well—there will come into your life the same dynamic Power which came into mine. The shackles of defeat which bound me for years went a-shimmering—and now?—well, I am President of the News Review Publishing Company, which corporation publishes the largest circulating afternoon daily in North Idaho. I own the largest office building in our City, I drive a beautiful Cadillac limousine. I own my own home, which has a lovely pipe-organ in it, and my family are abundantly provided for after I'm gone. And all this has been made possible because, one day, ten years ago, I actually and literally talked with God.

"You, too, may experience that strange mystical Power which comes from talking with God, and when you do, if there is poverty, unrest, unhappiness, or ill-health in your life, well—this same God-Power is able to do for you what it did for me. No matter how useless or helpless your life seems to be—all this can be changed. For this is not a human Power I'm talking about—it's a God-Power. And there can be no limitations to the God-Power, can there?"

For one cent spent on a postal card, this secret will be revealed to anybody—or, at least, the first and cheapest steps can be taken. The present population of Moscow, Idaho, is 6,000, a rise of nearly 2,000 in ten years, much of which may well be due to the business brought by Dr. Robinson. The circulation figures for *The Daily Idahonian* are not given in *The Editor and Publisher*. But the biggest paper in the state has just 20,000, so Dr. Robinson is a booster as well as a mystic.

so many hundreds of generations of experience had made second nature to the human race. The optimism of poets like Shelley, their belief that

"the world's great age begins anew,"

was, after all, tempered by a fear that it might turn out to be another historical confidence trick.

"The world is weary of the past,
  O might it die or rest at last."

Such pessimism was of course not at all unknown to Americans, to great Americans. It was Thoreau who observed with justice that most men live lives of "quiet desperation." It was the author of *Huckleberry Finn* who wrote *The Man That Corrupted Hadleyburg.* It was the American on whose life and example most hagiographical talent has been expanded whose favorite poem began:

"O why should the spirit of mortal be proud?"

And it was again Lincoln who, after the fall of Richmond —when it was obvious that the Civil War was drawing to a triumphant close, that, as Whitman was to write:

"our fearful trip is done,
  The ship has weathered every rack,
    the prize we sought is won"—

made no such triumphant comment, but repeated, with all his melancholy emphasis, a very different passage of poetry:

"Duncan is in his grave;
  After life's fitful fever he sleeps well;
  Treason has done his worst; nor steel, nor poison,
  Malice domestic, foreign levy, nothing,
  Can touch him further."

But the American tradition most effectively publicized is not disposed to worry over

> *"the dead,*
> *Whom we to gain our peace, have sent to peace."*

That life is not reducible to formulas, that there are bound to be sorrows and disillusionment even for the best prepared, for the new elect who have had the right eugenic ancestry, the proper education, the necessary contacts—these ideas are heresy in modern America. The man who has cured himself of B.O. and halitosis, has learned French to surprise the waiter, and the saxophone to amuse the company, may, as Heywood Broun said, find that people still avoid him because they do not like him.

But is it a heresy entertained by a few cranks only, or in fact half-believed in by a great part of the population? In a country where it is news, comforting news, that "Life begins at forty," some skepticism must have crept into the national viewpoint. Some people must have been thinking that life comes to an end when the first illusions, the first hopes, the fresh power of youth, are exhausted, that American life is designed for boys and young men, for girls of course, too, but not for adults. If this belief is or was widespread, one reason is to be found (as critical Americans have pointed out) in a view of life in which success is identified with competitive success—not with attaining a fixed standard, but with winning a place in the first ten of every hundred. As far as this view *is* accepted, it condemns the vast majority to failure, since ninety per cent must be ranked as unsuccessful. It is true that the man who is successful in one line may be unsuccessful in all others—and much American advertising is devoted to making some man anxious about his appearance, his fluency in speech, even his smell, who yet has valid economic or professional grounds for complacency. On the other hand, the man who is unsuccessful in his business or profession can find some compensation through buying culture or some other non-priceable good. He can be induced to look forward to a secure old age by an insurance company, or to a new and vigorous middle age by the advertisers of religions, education, body-belts, or what-have-you. But the American man-in-the-street is descended not from buyers of wooden nutmegs, but from sellers of them. He takes advertising seriously, but not so seriously as all that. He is not surprised to learn from Mr. John R. Tunis that the economic record of a Harvard "class," twenty years on, makes depressing reading—if from a higher education a large cash income is anticipated. He remembers catastrophes like that of 1929, following which the current hotel joke was the question put by the clerk: "What do you want a room for—sleeping in, or jumping from?" The anxieties of the American businessman, his needs for health farms, like the need of his wife for psychoanalysis and yoga, make another standard national joke. The fresh, boyish, unlined, happy, and, in the good sense of the term, ingenuous faces of the young American soldiers whom one used to see in the London Underground are replaced in twenty years' time by faces as marked by "the contagion of the world's slow stain" as those of the sharp-faced, acute, cynical Cockney soldiers were, if not from birth at least from adolescence. Even today, the bulky, gaily clad American airmen seem innocent and hopeful. Yet the world cannot be made safe for boys and girls, no matter how hard parents and society may try. They cannot even be fitted for the world, for that world will in part be made by them and altered by them.

It is perhaps the competitive strain of American life that accounts for the excessive gloom of current American letters. Just as an American advertiser is not content, like his English colleague, to tell you that "XXX is good for you," but insists that "XXX is better," on sale at the "better" bars or five-and-tens, the American novelist insists on telling you that things are worse and getting worse all the time. A great deal of this literary pessimism is mere fashion; the black paint is shot on by a paint-gun in the literary assembly line. In most cases it is merely Eddie Guest and Harold Bell Wright in reverse. But in the case of the better writers it is more than that: it is a resentful criticism of American life as being full of promises that no society can, in fact, keep. It is not valid criticism of much American literature that it takes a gloomy view, that it shows the unhappy side of American life. If it does, if it is bitterly critical, that is no novelty; so were many admitted past masters: Howells in his political novels, Henry James in his life, the Western agrarians of 1900 in their gritty pictures of life on the farm or in the small Kansas or Nebraska town. If Aldous Huxley is right in attributing German inability to handle the problem of modern personal life to the rarity of good German novels, Americans ought to be grateful to their novelists, who provide them with abundant precedents for all possible emergencies. And it would be a fraud on the public not to provide a sufficient number of ugly, awkward, dangerous, and painful situations, for we shall none of us miss experiences of that type. A happy literature is a dangerous drug.

But the pessimistic American writers, from Dreiser to Mary McCarthy or Carson McCullers, have, in fact, helped to break down the American view of life into still unreconciled attitudes. The optimistic religion of business and progress proved inadequate, and with its collapse other parts of the national religion were at least shaken. The standards of family morals, of sexual behavior, were affected. It is true that a great deal of the alarm over the dangerous immorality of modern American letters was silly. The book censors who hunted for improper words were no better employed than the beach or movie censors who measured plunging necklines like so many erotic geologists or sweaters with the eyes of a lubricious geometrician. Nevertheless, the censors, however stupid, were vaguely registering a great change, the invasion of sexual morals by the competitive standard that had conquered business.

Advertising and fiction alike told boys and girls that sexual happiness was theirs on pretty reasonable terms. Mr. James J. Walker was wrong when he said that "no girl had ever been ruined by a book," though he was right in thinking that no girl would be saved by idiotic censorship, especially if it left advertising sections alone, as being business and not art. For literature and advertising both presented possible lines of conduct that had been "unthinkable" (though, of course, thought of) a generation before. They offered precedents for action that came home to the young and produced more strains, more differences between the fiction of American life and the fact. And as another unsuccessful municipal politician could have told ex-Mayor Walker, it was nothing new:

> "*Galeotto fu il libro e chi lo scrisse:*
> *Quel giorno più non vi leggemo avanti.*"

Again, what was mere nonsense for boys and girls, whatever ethical dangers it involved, was dangerous for adults, for either it bred in them an easy optimism, the view that the shortest way across was the best way round; or it bred a premature pessimism and added to the amount of dissent from the official Panglossian religion that all was for the best in the best of all possible republics—or would be as soon as That Man was out of the White House. More people than was really necessary reacted, reacted by divorce, by neurosis, by an affected gloom that was no more impressive or convincing than so much real-estate optimism. And it was not a moment too soon that one of the acutest American sociologists issued his manifesto called *Let Your Mind Alone*.

But literary pessimism was not merely pessimism about this "so-called human race," merely doubts about "how to tell man from the apes." It was pessimism about that part of American life which had, historically, best justified American optimism—American economic prospects.

Literary pessimism about American life was not an invention of the twenties. Around 1900, the long depression years had had their reflection in regional novels that described, with depressing fidelity, what it was like to live in Ed Howe's Kansas or Hamlin Garland's "Middle Border." But for all their sincerity, for all the gritty verisimilitude of their style, the prairie novelists did not seem to get to grips with any general human problems. Of all the ills their heroes and heroines had to endure, there seemed to be few that dollar wheat wouldn't have cured. A much better novelist, Howells, was driven to writing socialist novels of the future by anger at the American present. Jack London predicted the rise of fascism, and there were plenty of literary spokesmen for the age of Wilson's "New Freedom." The "novel of social significance" was not new when it became the rage in the thirties.

But what *was* new was the general agreement among the new leisure class created by the new American economy—the women, and the sons of the successful pioneers —that life in Gopher Prairie, in Zenith, in New York, even in Paris, was hard to live. That pessimism was often affected and not of the highest quality. Indeed, the classic of this age, *Babbitt,* was not a pessimistic book at all, for George F. Babbitt survives his soul-killing experiences as a human being who would not have been improved in any sense of the term by living in the rue de la Huchette of

Elliot Paul's imagination or even in the precincts of Saint-Germain-des-Prés.

On top of this literary pessimism came the genuine pessimism bred by the depression. Here the writers were representing a general national mood and one that still colors much of American life. For behind a good deal of optimism is the memory of the great collapse, and behind a good deal of apparently thoughtless determination to have the best of both worlds in war and in peace is the terrifying memory of the years in which the American dream seemed to have become a nightmare: a nightmare of unemployment, of bankruptcy, bankruptcy of individuals, of great corporations, of cities, of states, an age of the destruction of normal economic expectation, the most fatal failure of a capitalist society. No novels or plays could exaggerate the indignation, the shock felt by millions of Americans at the coming, not of hard times, but of a general collapse of leadership, a general betrayal of confidence. "Sez you" became the cry of millions who had been well-behaved, credulous, good citizens, dutifully keeping both feet on the ground—only to find the ground giving way under them.

This was reflected in literature, in plays, even in films. It was reflected but exaggerated. There was a sudden wave of literary revolutionary affectation. Communism was pretty nearly the only wear and a very high proportion of young American writers either passed through the party ranks or were "fellow travelers." A few stayed. It was the time in which a reportage of fairly normal labor riots and strike incidents could be solemnly published under the title *America Faces the Barricades*. It was the incubation period of the New Deal.

There were external reasons why this literary extremism did not last. The control of the American Communist Party was not much more intelligent than that of any other Comintern branch, but the American heretics and schismatics were not like their timid English brethren, content to go into the garden and eat worms or dirt. They spoke up in meeting. They denounced and deplored and, in the old tradition of the mourners' bench at a frontier camp meeting, confessed their own sins and the sins of the unrepentant. There were half a dozen heresies apart from the great Trotskyist schism.

And with the first turn of the tide in 1933, the revolutionary temper of the American people turned out to have been a case of wrong diagnosis. It was only depression measles. It was no longer "Farewell to Reform" but Good-by to Revolution. The revolutionary intelligentsia scattered in all directions—some into the New Deal, some into pure letters, some into pessimistic conservatism, at least one into the embraces of the Dies Committee set up to smell out Communism with the zeal and technique of a witch-doctor at work in a kraal in darkest Africa.

The pessimists were replaced by the far more interesting preachers of historical optimism. And that optimism (a sign of the times) was based on the American past as well as on the American future. There was a cultivation of literary archæology; a change from little periodicals on the Left Bank to forgotten Southern and New England masters. Historical novels, historical films, primitive American art, primitive American thought, were given a new value by the need for restoring American self-esteem as well as by the spectacle of Hitler's Europe or the Russia of the great purge.

The movement was, up to a point, healthy. It was better than precious imitations of European preciosity. But it was forced to ignore too many truths to be wholly healthy. Early American art was interesting, but it was not much more than that. Where it was most successful was in the adaptation of European models, in Richmond or Charleston or Salem. There were admirable architects and craftsmen in eighteenth-century America, but that was all. Gilbert Stuart is a good painter, but he does not compare very well with his contemporary, Goya. Shaker craftsmanship was sound, but a Shaker village did not compare very well with Fountains Abbey or La Chaise-Dieu. For all that Mr. Van Wyck Brooks or Miss Constance Rourke could do, the American record in these fields of achievement was mediocre.

There was more to be said for a cultivation of really primitive art, of American folklore. But, again, there was too much forcing of the issue. The Americans were the heirs of English, Scottish, Irish folk song, but they did not increase their inheritance or improve it. *Frankie and Johnny* is an amusing ballad, but it is not *Helen of Kirkconnel*. Perhaps, as an eminent authority has hinted, the numerous unprinted folk songs do the American genius more credit; but even in this field there is no great originality and there are still importations from the Old World like *John Glaister*. As far as the man-in-the-street is concerned, the situation is further complicated by the synthetic character of much of the folk song he hears and likes and thinks of as deeply and traditionally American. Primitive art that is not really primitive is boring in the not very long run. When on a vaudeville circuit a modern cowboy asks with false naïveté whether the stars he sees are "big peopled worlds like our own," he is competing not with genuine folk song but with Leopardi. He cannot long stand the competition of:

> *"a che vale*
> *Al pastor la sua vita,*
> *La vostra vita a voi?"*

When a nation is at such a stage of sophistication as the Americans have reached, it is idle to try to fob them off with songs their mothers would have sung to them if the industry had been as well organized as it is now. All that the modern ballad-makers can do was better done by Stephen Foster than it is ever done today.

So we have to fall back on the real artists, on the men and women who are willing to follow their spirit where it listeth. And it is hard to discriminate, hard for the critic and hard for the common reader. Even the toughness and brutality, the crudity of language may become as much of a convention as the prudery of a generation ago. Mr. Cole Porter has truly asserted:

> *Good authors, too, who once knew better words,*
> *Now only use four-letter words, writing prose*
> *Anything goes.*

But there was a great deal to be said, too, for the young woman who remarked: "Oh, I never thought anybody *said* those things. I thought they only appeared in books!"

This is not the place (or it would be as easy as it is tempting) to praise contemporary American literature, so abundant, so varied, so courageous, so entertaining, so much the senior partner now in the English-speaking world. But it has not yet done what is necessary for national unification. It has not provided what Mr. G. M. Young rightly credited Mr. H. G. Wells with providing a generation ago in England, a new *Cortegiano,* a picture and standard of the modern world that neither crushed energy and optimism nor was so sugar-coated and irrelevant as to drive the young off in angry derision.

7

IN AMERICA the role of the farmer has been almost as important historically as it has been emotionally. The land that was settled, cleared, tilled has been the creation of the farmer, in most areas a creation that is quite recent in time. In Europe the basic work was done hundreds, even thousands, of years ago; some historians may recall the primitive settlers, the makers of the first efficient plows, or such restorers of material and spiritual culture as the monks of Monte Cassino. But all that is remote. In America there are many men still alive who remember that last great western push of settlement on to the Great Plains. Settlement in the cut-over timberlands of northern Minnesota or Wisconsin is quite recent. Even regions that had seemed to be doomed to total abandonment like Vermont have had a new lease of life as milk-producers. A high proportion of the immigrants who have settled on marginal abandoned lands—like the Poles in Wisconsin or in the tobacco lands of the Connecticut Valley—have preserved, for one generation at least, the peasant attitude of reverence for the soil. Americans who have migrated to the city from the countryside or the small country town have inherited many rural habits of mind. And the rural bias of the American people has been reinforced by a political system that overweighs the rural vote in federal and still more in state elections, and by a historical tradition that has been adequate for a farmers' republic, for the egalitarian, free, rural democracy of Jefferson and Jackson. For an American, therefore, even if he is a city-dweller, there is something especially outrageous in the long decline in relative economic importance and in social stability of the American farm population. That less than half of the American population should now live in rural areas, that much less than a quarter of the population should be living on farms—this is novel, disconcerting, improper. And the American farmer is more or less consciously exploiting a situation in which his own natural desire to get a "reasonable" share of the total national income is politically supported by not very clear-minded town-dwellers, as well as by quite clear-minded statesmen and sociologists who hold that a contented and numerous rural population is a necessity for a healthy republic.

It would be unrealistic to underestimate the power of this rural bias. The conquest of the United States by the plow has been the most generally approved American victory. It is only today that critical experts are beginning to wonder whether the plow has not been an enemy of the American land and, more confidently, to ask if American policy is to be devoted to keeping a large population employed at a low economic level on the land or to producing from that land the largest quantities of needed crops? Ships loaded with wheat, little metal gasometers filled with corn, mountains of rancid butter, all paid for by the taxpayer, are a tribute not only to the political power of the overrepresented farmer, but to a rural myth. Much of American farming is as idyllic and as uneconomic as the dairy at the Petit Trianon. Such skepticism has to fight a centuries-old national tradition that makes of the advancing farmer the great folk hero. Not until the independent settlers had made the forest, then the prairie, then the High Plains, into plowland, was the great American folk-movement over. The ballads of the nation fight the figures of the agronomists. So far the ballads have it.

For the winning of the West, the making of all America, bred its legends, not only the legends of the great pathfinders or great Indian fighters, but of the bringers of the gifts of civilization. There was the legend of Johnny Appleseed, that John Chapman who carried his apples all over the West, most famous of those who

> *In the days of President Washington,*
> *The glory of the nations,*
> *Dust and ashes,*
> *Snow and sleet,*
> *And hay and oats and wheat,*
> *Blew west,*
> *Crossed the Appalachians.*[1]

And with the wheat and the hay and the apples came civilization:

> *A ballot-box in each apple,*
> *A state capital in each apple,*
> *Great high schools, great colleges,*
> *All America in each apple.*[2]

Americans like Johnny Appleseed, like the bold South Carolina woman who introduced indigo culture, like John Rolfe, who did more for the future by curing Virginia tobacco than by marrying Pocahontas, like Edmund Ruffin, who found the way to restore the wasted lands of tidewater Virginia, like a hundred plant- and cattle-breeders—these were the American equivalents of Pallas and Flora and the other Greek and Roman benefactors of the husbandman. To the prairie farmer's clever son, the *Georgics* were the most relevant Latin poetry—and one clever daughter of a pioneer professor has told us what Virgil meant to her in raw Nebraska. Miss Willa Cather, who has combined the *Eclogues* and the *Georgics* in *My Antonia,* is only the most accomplished prose Virgil of the great settlement.

[1] Quoted by permission of the publisher from *Collected Poems of Vachel Lindsay* (New York: The Macmillan Co.; 1925).
[2] Ibid.

The corn, the maize higher than a man's head, was the oldest and most representative American crop. "Out where the tall corn grows" was a true folk song and it is fitting that the opening song of the nearest modern American approach to folk-art, *Oklahoma!,* should be a celebration of corn "as high as an elephant's eye." The annual cornhusking championship was the true Olympic festival of a farmer people. It is probably pure sentiment to regret the passing of the tall corn; in some regions, at least, it is profitably replaced by shorter and more useful and economical though less impressive corn plants. The great combines on the Western plains, as well as other labor-saving devices, have reduced to a mere battalion the once great army of migratory harvesters who, under the derogatory title of "hoboes" or the even more dangerous epithet of "Wobblies," moved from state to state with the harvest. Their songs are going too:

> *You advertise in Omaha,*
> *"Come, leave the valley of the Kaw."*
> *Nebraska calls, "Don't be misled,*
> *We'll furnish you a feather bed!"*

But the Rock Candy mountains of the hoboes, like the revolutionary dreams of the I.W.W. (the Wobblies), have passed beyond the horizon as the American farmer has adjusted himself slowly and reluctantly to a new mechanical world in which the old laws seem to have been repealed.

First of all, the American farmer's share in the national income has not only fallen as the proportion of farmers to the total population has fallen; it has fallen even lower than mere proportions would suggest. The farmers, as a class, underwent all the downward pressures of American life in the period between the two wars, but they have only in a slight degree benefited by the boom times. During the first war, the farmer, like everybody else, got a greatly increased cash income (though not nearly so much as he thought he should have got; price-fixing was as unpopular then as now—as the Democratic administration learned at the 1920 elections). There was a general discounting of a rise in the value of farm land that had doubled the amount of agricultural mortgages between 1910 and 1920. But the farm income, which in 1919 was $17,000,000,000 odd, fell catastrophically; and even when good times had returned for industry, it was only $12,000,000,000 in 1926. When the great collapse of 1929–33 began, it was again the farmers who took the worst rap. Farm income in 1931 was less than a third of farm income in 1919.

It was no wonder that the American farmer, his whole security endangered, his whole normal expectation of profit made ludicrous, should have been embittered, angry against all the forces, occult and open, that seemed to make sure that he always got the wrong end of the bargain. He was not prepared (who would have been?) to accept the fact that the tide of economic development had turned against him. For instance, the Midwest farmer's basic problem was to decide in any given year whether to feed his corn crop to his pigs and sell the pigs, or to cut down his pig production and sell his corn. The majority of farmers were sure to guess wrong. For if the majority bred pigs, pigs were cheap and corn dear; and if, next year, the majority sold corn and neglected pigs, pigs were dear and corn cheap. To play the game against the "corn-hog" cycle required foresight, respect for statistics, and either a successful determination not to do what your neighbors did, or a highly organized system of co-operative marketing and production. For the majority, whose decision was the main price determinant, only the second solution was open. And the American farmer was highly individualistic, a slow and skeptical cooperator, always ready to take a chance to beat the market— a state of mind bred in him by political and social institutions and by a highly variable climate. For a catastrophe that destroyed crops in one region might have no effect in another which would benefit by the short supply. Farming was a gamble, and that was the way the American farmer liked it.

It was natural, too, that the farmer should have looked out for foreign as well as for domestic devils. Though he did not really appreciate it, his competitive power in the overseas markets was being weakened. For one thing, with the development of groundnuts in West Africa, the slow, indirect way of producing fats through lard was made expensive. Indeed, the cottonseed oil of the South was a dangerous competitor of Iowa lard *inside* the American tariff wall. And that wall made it harder for the potential customers of the American farmer to buy what he had to sell—in direct competition with Canada, Australia, and Argentina and in indirect competition with all the subtropical products made available by modern technology and made additionally formidable competitors by changes in dietary habits.

For two generations, the American farmer by voting the Republican ticket and supporting a high-tariff policy had shown notable disinterestedness, if cloudy economic thinking, for he thus helped to pay the high price of industrializing America. By the 1920's, he was still voting the Republican ticket and supporting very high tariffs indeed, but he was no longer content to let it go at that. He knew that protection for his basic crops was superfluous; what he wanted was a share in the total national income proportional to his numbers (which could be computed) and to his social and political merits which were more open to dispute. So he supported schemes like the McNary-Haugen bill, which was the first serious attempt to use the taxing power of the Union to compensate the farmer for his tariff-induced losses. But it was now questionable whether the traditional roles had not been reversed and whether American industry, now interested in its export market, was not having to pay the costs of keeping alive American agriculture on a scale to which the nation was accustomed. The bean-growers of Michigan could be protected against unfair foreign competition, but of what profit was that to the automobile industry of Michigan, which needed markets, not protection? But the farmer (with a great deal of non-farm support) continued the attack, and the refusal of the Republican presidents to sanction such subsidies to the farm interest helped to produce that revulsion against the Grand Old Party which led millions of American farmers to vote in 1932 and in 1936 with no grateful regard for the fact that the Republican Party had saved the Union two generations or more before.

But the prices of crops were not the only worry of the farmer or of the nation. The very existence of the land was at stake over wide regions. The explorers of the early nineteenth century had marked the region west of the Missouri "the great American desert." It was roughly all the land west of 100°; it was marked by the change in its rainfall and in its vegetable cover. East of 100° was the tall-grass country that got the necessary twenty inches of rain a year; west was the short-grass country that could not rely on the necessary rainfall, a region in which the native grasses were hammered into a moisture-holding mat by the feet of the millions of buffalo and totally undisturbed by the nomadic Indians, who lived off the buffalo. But as the tide of settlement moved west, these lands designed for buffalo and then for cattle were coveted by the would-be settlers brought in, with their new plows and reapers, by the new railroads.

A series of exceptionally wet years made the fears of the geographers seem folly or treason. There were some individual catastrophes. There was the famous story of the pioneers who had set out for the West with the legend painted on their wagon "Pike's Peak or Bust," and who came back with the legend revised to "Pike's Peak and Busted." There was the story of the westward-moving optimist who met the eastward-moving pessimist. "This would be a fine country if it had water." "So would Hell!"

But not until the end of the eighties was there a serious recession of settlement in western Kansas and Nebraska and in the Dakotas. There are counties in those states whose population has never been so high as it was in the census of 1890. It was discovered that there *were* limits to settlement; that the rainfall was often inadequate; that the belief that plowing itself increased the rainfall was a booster's error, made in more or less good faith.

The economic equilibrium established round 1900 was badly upset by the First World War. The demand for wheat was immense; prices were high; more and more land was plowed up, including land that should never have been plowed. All the postwar sorrows of the American farmer fell with especial weight on the shoulders of the farmer on the new Western frontier between the well-watered and the semi-arid lands. Low prices hit him worst; he had fewest capital resources; he was farthest from domestic markets; was most at the mercy of world prices as recorded in the Chicago wheat pit or in Winnipeg or Liverpool. In these states the radical political movements —Farmer-Labor parties, the Nonpartisan League, radical dissent within the Democratic Party in the southern section, in Oklahoma and Texas—upset the old political system. There was a return to the spirit of the insurgent nineties when Mrs. Lease, the "Kansas Pythoness," advised her fellow citizens "to raise less corn and more hell." Old established radical dynasties like the La Follettes; new figures like Governor Floyd Olson in Minnesota and Senator Nye and Governor Langer in North Dakota; returning figures from the past like "Alfalfa Bill" Murray in Oklahoma, expressed this discontent with an economic system that was a purely negative lottery: all blanks and no prizes.

But the worst times came with the general depression, with the general collapse of rural credit, with the foreclosures on a great scale that marked the collapse of farm values and, even in so rich, well-farmed, and well-ordered a state as Iowa, led to something like a *jacquerie*. Far worse was the situation of the High Plains farmer. For nature took a hand and inflicted a series of catastrophic droughts, droughts that got the attention of the most urban-minded Americans. For the dry, loose soil of the marginal farms simply blew into the air. Hundreds of miles away in Minneapolis, the soil from Dakota farms piled up on the carpets of the houses, and over a thousand miles away it darkened the sky in New York. Away to the south, in western Texas and Oklahoma, it was a case of farm lands turning to sand; and the poor, ill-educated, ill-equipped marginal farmers there began that long, uninspiring trek westward to California. The "Okies" of *The Grapes of Wrath* were a novelty in American history, mostly defeated, dispirited fugitives from soil that had been opened to settlement only in 1890 and was desert by 1934.

Farther north, things were not quite so bad. The Scandinavian farmers of the Dakotas had more technical resources and more capital. Even in the worst year of all, 1934—when the rolling country west of the Missouri looked, at a distance, like a Scottish moor covered with a kind of heather that was, in fact, wheat stunted to a few inches by the drought, when the dying cattle were shipped hundreds of miles east by the federal government to water—there was no despair. "A good year will set us all right," a Swedish farmer told me when I spoke of the theory that arable farming would have to be abandoned altogether. And an Irish settler, a veteran a hundred miles farther west, said this was bad, but not so bad as the grasshopper year in the seventies when he had brought horses up from Nebraska and could not water them for three days because every water-hole was full of dead "locusts."

But no amount of courage could make it less of a disaster. The whole credit structure collapsed. Such exhibitions of state pride as the skyscraper capital of North Dakota that soars out of the plain at Bismarck seemed doomed to be an American equivalent of the statue of Ozymandias. "They say we must pay our debts, but they tell you that they understand why you can't pay your war debts," said a Swedish farmer to me that year in the scorched country west of the Missouri. "If you can't pay, how can we? And our debts are just as much war debts as yours. We contracted them to raise crops for you. The government wouldn't let wheat prices rise, but it let them fall all right. We won't quit and we won't pay."

Even in less desolated regions, there was the same anger, the same sense of frustration, the same nostalgia for the good days before Europe went mad and the American land ceased to rise in value every decade and ceased even to stay put. For this last outrage of all, the blame was imputed to the East—and Europe is part of the East.

The American farmer and all American society had been taught for over three centuries to have a sacred respect for the land. This did not prevent its being exploited, mined rather than farmed; but trust in the American soil, the producer of good things, *magna parens frugum,* was as lively in American as in Roman breasts. That land, it must be remembered, had never known what Europe has so often known and Asia knows nearly all the time, the terror of a great famine. Many Americans have gone hungry in the past, some go hungry now; undernourishment as well as stupid nourishment is endemic in certain regions. But America has not gone through an experience like that of

Ireland in 1846-7 or that of Ukraine twenty years ago. To find the American soil revolting, refusing to bear, blowing away, having to be abandoned (in Oklahoma only a generation after the first settlement), was the most disturbing sign of all those that pointed to a need for a national stocktaking. The decade between 1920 and 1930 was the first in American history (since the white man came) in which the forest area *increased*—and that meant less an intelligent replanting of cut-over land than the natural springing-up of scrub. To have to take thought for the morrow of the whole American land, this was a reminder that even the United States was not exempt from the general limitations of our human dwelling-place.

It was a disillusioned, often embittered, and still more often puzzled farmer who had to make the great reorientation to the first war. The job of making America was his; his were the hopes of most representative Americans. He found that America would not stay made, that Nature and unknown, remote, and evil forces still combined to thwart him. He was saved from expropriation by the "Triple A" programs of the first Roosevelt administration. For the moment he was grateful. "Landon won't carry a county west of here," said a prominent Republican in a Middle West state in my hearing in 1936; "Henry Wallace will carry them all."

But the Republican Party (of which the speaker was a senatorial ornament) came back all the same. For the farmer didn't like not growing crops, killing young pigs, adjusting his methods of farming not to his own guesses and hopes but to remote statistical calculations in Washington. As long as he had no other cash resources, the federal checks were gladly, even gratefully, received. But when he got a chance to make money again by growing as much as possible, he jumped at it. And then to learn that he had to submit to more rigorous controls, do without tractors sent to Britain or Russia, do without sons and hired hands sent to Guadalcanal or Iceland or Libya—this was to have another lesson in the perverseness of the nature of things and a new temptation to look for the devils who were in part, at least, responsible for this new disaster. One of those devils was of course Hitler; another and much more hated one was Tojo, or any representative Japanese; but others were Americans—above all, the remote "bureaucrats" who didn't know the life of a dirt farmer and his needs and deserts.

Farmers have long supplied the soldiers for most societies. But in all countries farmers dislike war, however resigned they may be to it. Its waste seems to them (as it does to women) a contradiction of all the habits of normal, healthy, and beneficent life. And two wars in one generation, two wars not at all obviously connected with the needs of the farmer in the Great Valley, made a demand on critical imagination that could not be met, at any rate in full. Patriotism, national pride, the acceptance of the legitimate authority of the United States, these were in many cases substitutes and adequate substitutes for that complete grasp of the ideological issues of the war that comes easily to editorial writers. Thinking his the most important national activity, convinced that all other forms of economic life are parasitic on his, the American farmer (or any farmer) was resigned to war but skeptical about its conduct. So he did not take kindly to economic controls; they were worse than the draft that took his son. He knew the limits of planning (can *they* control the rainfall?). But it must be remembered that in the rural areas there was less opposition to the Second World War than to the First; there was less than there had been to the Civil War, in North and South alike. And the American farmer has got hold of one truth at last. "It takes more than one to keep the peace" is a more useful maxim than that "it takes two to make a quarrel."

And converting the farmer was very important indeed. For the American city did not reproduce itself. It used to live off immigration from Europe and the country; now it must live off immigration from the country, and in every American city and town a very large section of the population are still farm boys in sentiment, still in touch with the land, still half-convinced that only farmers really know the answers. It is, in part, his conviction that he is the sole indispensable citizen, as much as his share of the general human belief that the world owes him a living, which allows the traditionally independent American farmer to rely so completely on political action to keep him at the economic level to which he thinks he is entitled. All other economic classes are parasites by definition; a farmer producing *anything,* no matter at what cost and how little wanted, is serving the deepest interests of the commonwealth. It is a belief that not only comes naturally to the farmer but is half-believed in by the urban voter. But only half-believed in today.

More than half of the American people now live in areas classified as "urban," and if some of those areas are urban only in a census-taker's mind, many residents in technically rural areas are really city-dwellers. The devotee of the old New England rural life of Bronson Alcott's boyhood who sought it round Westport, or even Southport, Connecticut, would be wasting his time.

The new roads and the new cars, and the closer integration of national life that these have made possible, have led to a very rapid sophistication of the remaining rural population. Reuben, the hick farmer of vaudeville, is a fiction as dated as a Keystone comedy. Even small country towns have been urbanized in appearance and in temper. Movies, advertising, mail-order houses, ease of travel have undermined the cracker-barrel on which the traditional rural philosopher sat. The last great effort to impose rural moral standards—prohibition—failed, and legal puritanism now finds its political driving force in urban Catholicism, not in rural Protestantism. The pin-up girl, not booze, is the enemy to be extirpated by the arm of the law, but the dangerous seductions of *Esquire* are not burning topics in the corn belt.

The urbanization of the American country has followed fairly closely on the urbanization of the American city, on its coming-of-age, its acceptance of the facts that a city is not merely an overgrown village and that city life is a new way of life to be learned. And it is in the American cities, outside of New York and a few of the older Eastern regional capitals, that the coming-of-age of the American way of life can be most easily seen.

The American cities were and are very unlike English cities. There is no real capital; New York may be a playground for socially ambitious Westerners, or even for Bostonians or Philadelphians anxious to relax a little; but persons whose position on the Main Line or in Beacon Street is secure do not seek to climb to Fifth or even to Park Avenue. Distances are too great for social centralization, and the idea of Washington as a social center is older than the New Deal though not much. A city like Seattle, like Louisville, like Cleveland, like Milwaukee, has bred its own society, imposed its own standards, refusing scions of great Boston dynasties admission into the best brewing circles of Milwaukee, not taking too seriously the visitors to Louisville, for whom it is merely the home of the Kentucky Derby.

The towns grew few or none of the English provincial-town complexes. They knew they were not so big as New York (the only American city that can afford to call itself *little* and *old*) or even Chicago, but they had their own standards, their own society. Mark Twain settled down in Hartford; Howells had doubts about quitting Boston for New York; so great a newspaperman as William Allen White stayed in Emporia all his days; and as for persuading a citizen of San Francisco that he would gain anything by moving elsewhere—why, confusing him or her with a mere "Angeleno" could hardly be more offensive! The cities, large and small, became more attractive as streets were paved, water brought in, capital spent on civic improvements. The days are long past when there was justification for the New York reporter who was sent to cover a fire in Rome, New York, and wired his office: "This town seems to have been built in a day."

For one thing, towns have become much cleaner, much more habitable. That adjustment of the American people to the American climate which modern wealth and technology have brought about has made the cities habitable in a way they were not a generation ago. Improved local transport, for instance, has abolished the horrors of the horse car in winter. No longer do pigs scavenge on upper Broadway, and if Philadelphia's water supply is still very bad, the city has a subway.

The dirt, untidiness, lack of unity of the American city were necessary aspects of its fantastic growth. No doubt corrupt municipal politics accounted for a good deal; so did the recent rural habits of most city-dwellers. But it was, above all, a case of priorities. Not everything could be done at once. The cities were too busy growing not to sprawl. It is obvious that the Baltimore of Mr. Mencken's and Cardinal Gibbons's boyhood must have been a charming place to live in, but on a hot day the smells must have detracted from the charm as they still do in places like East St. Louis. Booth Tarkington's Indianapolis, Tom Johnson's Cleveland, the Chicago of the early Dreiser, full of energy and civic pride—these also were primitive in a good many ways. Primitive, but not provincial.

The consequences are not merely agreeable for the city-dwellers; they are important for the world. For they encourage the regional feeling, the regional diversity of the American people. They make it almost as silly as ever to look to New York or Washington, or even to Chicago or Hollywood, to find out what the American people are thinking. Great areas may be thinking nothing; great areas may be thinking totally different things. "Almost as silly," for of course there has been a great deal of integration. Radio and television; the movies with their influence on the tastes of the multitude and their reflection of what high-paid guessing experts think the public wants; the national columnists, syndicated in newspapers and magazines all over the country; the lecturers, telling the same tale from Sandusky to San Diego—all these have made it easier to estimate what the American people think or will think. But they have not made irrelevant the important truth that there are no provinces, no areas ready to take a lead from a center, no universally accepted body of makers and molders of public opinion.

The great American cities have their own great newspapers, as the greatest British cities have. But there are hundreds of small city papers, too, some of which may be more important in their area than any metropolitan paper is in its. "I don't care what the London *Times* said of me —I'm waiting to see what the *Skibbereen Eagle* says." The Irish M.P. who was being epigrammatic in London would have been uttering the merest platitude in Washington.

The local magnate is not often thinking of how quickly he can get away to some region where his origin is little known and settle down as a country squire. It is true that, once the connection with the grass-roots is cut, he may do just that; but if he does he loses all power and prestige in the region from which his fortune came.

More often he and others like him will be the founders or benefactors of local museums like the admirable one in

Seattle or the magnificent one in Kansas City. The local universities, state or private; the local municipal universities like those in Cincinnati or Louisville; new city universities like those in Detroit and Kansas City—these are centers of local pride, of local opinion, of local controversy. So are the local preachers and the local politicians.

Sometimes the prestige of the city outside its own region may be more or less accidental. It is certain that not many people would have heard of Rochester, Minnesota, if the Mayo brothers had not established their famous clinic in their home town. The New Yorkers had to come to them as other New Yorkers had to go to Reno. Rochester, New York, owes a good deal of its importance to the munificence of George Eastman, who gave great endowments to the university, founded the great music school, and gave a subject to Mr. Paul Horgan for *The Fault of Angels.*

Literature reflects this healthy provincialism. Not only are there good regional novelists and poets but, odder still, there is no taboo on fictional crime outside New York and its neighborhood. Some of the best modern American crime stories are located round Duluth; Mr. Dashiell Hammett's hero practices in San Francisco; Perry Mason works inside the law in Los Angeles County; there are eminent fictional crime-detectors at work as far apart as Dallas and Cape Cod.

There is a great professional orchestra in a city so geographically remote as Minneapolis, which also served as the home town of a most admired American Shakespearean scholar, well over a thousand miles, both of them, from New York or the Folger Library in Washington.

It is this regional autonomy that justifies, as far as it can be justified, the locality rule in politics. The law that prohibits an American citizen from representing in Congress a state in which he does not live and, in effect, limits the members of the House of Representatives to men and women living in the actual districts concerned, is a serious handicap to Congress as an efficient maker of national policy. But how natural, how inevitable it is in the United States! The case of Canada shows that a large, federal country need not impose this self-denying ordinance on its voters; but once it has been imposed, how hard to get it repealed, in law or practice!

So it goes; the local radio stations, even if members of a chain, have their own local clientele to consider and please. The local department stores have their own view of what fashions are suitable for Fort Worth or Cleveland, and New York would be rash to assume that local taste does not matter. Local pride backs local talent.

It is an old story, of course. Inland cities have been pioneers in many things. St. Louis was the first center of Hegelian studies in America—and even in the eighteenth century the little French frontier town was quite as much abreast of the intellectual times as was a French provincial town like Clermont-Ferrand. Chicago was, for a few years, the poetry capital of the United States, and Hollywood is a permanent rival of New York in all fads, fashions, and follies. New England cities like Hartford, Springfield, Worcester have not surrendered their autonomy of judgment to New York, much less to Boston. Civic pride and rivalry keep more places than Fort Worth and Dallas on their toes, often with admirable results. There is a story of a priest and a parson arriving in Dublin in a very crowded week and having to share a bedroom; the maid found them in the morning, each asleep on his knees beside his bed. American cities, in the same predicament of rivalry, are found awake, not asleep—though the rivalry may not produce uniformly good results at the same time. Thus, as far as I know, Cleveland and Cincinnati have never been in a state of municipal reform simultaneously; but each has had its reforming zeal given fresh edge by the contemplation of its sinful rival—which is the next best thing.

All people who have serious business to do in America, sellers and buyers of all things, cars and radio time, politicians and religionists, know that you must never forget that the American, more and more a city-dweller, is convinced that he is a citizen of no mean city. And more and more he is right. He can remember, for example, what the Chicago lake front, now so splendid, was like before the Field Museum, the Planetarium, the Stadium were built on the slob-land between the Illinois Central tracks and the lake. He can remember the Jersey marshes before the fantastic Pulaski Skyway, like an H. G. Wells vision, swept over them. (They still smell horribly.) Smaller cities have similar sources of pride, like the highly unfunctional sky-scrapers of a city like Beaumont, Texas, or the Huey Long Bridge at Baton Rouge. True, the center of many cities is "blasted" by slums and made impassable by traffic jams. Businesses, as well as homes, take refuge in the suburbs. New office buildings lead to new congestion and slums crowd round the foot of the skyscrapers as they did at the foot of the Acropolis or round the medieval cathedrals. But each city is, for its own region, a capital, a source of opinions and taste. Each city and each region is "from Missouri"—it has "got to be shown"; and until it has been shown, it is worse than useless to go on the basis that all the best people in New York or Washington think that way already. The United States is not and will not be a vast Metroland. It is a nation of cities and of countrysides, spread over three million square miles, and so it must be hard to interpret and to unify, even in a great crisis. And even when it is really unified, each region will crab the deeds and the words

of the others, especially of its nearest neighbors. The job of
the leaders (and a most difficult job) is to hold together:

> *this land,*
> *My own Manhattan with spires, and the sparkling*
> *and hurrying tides and the ships,*
> *The varied and ample land, the South and the North*
> *in the light, Ohio's shores and flashing Missouri,*
> *And ever the far-spreading prairies cover'd with grass*
> *and corn.*

To repeat, it is hard to do, and it has to be done by persuasion and not by coercion. But for a great cause, it can
be done.

8

THE FRAMERS of the American Constitution put as their first aim the provision of the political means to "a more perfect union." They did not aim at perfect union, at the ironing-out of all regional differences, at the destruction of all regional independence. One of the organizers of the movement that led to framing the Constitution did, indeed, want complete union, did want to abolish local autonomy. But the ideas of Alexander Hamilton were so remote from any possibilities in the America of 1787 that they were more or less politely ignored by his colleagues, and Hamilton left the Convention in disgust. When the Constitution was put before the people, Hamilton was an effective fighter for it, and as the first Secretary of the Treasury he helped to get the machine running. But he was not a maker of the Constitution, because he thought it was not good enough, that what the United States needed was complete union, the fusion of the thirteen states into a unitary body politic.

Although Hamilton did not get his way, it was not necessarily a silly way. For the weak federal government that went into operation in 1789, like the strong federal government in operation in 1956, was a clumsy method of carrying on the business of the American people if all that is to be done is to carry on that business. It is clumsy to have the machinery of government in forty-nine units: the States, and the Union. It is clumsy to have the powers of the federal government loosely defined, so that they are constantly matters of controversy, so that many things are not done because it is uncertain what organ of government has the legal power to do them. It is at best inconvenient that the uncontested powers of the federal government are divided among a President, a Senate, and a House of Representatives, and that the question *what* power is *where* is decided by the majority of a Supreme Court of nine members. A government so organized must often be slow and uncertain in its action, indeed sometimes be incapable of action or, at any rate, incapable of action in time to meet the situation. The existence of an irreducible minimum of power in forty-eight states causes grave inconvenience, since it means that law and political practice vary from state to state. And some of those states are small in area, or in population, or in both; some are also the results of historical accidents; some break up the natural unity of geographical areas in a way to horrify a geopolitician or a political realist of the type that abolishes ancient European nations in an editorial. It is absurd that the empty mountain state of Nevada should be able both to make a good thing out of its lax divorce laws and its legalization of gambling and to hold the United States to ransom to buy its other main asset, silver, at an exorbitant price. It is absurd that the three counties that make up Delaware should be empowered to charter corporations to do business all over the Union on terms more profitable to the corporation's controllers than to the body politic. It is absurd that the New York harbor area should be under the control of two states *and* the federal government, and that the pride of Arizona should hold up, for years at a time, the development of water-power that southern California badly needs.

But to cure these absurdities it would be necessary to impose on three million varied square miles a central authority strong enough to suppress local objections. But such a government would have a pretty free hand in deciding what local objections it decided to suppress—and such a government would be too strong for local liberties, so the American people decided in 1789 and have kept on deciding since.

The standard of comparison we should apply to the degree of success with which the American people have achieved "a more perfect union" is not that of a comparatively small, unitary country like Great Britain or New Zealand. We must look at countries with something like the same problems of space to deal with. We must look at Russia, at Canada, at Brazil, at Australia. And if we do look at them, we find that the Soviet Union with its central Russian mass and its control by the Communist Party machine, and Brazil with its dictatorships—that both of these are, from the American point of view, buying union at the expense of liberty. On the other hand, Canada and Australia, while free, are not, by American standards, united; neither, for example, dared to exercise in World War II that most difficult power of government, the imposition of general conscription for service all over the world. Australia is repeatedly in the throes of attempted constitutional reforms designed to give the federal government temporary powers adequate for the times. And Canada, despite the formal powers of its federal government, has had to allow Quebec to exercise a power of nullification which, in kind if not in extent, is like that claimed long ago for South Carolina by John C. Calhoun. South Africa, with a formally unitary government, is divided three ways by race conflicts, by bitter historical feuds, and by possibly insoluble economic and racial problems. Should the world demand for gold and diamonds fall off, the Union of South Africa might have to face, all over again, problems that optimists think were "solved" in 1909.

To have created a free government over a continental area without making a sacrifice of adequate efficiency or of liberty is the American achievement. It is a unique achievement in world history.

And because that achievement is tied up in fact and in legend with the Constitution, with the political system which makes the Constitution work, with a long historical experience (long, as modern political history goes), the American people are entitled to more than tolerance: they are entitled to sympathetic understanding in their worship of their own system of political and social institutions. And sympathetic understanding must begin with understanding of the obstacles to unity that faced and still face the People of the United States.

Part Two

UNITY AND LIBERTY

*"May the Great Ruler of Nations...
inspire a returning veneration for that Union which,
if we may dare to penetrate His designs,
He has chosen as the only means
of attaining the high destinies
to which we may reasonably aspire."*

—PROCLAMATION OF PRESIDENT JACKSON
TO THE PEOPLE OF SOUTH CAROLINA, 1832

1

"WE THE PEOPLE of the United States, in order to form a more perfect Union, establish Justice, insure domestic Tranquillity, provide for the common defence, promote the general Welfare, and secure the Blessings of Liberty to ourselves and our Posterity, do ordain and establish this Constitution for the United States of America." So runs the preamble to the American Constitution. When that Constitution went into operation in the grand climacteric year of 1789, the "more perfect Union" aimed at was the political and economic unity of thirteen states, stretched in a thin ribbon from Nova Scotia to Florida, bounded on all sides (on land) by the territories of King George III of England and King Charles IV of old and new Spain. The more perfect Union now covers the whole area from Pacific to the Atlantic, three million square miles. The Spaniards no longer hold St. Augustine or the British Detroit, and no one, now that Colonel McCormick is dead, worries about threats to the territorial integrity of the Union from its Canadian or Mexican neighbors. The forty-eight states, as well as such outlying dependencies as Alaska (so near to Siberia), Hawaii (too near to Japan), Puerto Rico, and Guam, and such linked political associates as the Commonwealth of the Philippines, have been welded together in a fashion that would have seemed miraculous to the Founding Fathers. During the war no one doubted the durability of the Union or its power to expel the Japanese from Manila or from Wake Island.

But there is a sense in which the "more perfect Union" has yet to be achieved, for the American people are not yet a unity, are not yet mingled in a true community of common purpose, common standards, mutual trust. In 1789, the population of the United States was overwhelmingly British in origin. French Huguenots had played a very important part in the political and intellectual life of the colonies, especially in South Carolina. German settlers had played a statistically more important part, especially in Pennsylvania and New Jersey. Dutch settlers had played a very important part in what was once New Netherland and is now New York. There were a good many Scots and still more "Scotch-Irish"—Ulster Presbyterians. There were a fair number of "mere Irish" like General Sullivan and Charles Carroll of Carrollton. And there were a good many Welsh. But, though the English strain was most dominant in New England, it was dominant everywhere.

In the nineteenth century, thirty million immigrants entered the United States, and increasingly they came from parts of Europe that had contributed little to the population of the thirteen colonies. It is doubtful if the beneficiaries of the Constitution today, the present "People of the United States," are in a majority of cases the posterity of the American people of 1789 for whose descendants' liberty such thought was taken.

The three most important racial groups of recent immigrant origin are, at the moment, Germans, Italians, and Poles in that order. And although there were in America a few Italians like Jefferson's friend Philip Mazzei, and although the Polish leaders Kosciusko and Pulaski played an important role in the American Revolution, there were, for all practical purposes, no Poles and no Italians in the United States of 1789. And although there were many Germans, natives like Muhlenberg or newcomers like the Baron von Steuben, the Germans in 1789 were a small though not negligible minority. Anyone with a knowledge of the light that family names cast on Irish history can see that, in the very Protestant America of 1789, there were many Irish whose recent ancestry must have been Catholic. Nevertheless, the United States in 1789 was above all English and Protestant.

In the century and a half that has passed, a great work of assimilation has been accomplished. No names could be more thoroughly American than Dwight Eisenhower, Chester Nimitz, Franklin Delano Roosevelt. In a Midwestern town a degree of unity is achieved that includes everybody, of no matter what racial origin. Or almost everybody. For the Catholics, the Jews, and the Negroes are still, to some extent, regarded as being outside the local community life, and so are the recent immigrants whose language, habits of life, and economic status remind the spectator that it is less than a generation since mass immigration stopped. So, too, are Southern poor whites, pushing north into the new industrial towns where the "old-time religion" has to struggle hard and not always successfully to keep its place, where the colored population has (from a Southern point of view) forgotten its place, and where so many aspects of town life, from the high-school curriculum to the standard diet, underline the difference between the rural "Anglo-Saxon," Protestant South and the new America in which all the peoples of Europe have contributed blood and habits of life and speech.

There is an apparent paradox in the contrast between the remarkable physical uniformity of American towns and their variations on the moral and psychological sides. Outside the South and the far West, the traveler getting off a train in the dark or driving into a town from the airport might well be in doubt as to what state, even what region, he was in. The towns look remarkably alike. The red fronts of the "Great Atlantic and Pacific Tea Company" are common to all. An expert in the distribution of the chain stores might guess something from the name above the

"Five and Ten," for it is only in England that Wool-worth's is always Woolworth's. The classical façade of the local banks, the neo-Gothic of the churches, the elegant brick and granite of the new post offices—all are lacking in local flavor. Is this Indiana, or Ohio, or New York State? One might get a clue to its being a Southern town from the number of Negroes and from an indefinable air of something that it would be unkind to call slowness and, sometimes, too flattering to call leisure; or to its being in the West from the aridity of the landscape and the semi-cowboy character of the male costume; or on the Pacific slope, from the geniality of the climate and the exuberance of the population. What is surprising, however, is not the amount of variation but the uniformity achieved over three million square miles.

The physical uniformity, true, conceals a good deal of racial variety. In New England, that block of church and school and convent is a citadel inside which the *Canadiens,* the "Canucks" of their "Anglo-Saxon" neighbors, barricade themselves against denationalizing forces and preserve in Maine or Massachusetts the ethos and the language of Quebec. In Minnesota, Swedes keep alive some of the old ways they learned in Scandia, and in their Lutheran churches and denominational colleges resist complete cul-tural assimilation. Whole cities, like the Polish enclave of Hamtramck in the midst of Detroit, are ruled by one racial group and seem to the zealots of mere uniformity to be "un-American."

But more common is the town in which a dozen groups have to live together in close contact, in which a street of Germans borders on a street of Irish, in which the Italians and the Greeks are mingled in school and market, in which Jew and Gentile have to learn to get on together. It is in towns like these that the problem of Americaniza-tion is most acute, in which the well-meaning efforts of

Rotary Clubs and women's organizations fail in face of the facts that seem to suggest that, whatever the legal fiction may be, there *are* first-class and second-class and even third-class Americans, that there is a scale descending from the "old stocks" down to the Negroes.

They are all Americans; from the European point of view, in what they have in common—in speech, in appearance, in habits of speech and posture, in ways of life and views of life—they are all much alike. The American Pole is more like the American Finn than either is like a pure Pole or pure Finn. America denationalizes quickly. Does it nationalize?

At times there is a temptation to say "No." Then American society seems like a pipe line; in it the different kinds of oil are all moving in the same direction, but they do not mix, except at the edges; they are all moving to produce a common American refined article—but the Bayonne in which this job of political and social cracking is to be done either does not yet exist or is not equipped to handle more than a tithe of the crude oil coming in from a dozen different sources.

Not all Americans are at home in America or are accepted as first-class citizens. America, like other older countries, has not completely succeeded in uniting all its people on a basis of freedom and equality. Its political and social tradition, which has so successfully set out to make men and women proud and glad to be Americans in this world, has not dealt or attempted to deal with all of human hopes and fears.

Nor is this all. American unity has, in a sense, decreased as the original religious homogeneity of the thirteen states has been diluted by non-Protestant, non-Christian elements. America is now the capital of world Jewry, and anti-Semitism is one of the problems that perplex the wise American, Jew or Gentile, and tempt the demagogue, lay or clerical. In New York the concentration of nearly two million Jews has made it possible to pretend to ignore, over the large areas where none but Jews live, that outside those areas there are present the elements of jealous hatred which are the standby of the anti-Semite. Whether Jew or Gentile is exclusively to blame is not a subject for inquiry here. "Restricted holiday camps" that exclude Jews are neither the cause nor the result of camps advertising "dietary rules strictly observed" that exclude Gentiles. There is anti-Semitism among the Negroes of Harlem, one "under-privileged" people set against another. And there is the old cleavage between the old, assimilated, modern-minded Jews and the mass of "Jews without money," often bringing from the ghettoes of Poland the qualities bred in ghettoes which are not socially valuable in the modern world. Whether American Gentile society is so rich in social talent, in artistic taste, and in intellectual power as to be able to afford, in the long run, the snobbish exclusiveness of many clubs and fashionable suburbs is open to question. What is not open to question is the danger to American social and political life inherent in the exploitation of anti-Semitism by crypto-fascist organizations, as well as by bigoted devotees of peace and international brotherhood. Colonel Lindbergh may have been only obeying a memory of his father's vehement intolerance when he hinted that the Jews had better behave themselves (in the father's case, it was the Catholics who were warned). But the priests and ministers and senators and congressmen who have, in the not very remote past, accepted, more or less willingly, the aid of rabid anti-Semites have a great responsibility before the American people and before the other minorities who will learn, if they do not know it already, that when American frontier intolerance gets its head, it does not require much rational justification. The Poles in Detroit who treated the Negroes of Sojourner Truth as the Germans in Poland

127

treated Poles; the soldiers in Los Angeles who beat up the Mexican "zoot-suit" wearers; the woman who wanted the speaking of Spanish forbidden in Los Angeles; the Ku Klux Klan who came in to profit by the pathological situation largely created by Catholics in some Midwestern states; the Protestants who, for whatever innocent motives, are ready with facile charges against Catholics—all are enemies of American union.

There are patches of the United States where settlers of one origin have concentrated so thickly that they have been able to carry over into their new environment a good deal of the spirit and tradition of the old. The German Pietists of Pennsylvania, the German Catholics round St. Meinrad's Abbey in Indiana, the Dutch in parts of Michigan, the Scandinavians in Minnesota and North Dakota, and, most tenacious of all, the French Canadians in so many New England towns and villages—these in greater or lesser degree have resisted the complete transformation of their lives by Americanism. But not all emigrants have any very kindly memory of the homeland. The Pennsylvania "Dutch" (i.e., Germans) have no living memory at all of Germany; many of the Dutch have no kindly memory of the Holland that persecuted their rigorist ancestors. Many of the Germans believe truly, and more believe falsely, that their ancestors were driven from Germany after 1848 because of their liberal or radical political views, intolerable in a country where reaction was triumphant. True, an affection for Germany could survive such an ordeal, as it did in the case of so eminent a German-American liberal as Carl Schurz, who forgave Bismarck's Germany much that he would have condemned in the contemporary United States. And one very distinguished American scholar has told me how his father, normally completely indifferent to the land of his birth, developed a good deal of German patriotism in the war between 1914 and 1917 as he got more and more tired of hearing all Germans described as Huns.

The unifying role of the Christian tradition in America has been less important in this century because of the character of the religious conquest of the frontier. The religion that followed the pioneers was emotional, uncritical, unintellectual. The old New England Puritanism, with its insistence on learning, with its emphasis on the provision of a clergy that could use and a congregation that could accept an elaborate theology and epistemology, had no competitive chance on the frontier against the Methodists and Baptists. Petrus Ramus could not fight Peter Cartwright. So typical a New England experiment as the foundation of Illinois College failed, in a sense; it had to be transferred from the Congregationalists to a more emotional religious denomination. Indeed, the optimistic, humanistic culture of Emerson was more successfully exported to the frontier by missionaries like Emerson himself than was New England religion in the more technical sense.

The Anglicans and Presbyterians did a little better but not much; Bishop Chase and Kenyon College were very important forces in the civilizing of Ohio, but Bishop Chase was not Bishop Berkeley. Princeton was more of a religious power house for the South and West than Harvard and Yale were, but for too long Princeton College remained wedded to a sterile, old-line orthodoxy that was unattractive to the ebullient temper of the frontier and curiously high and dry compared with the atmosphere of its Scottish academic parents. President McCosh was not quite adapted to the age of the two Cairds in Glasgow, or even of Principal Tulloch and Principal Rainey in St. Andrews and Edinburgh.

The old, humanistic culture of the South had died; it lacked the moral energy that the frontier situation called for. And when a Congressman objected to the purchase of Jefferson's library by Congress, on the ground that it contained too many books by Voltaire, he was expressing a popular opinion. Only the immense prestige of Jefferson could have secured protection for his ideas and, as it was, his new University of Virginia had to abandon its original plan of employing Thomas Cooper, that dangerous Deist.

Religion became a matter of conduct, of good deeds, of works with only a vague background of faith. It became highly functional, highly pragmatic; it became a guarantee of success, moral and material. The world of which Henry Ward Beecher on one side and Colonel Ingersoll on the other were such representative specimens was not quite the world of Harnack and Renan, Newman, Liddon, and Gore, Loisy, Denifle, and Denny. Theological schools turned from theology to a form of anthropology—a moralistic and optimistic form, but anthropology all the same. That "the proper study of mankind is man" was the evasion by which many American divines escaped the necessity for thought about God.

In the twentieth century this policy suddenly ceased to be adequate. The fight over "fundamentalism," whether it took the form of the so-called "monkey trial" at Dayton, Tennessee, or the listing of "evolution" as one of the serious causes of stress between daughters and parents in Muncie, Indiana, or the fight in the Princeton Theological Seminary over the place of orthodox Calvinism in the last home town of Jonathan Edwards, was a fight over a very real problem. In the making of America, views about the relationship of God and Man had played a great part. If the God of the first settlers, and the God of the frontier who had converted so many tens of thousands in the straw pens of so many camp meetings, was no longer the God of the new universities, of the new technology, what was to replace Him? Could anything replace Him but "Democracy" made into an object of worship, or business, or success? Nobody knew; nobody knows, yet.

And this conflict hindered assimilation, because it weakened an old bond of understanding if not of union. Into this Protestant world millions of non-Protestants were pouring. There were, for example, the poor Jews. They were rapidly being torn away from the ways of life learned in eastern ghettoes but not provided with new ways of life by an American society itself perplexed and drifting. The earlier Portuguese and German Jewish immigrants had moved into a society that was far more confident of its aims and standards. As far as the Jewish immigrants were orthodox, they were moving into a society that shared with them a common literary inheritance. Americans whose parents called their children not merely by common Biblical names like Abraham but by rare Biblical names like the Arunah and Azariah of the founder of the Baltimore *Sun* knew something about the Jews, were capable of a certain sympathetic understanding of the synagogue which was not possible a generation or two later, when Jew and Gentile alike had forgotten the Old Testament and when Galushas and Isaacs had become Earls and Miltons.

Of more importance was the maintenance of a nearly complete barrier between the non-Catholic five sixths of the American people and the Catholic sixth. For while the Jewish immigrants in the majority of cases left Jewish orthodoxy behind in a generation or two, a very large proportion of the Catholic immigrants kept to Catholic orthodoxy. There were, of course, cleavages in American Catholic families like those in Jewish families. The uprooting of the shady hero of *I Can Get It for You Wholesale* is a special Jewish case, of which Mr. Farrell's pursuit of a way of life for a Chicago Irish boy brought up as a Catholic, and Mr. Dreiser's pursuit of a way of life for an Indiana German brought up as a Catholic, are more attractive examples.

But from the political and social point of view, the Catholic problem is one of segregation, voluntary or involuntary. It is to be seen in its most striking form in New England, especially round Boston, where the Irish population, now settled there for a century or more, still carries a chip on its shoulder and is often represented in public by too noisy spokesmen who would quickly be taught their place in Dublin, in conversation and gossip if not in print. It is reflected in an attitude toward the culture of the modern world which startles any European observer and, in private, provokes hostile comment that recalls the atmosphere of a society in which anti-Semitism is beginning to be a real danger.

There is the memory on the one side of the hard life in the mills, of the poor bargaining position in which their illiteracy, their poverty, and their inexperience of the industrial world left the first Irish immigrants. There is, on the other side, the memory of the excessive pugnacity, even when sober, of the newcomers, as well as of the social problems created in what had been a homogeneous society by the arrival of hundreds of thousands of people with a different economic and social background and a different religion. This last difference was and is more important than it suits either side to admit. There is a real conflict of traditions. The New Englanders saw themselves as pioneers of religious freedom and, though a few Quakers like Whittier might have their doubts and a few domestic critics like the Adams family might see the picture a little out of focus, in general this view of the past was accepted. But to the incoming Irish it was very different. The old Bostonians were the people who burned down the Charlestown convent, in part because of the stirring preaching of orthodox divines like Lyman Beecher. They were the people who welcomed the happy combination of religious propaganda and pornography known as *Maria Monk*. They were the heirs of the Puritan and Whig tradition in England. Cromwell was one of their heroes—whereas, for the Irish, Cromwell was the man of the Drogheda massacre and of the Hitleresque slogan "To Hell or Connaught." The Irish remembered the breach of the Treaty of Limerick, while the New Englanders remembered the Revocation of the Edict of Nantes which gave Boston the Revere family. The more enlightened and learned New Englanders were capable of sharing Voltaire's indignation over the execution of Calas, but the Irish were more likely to remember Oliver Plunkett, Archbishop of Armagh, judicially murdered by the party whose greatest ornaments were Isaac Newton and John Locke.

So admirable a man as John Jay Chapman acted more like a New Englander than a New Yorker when he tried to teach the Bible and influence the Irish slum children of the Bowery, forgetting that they saw the religious history of modern times (as far as they knew anything of it) from a viewpoint quite other than that which came naturally to one of Huguenot ancestry. And if they shrank from his simple Bible-teaching, it was because they believed that in the lifetime of their fathers and mothers the Catholic Irish had been subjected to the most formidable dragonnade of all, the ordeal of conversion by famine. They may have been wrong, but there is no evidence that John Jay Chapman ever tried to find out why he was so coldly received, any more than the readers of *The Protestant* did. (Some of the writers knew quite well what they were doing.)

Even the German Catholics, who had had a much easier time than the Irish, had not been the recipients of much sympathy when Bismarck put their bishops and priests in jail with the approval of the liberals of the time —except really acute ones like Walter Bagehot. And no Catholics noted much real enthusiasm among liberals for the cause of religious liberty in the state of Vera Cruz or

Tabasco during the height of the Mexican revolution. Nor did the argument that the Mexican Catholics must have deserved this treatment impress them as conclusive, any more than the same argument pleased liberals in the mouths of defenders of Hitlerian persecution of the Jews—or Catholics.

The average American Catholic does not think of himself as being on the side of the Inquisition; he thinks of himself as being a victim of persecution. The tone of a paper like the Brooklyn *Tablet* strongly suggests that the inquisitional temper is there all the same, but the Manhattan liberal press gives the Brooklyn *Tablet* more ammunition than its directors realize. It is, for example, a mistake to launch an attack on a priest suspected of fascist leanings, sign the attack with a markedly Jewish name, and forget to give the priest the customary title of "Father." It is also a mistake, if you want to win intelligent Catholics, to imply that they have much more control over and more responsibility for their co-religionists in Spain or Boston than Union Seminary has for the antics of serpent-handling Protestant zealots in Tennessee. It is probably also a mistake to protest against the necessarily Christian character of any non-commercial celebration of Christmas in the schools of White Plains.

Whatever the causes, the barrier is there. The Catholics' policy of supporting (entirely out of their own funds) schools of all grades and colleges and universities professing to be in competition with the great state and private universities has led to grave suspicion among the non-Catholics. Since all or practically all the teachers in Catholic schools are Catholics, while in New England, New York, and Chicago they constitute a great proportion of the teachers in the ordinary state undenominational schools as well, they seem to be, at considerable expense to themselves, both insulating their own children and influencing the children of others. In a New England town like Holyoke it may cause serious ill-feeling if it is suspected that appointment and promotion in the public schools is under Catholic control, since, as far as ecclesiastical authority prevails, there will be no Catholic children in those schools. Of course, this clerical ideal is never reached and the Protestant would-be teacher in New England is better off than the Catholic would-be teacher in rural Kansas or Georgia. She has a chance of getting a job, the Catholic has none. But since the Protestant tradition is native and the Catholic tradition exotic, the grievance is very differently felt.

Catholic suspicion, Catholic resentment, Catholic conviction that Catholics will not get fair play produce an indifference to influencing public opinion that is bad for the democratic process. The Catholic spokesmen appealing to their own people are victims to the American passion for oratory and vehement public polemics. There is not much in common between the controversial methods of Cardinal Newman and those of Bishop Fulton Sheen. The American public, the American politician, the American newspaper has to allow for Catholic opinion because there are so many Catholics, not because Catholic opinion has any interest as such. And Catholics do not explain nearly so often as they denounce and deplore.

Even if they did explain more, they might not do it very well, for the Catholic church in America is still, in the main, a church of poor people not interested in refinements of doctrine or apologetics. Thus when an American seminary professor was asked to contribute to a co-operative Catholic work of learning published in England, his contribution was so old-fashioned that it would have caused a mixture of amusement and distress in the Catholic faculties of his ancestral home in Germany. Not thus did the theologians and exegetes of Bonn or Freiburg or Munich write. The English editors had, in fact, to scrap the volume and get it rewritten. And it is permissible to wonder how many Irish-American bishops would appoint (if they could find one) so learned and critical a Hebrew scholar as Dr. Kissane to a chair in one of their seminaries. He is sound enough to be President of Maynooth, but is that enough for American Catholicism? It is probable that the bishops, in intellectual matters, are more tolerant than many of the faithful. (The late Cardinal O'Connell went out of his way to give an audience to a convert assailed by the trigger-happy laity of his city of Boston.) And the standards of some American Catholic colleges and universities have risen very rapidly indeed in recent years.

But it is unfortunate that the American Catholics are, by their training, so ready to suspect the worst of their neighbors and that their neighbors suspect the worst of them. On the one hand, the politicians, priests, and publicists see infidel, Moscow-fed hands clutching everywhere; on the other, more Americans than are quite conscious of it have fed on the mythology to which Mr. Upton Sinclair used to lend assent.

It is especially a strain in the field of foreign policy. For there a real conflict of policy, of prudence, of judgment of the realities may be made impossible by Catholic suspicion on one side, by Protestant suspicion on the other. A policy which, whatever its motives, may end in the destruction of the possibility of Catholic life in Poland, for instance, or the physical destruction of Rome, will be seen very differently by those who care for the fate of Catholicism and those who don't. The American Catholic, with a good deal of naïveté, tends to make the attitude of a foreign government toward the Catholic church a touchstone of its decency, as Jews do the treatment of Jews. The American Catholic, too, reads too easily the term "Catholic" in terms of his own experience. That "Catholic" may mean very different things in Boston and Buenos Aires,

St. Louis and Rome, he is slow to believe. The formal unity of doctrine is interpreted as involving identity of practice and devotion. The possibilities of American action are seen in naïvely American terms. That they are naïvely American *Catholic* terms does not make the attitude less American.

2

IN ALL DEMOCRATIC COUNTRIES there is a fashionable readiness to sing "frustrate their politics, confound their knavish tricks." It is not to be taken too seriously, either as a judgment or as an expression of popular sentiment. Indeed, it is one of the attractions of a democratic society that it gives a place to the natural human emotion of critical resentment by the ruled of any pretension to infallibility in the rulers. A democratic society is one in which "the populace rise at once against the never-ending audacity of elected persons." And in general the American, if he does no more than deflate his rulers by irony, does that.

But however pleasant and reviving this practice may be to the irritated if not oppressed citizen, it conceals from the superficial and cynical observer some important truths. Above all, it conceals the truth that the United States was made by politicians. It was a comparatively small group of politicians who organized the popular rising against the authority of George III. And some of those political leaders, Sam Adams for instance, might not have been totally at a loss in Mr. Crump's Memphis, Mr. Hague's Jersey City, or Mr. Pendergast's Kansas City. It was a group of politicians who created the demand for the new Constitution, who drafted it, who made it work. It was a group of politicians round one of their number, Alexander Hamilton, who provided the new Union with adequate financial resources and powerful vested interests; it was a group round another and more capable politician, Jefferson, who provided the necessary diplomatic and constitutional facilities for the rapid expansion of the American farmer to the West. It was politicians who postponed the outbreak of the Civil War, and it was one politician, at that time a rather obscure one, more or less accidentally elected to the office of President, who decided that the Southern states should not be allowed either to secede peacefully or to stay in the Union on their own exorbitant (as President Lincoln thought) terms.

Indeed, the role of the American politician and party is best exemplified by the history of the years leading up to the outbreak of the Civil War. It was not till the parties began to break down, till the Whigs disappeared and the Democrats were torn by schism, that civil war became practically certain. When in 1860 the Southern Democrats refused to accept Stephen Douglas as the party candidate, when the Douglas Democrats in the North refused to admit the right of the South to veto the will of the majority of the party, the case became really desperate. Churches, learned societies, clubs, these had split already. There was the atmosphere of civil war in the Senate when Senator Sumner of Massachusetts first attacked Senator Butler of South Carolina with virulent rhetoric and was then nearly beaten to death by Representative Brooks. There was actual civil war on a small scale in Kansas, where that eminent, zealous, and murderous land-speculator, John Brown, slew his enemies and, a year or two later, was captured by Colonel Robert E. Lee when he tried to instigate a servile war in Virginia. John Brown was an assassin to the South, a martyr to much of the North. But not till the Democratic politicians could no longer even pretend to cooperate, not till Lincoln, a politician of politicians, refused to accept compromise on the fundamental issues, was all hope gone. What the politicians could not do, no one could do; then it was a question of war, the final argument of kings and commonwealths. It was the political passions of the politicians, the political interests of the parties, North and South, that made the problem of reconstruction in the South after the Civil War almost insoluble.

It may be argued that before the Civil War the main direction of American policy was in the hands of the Supreme Court. In a sense it was; the Court alone had the continuous authority that was needed. But the Court succeeded as far as it was politically minded and wisely politically minded. It had to remember what its greatest chief said: "We must never forget that it is a *constitution* we are expounding."

When the Supreme Court disregards the implications of this famous dictum of Chief Justice Marshall, and either takes refuge in a kind of high and dry constitutional pedantry (as it did between 1933 and 1937), or plays politics too openly and usurps the functions of other departments of government (as it did in the Dred Scott case in 1857), American reverence for the Court is badly strained and its utility diminished. And utility is the justification for the Court, as it is for Congress and the President; all must contribute to the unity and peace of the United States.

This overriding purpose justifies one aspect of politics that the pedantic purist often condemns, the catering to minority groups. In the Supreme Court itself, it is normally politically desirable that there should be at least one Catholic and one Jewish justice, that the South and the West should be represented, and that the Court should not be exclusively of one party. This is desirable because justice must seem to be done, not merely be done. It does not mean that the Court will divide on these lines. But the role of members of the Court, once appointed, cannot be foreseen. The most revolutionary decision of modern times, the decree against school segregation, was handed down by a unanimous Court presided over by a former Republican candidate for the vice-presidency and including a former Democratic Attorney General from the heart of Texas. It is possible that had Mr. Byrnes stayed on the Court instead of, by a roundabout route, becoming Governor of South Carolina, he would have joined his brethren in their unanimous judgment.

At a much lower level, the practical politician has to "seed" his list of candidates for all kinds of offices. In a polyglot city like Cleveland or Detroit, he must see that all important national groups are represented, possibly at a loss of formal efficiency, but at a gain in solidarity. To ignore the gain is to ignore simple facts of human nature that were not ignored at Versailles, except by mere academic critics. For a Pole or a Slovak to see one of his own kin as a judge or alderman or congressman is to be ready to believe that American democracy has some meaning. For a Negro to know that there are Negro congressmen, federal judges, generals, is no doubt to be led to think that there are far too few, but how much better than there being none at all! For the grievance of exclusion from the jobs is a very real grievance, and to diminish the sense of grievance of minorities which are otherwise underprivileged is to promote the unity of the American peoples. The politicians have done this more consistently and better than any other class of Americans. The generous naturalization policy, and, in the old days, the privilege of voting without naturalization, made it profitable for the political managers to cultivate voters who, in other ways, were made to feel snubbed in America. As Charles Eliot Norton pointed out, the haughty attitude of the old New Englanders toward the Irish immigrants was bad for the political and social health of Massachusetts. But the politicians could not be so snooty as the Brahmins. Henry Adams might ignore the forces that were transforming New England into New Ireland, but his brother, John Quincy Adams II, the Democratic leader of the state, could not do so. Neither could the ambitious pupil and friend of Henry Adams, young Mr.

Lodge. For he needed, in emergencies, enough Irish votes to offset the influence of politicians like Patrick Collins. Senator Lodge might regret to see the Irish tide lapping round Nahant, but there were voters to be won over by judicious twisting of the British lion's tail.

Of course, there was another and less desirable result of this cultivation of minority groups. As Lodge himself pointed out in 1919, the existence of strong racial minorities in America made the adoption of any positive American foreign policy dangerous and difficult. And it is true that racial feeling plays some part in the views of the American people about the outside world. Negroes cared about Abyssinia. The Irish dislike of England is not what it was, but it has not completely disappeared. American Poles were less likely to believe all that intellectuals told them about Russia than were American Czechs. And politicians know all this, have to allow for all this. It may make them despair of Europe, where there are no skilled manipulators to adjust the *amour propre* of competing racial groups. But although they may despair of doing anything with the warring nations of the Old World, they at least do not believe that the day of nationalism is over. They know it is not over in Chicago, and they reasonably doubt whether it is over in Prague or Warsaw. But in the meantime they go on with their indispensable job of making minor concessions, often very formal concessions, sometimes corrupt concessions, but all helping to turn Polish-Americans and German-Americans into good Americans—and reliable voters.

There is one region where racial and historical disunion is always a problem, is the cause of other problems, and is at moments the cause of a feeling of despair which, in face of any other American failure, would be premature and absurd. The South is analogous to the poor, feud-ridden, historically unfortunate border countries between

Germany and Russia. It is poor, it is backward, its private troubles irritate the rest of an optimistic people. It has its own version of the common tongue; it is statistically inferior in a statistically-minded people; in the great national crisis that saved the Union, it was the enemy. But the main Southern problem is the color problem. It is still *the* problem. Yet it is a problem on the way to a tolerable solution in a predictable period of time, as it was not as recently as ten years ago. Three things have happened to change the conditions that bred despair. First of all, the gigantic increase in American wealth has benefited, relatively though not absolutely, the Negro more than it has any other American, and the same change has eased many Southern problems by enriching the South, which has gained, again relatively to its previous status, more than any other section by the spread of industry. Secondly, the Second World War, the Korean War, and, above all, the cold war have forced to the forefront of the American mind what Gunnar Myrdal called "the American dilemma," the contrast between the promises of "life, liberty, and the pursuit of happiness" and the realities of American life for nearly a tenth of a nation founded on these promises. Unlike white South Africa, the United States is moving toward fulfilling the promises rather than to denying their applicability to the Negro. Lastly, political action, legal action, two traditionally sacred forms of the American way of life, have (reinforced by a reviving Christian tradition) exposed the betrayals of the American promises as deeply un-American and their fulfillment as not only tolerable but rewarding. The American white, even in the deep South, is turning away from his past with something like the relief of the heavy drinker going on the wagon. He is uncomfortable but relieved.

The South, naturally and rightly, resents the view that it created the problem because of its own original sin. Not only was the sin national, but the manner in which slavery was abolished made a problem which, at best, was terribly difficult, almost insoluble. The slaves were freed by the military defeat of *all* the whites, not just a small class of masters. Emancipation did not merely ruin the plantation owners—it disorganized the Southern economy at a time when all Southerners, black and white alike, were impoverished by a long, wasteful, and lost war. The victorious North behaved with far more economic ruthlessness than the victors of Versailles, and it imposed in the name of "Reconstruction" the rule of emancipated slaves, local renegades (the "Scalawags"), and imported adventurers (the "Carpetbaggers"). Their governments were not necessarily much more corrupt than those which at the time afflicted some Northern cities and states, but they were far beyond the means of the impoverished South. The North could get along with corrupt and wasteful governments that did nothing but plunder the treasury. But the South needed positive government, and it could not get it. Worst of all, the South did get that damnable gift, excuses. It was given a reason for being permanently sorry for itself, like Ireland and Germany. It was given a permanent excuse for all internal weaknesses and faults. It was excused from assessing its own share in its troubles. Only today is the South slowly accepting the fact that the sins of "damn Yankees" and "uppity Niggers" are not enough to account for all Southern troubles.

The white South was not merely united by a common tragic experience. It had acquired from that experience a new order of values that it did not share with the rest of the United States. In the South, the heroes were nearly all soldiers. With the exception of Mr. Jefferson in Virginia, the Southern pantheon was a soldiers' temple. No politician, not Patrick Henry nor Tom Watson, could compete for popular reverence with Lee and Jackson and even such politically ambiguous heroes as Longstreet. Even in Louisiana the new fame of the martyred Huey Long had to fight with the old fame of Pierre Toutant Beauregard. And the people who filled the society sections of the papers, the Coca-Cola magnates of Atlanta, the steel magnates of Birmingham, were outshone in glamour by the heroic dead. Richmond might be the city of "Pin Money Pickles" for the believer in sky signs, but for its inhabitants it was and is the capital of the Lost Cause.

This priority was reflected in the high estimate put upon the career of arms. A nomination to West Point is a great honor indeed in the South. And of the eight colleges that prepare officers in an admitted rivalry with West Point, six are in the South. It was in one of them, the Virginia Military Institute, whose most famous teacher was Thomas Jonathan ("Stonewall") Jackson, that the former Chief of Staff of the American armies, General Marshall, was trained. In the Second World War, long before the mass of the American people saw how deeply its future was involved, the South was interventionist. It provided far more than a normal proportion of the American volunteers who joined the Canadian army and air force. The South knew that war *could* settle a lot; it had settled the South. It knew that it was not enough to say that one Yankee could lick three Japs or Germans, for had not one Southern Rebel licked three Yankees—and look at the final result! There was, too, a deep sense of kinship with the British people, and there was party fidelity to Mr. Roosevelt. Most Southern Democrats might not think much of the New Deal, but this was an old deal, the deal of war. So Dixie took her stand long before the rest of the Union. And the Texan was unjust to his own state when he said that if the United States went to war, he thought Texas would, too. It was the United States that joined a war that Texas had already entered, all but the formal declaration.

3

THE POLITICIAN has to deal with "pressure blocs," and is often blamed for it. But it is only partially his fault that American politics is so largely a matter of pressure blocs, and—in addition—dealing with pressure blocs is a skilled job. It is a problem of political engineering, of estimating the pressure, the head of steam behind that drive, the kilowatt hours that such a project can rely on. It is not a mere question of taking a Gallup or a *Fortune* poll and discovering what a representative sample of voters will say if asked; the politician must guess what they will do, in the form of actual voting, in the form of support for lobbying, in the form of abstaining from supporting one party or individual and supporting another, in the form of casting the great, silent, and often decisive vote of the electors who stay at home on election day. He must estimate how hot the voters will feel in November about issues that appear to be burning them up in May. Two thirds of the senators must guess how hot the voters will feel—whether indeed they will feel anything—in November two years or November four years ahead.

But it is not only that. The role of all politicians, even when it is a mere matter of estimating the power of pressure blocs, has got harder in the last generation. In 1900, perhaps as late as 1912, the great traditional sectional divisions of the American people were still pretty much what they had been when the system broke down in 1860. There were the manufacturing states of the East. They had their own variations in sentiment and interest, but basically they wanted high tariffs and a strong central government. There was the South (then, even more than now, a region that was almost a nation). There was the Middle West, still, like the South, a producer and exporter of basic crops; there was the West, still mainly an exporter of minerals and cattle and wheat. But the new industrial revolution has made these simple lines of division no longer unalterable frontiers. Every state, or almost every state, has its important industrial interests, and those interests may lie as much in the export as in the import market. The agricultural interest is now (some hold) a burden on the total American economy, living off subsidies and tariffs without which it would be doomed to a serious contraction. And although hereditary voting—being a Democrat or a Republican because your grandfather was—is still one of the most potent forms of American ancestor-worship, it is more and more common to find voters usefully classified by age and economic level, the young and the poor tending to be New Dealers if not perfectly orthodox Democrats.

The politician is now assailed by half a dozen competing interests within his own state or region; and his party affiliation, his own political philosophy, may give him no help in making up his mind as to what is going to be good for the public and even for himself. Some of the lack of party discipline that has been marked in Congress is due to this genuine confusion of mind. It has mainly worked since 1937, the ending of Roosevelt's autocracy, to weaken the Democratic Party, but President Eisenhower has found himself as handicapped as was President Truman, and the congressional elections of 1954 were largely fought on the issue of which party had given and would give the President the most effective support. It is possible that the two historical American parties are going through a necessary period of disintegration and readjustment. It is an unfortunate coincidence that the whole world is going through such an adjustment, too, and cannot wait till the American party structure has been reconstructed before it undertakes to organize itself. Yet it may not be able to organize itself in any satisfactory fashion if the American internal conflict is not resolved some way, soon.

The separation of powers is laid down in the Constitution and is emotionally anchored in American political habits. But a development that is not constitutionally necessary and has no particular claim on popular support has made the separation of powers also a separation of personnel. The members of Congress (members of the House and members of the Senate alike) are more and more cut off from the Executive personnel. It is not only that with the decline of the "Spoils System" the administration of the federal government has more and more passed into the hands of permanent civil servants ("bureaucrats," as the politicians call them). But the political chiefs of the administration are hardly ever chosen from the personnel of Congress. Only one President in this century, Warren Harding, has been elected from Congress. Only one other, Mr. Truman, had served in Congress. Except for Mr. Dulles's brief period in the Senate (he was appointed to fill out a term and defeated when he ran for the office), no member of President Eisenhower's cabinet has served in Congress. Many senators have held executive office in their own states or cities. A few have held cabinet posts in the federal government. But in the main there is a pretty complete cleavage between the personnel of Congress and the executive. The case of the Republican nominees in 1940 was undoubtedly exceptional. But it is worth noting that the presidential nominee, Mr. Wendell Willkie, had never met the Republican nominee for Vice President, Senator McNary, before they were put on the same ticket. It is not surprising, then, that Congress (especially the Senate) should tend to be more critical than constructive, more legalistic than responsible in its attitude to current problems.

The Senate, as its name suggests, has a special place

for old men or, at any rate, for elder statesmen, who may, in fact, be fairly young though old in politics. It is supposed to and does take a long-term view. Elected for six years with a good chance (unless there is a party upheaval) of being re-elected, the average Senator may expect to be in office when the ordinary President has come and gone; and some of the senatorial irritation with Mr. Roosevelt arose from the unprecedented situation that he had been in the White House longer than most Senators had been in the Capitol. There are Senators who have served under Republican Presidents before General Eisenhower (though none of them is a Republican). These are exceptional cases, but the Senate does allow a good deal of play for the political veteran who gets elected over and over again—and it is easier to get elected over and over again from sparsely populated states than from populous states, and it is easier to get elected from states that never change their politics (like South Carolina, which is always Democratic) than from states like New York, Illinois, or Massachusetts where party fortunes oscillate and personality often carries the day or loses it.

The Senate sometimes seems to the voter too tender of mere seniority, too tolerant of voices from the past. It would not matter if the Senate were a land of faery:

Where nobody gets old and godly and grave,
Where nobody gets old and crafty and wise,
Where nobody gets old and bitter of tongue.

But it is not. And the Senate may seem lacking in simple, optimistic faith to commentators who are too well provided with it. The Senate, however, exists to be skeptical. It has never died as a corporate body, never been dissolved, never lost continuity since 1789. It has seen many more than four-and-twenty leaders of revolt, and has seen a good many of them settle down to very unrevolutionary ways in the Senate.

The Senate waits till it sees whether the American people is off on a real campaign, or on one of those short-distance crusades to which "Mr. Dooley" noted his countrymen's addiction.

It is this attitude of watchful waiting that earns the Senate such hostile criticism when it is applied to problems of international relations. For no treaty can be ratified without a vote of two thirds of the Senate "present and voting" —which means, in practice, that thirty-three Senators, possibly from what are called the "acreage states," the more or less empty commonwealths of the West plus a few others, may hold up an international program approved by the overwhelming majority of the American people, advocated by the President of the time, and eagerly awaited by that large part of the outside world which would follow an American lead if one were given. The long, maddening, and apparently endless delays of the Senate's procedure in such cases do not merely exhaust the patience and energy of the American voter, who may decide it is less laborious to let the whole project drop than to attempt to convert the irreducible minority of the Senate. It also has a natural if deplorable effect on the outside world, which comes, after a time, to the frame of mind of the man in the American hotel bedroom who heard another guest, in the room above, drop one shoe on the floor. He waited and waited and waited till his patience was exhausted, then called out: "Damn you, drop the *other* shoe!" At that stage the State Department has, regretfully, to inform the world that the United States has no other shoe because the Senate has refused to concur in the treaty negotiated with such anguish by the President and by the Heads of States less well provided with constitutional safeguards.

But however the Senate minority may use or abuse its prerogative, it must be borne in mind that there is no effective substitute for a treaty binding the United States continually and morally. Constitutionally, because no treaty has ever been invalidated by the Supreme Court and it is a doctrine of the Court that, within very wide and undefined limits, a treaty creates the necessary powers which it calls for. No "gentlemen's agreement," no "executive agreement," no "joint resolution" can do that. And, still more important, no substitute for a treaty can bind the conscience and coerce the will of the American people. It is the knowledge that this is so, that a treaty may not only bind the United States, but confer power on the federal government to implement the treaty by legislation, which accounts for the support given to the so-called "Bricker amendment." For the vigilant Senator Bricker of Ohio, conscious that any President can present the Senate with *faits accomplis,* wishes by a constitutional amendment to make "gentlemen's agreements" ineffective and to deprive formal treaties of any power-granting character. But despite the senatorial alarms and envy, the amendment has not got through. The American people, if not the congressional politicians, do not wish new fetters to bind the President (whom they have chosen) in the age of the H-bomb.

There are drawbacks to this situation, but it has to be accepted that it is far more useful to get a limited treaty with the United States than the most promising, vague, and undefined substitute for a treaty. The treaty will certainly be more limited, more cautious, less inspiring. But it will be valid and lasting. Nothing else will be.

The problem of international organization is naturally seen by Americans in the light of their own experiment and experience. They know how political institutions grow in directions unforeseen by their makers. Few of the Founding Fathers would recognize today—and only one, Hamilton, probably would like—the federal government as it has grown to its present predominance. It was against such growth that the South fought the Civil War. Under the shadow of the

Union, the states have shrunk in authority and prestige, and no amount of wishful oratory will ever give them back the sovereignty and prestige they owned yesterday. This process has been beneficial, inevitable (as that word is loosely used), irreversible. But it involved a great civil war testing the principle, as Lincoln put it when the war was drawing to a close, "whether any government not too strong for the liberties of its people can be strong enough to maintain its existence in great emergencies." The issue was already decided; the government of the United States *could* maintain its existence. But John C. Calhoun, had he lived to see that issue decided, would have asserted that the Civil War had proved that such a government would be too strong for the liberties of the states.

Only if an American leader or leaders can persuade the American people—and the Senate—that the fears of John C. Calhoun, however justified, must be defied, that the caution which dares not do anything because there is a risk of its turning out badly must be discarded, will the stability of the world, even for a generation, be underwritten by the United States. That hope for mankind is tied up with the problem of getting the American people, in its constitutional embodiment in the Senate, to accept the international implications of Thurber's law: "There is no safety in numbers or in anything else." But there are two orders of risk: the risk of certain disaster if nothing is done, and the risk of failure if something is attempted. This persuasion is a job for Americans. Above all, the job of converting the Senate is a job for Americans:

> *Only those who brave its dangers*
> *Comprehend its mystery.*

The sophisticated Easterner—indeed, the sophisticated American—when he looks at certain senators and, still more, at certain representatives, is likely to form a poor opinion of the discrimination of their electors. He supposes that the relationship between voter and politician is like that between the popular but silly preacher and his congregation as described by Charles II: "His nonsense suits their nonsense." There are cases in which this diagnosis fits the case, though it must not be forgotten that the voters may be perfectly well aware of the fact that their representative is not a totally serious character—but, then, is politics serious? One way to circumvent the wise man who considered making ballads more important than making laws is to get the laws and the ballads made by the same people. And good ballad-makers are harder to find than run-of-the-mill politicians. But it is also to be remembered that the sophisticated may be wrong, that the politician is not necessarily silly merely because he talks or dresses or thinks differently from the best people in the East, or even in the West. Mr. Bernard De Voto has pointed out how much Francis Parkman lost on the Oregon Trail by his Boston Brahminical superiority to the rough-and-ready frontiersman, who had not only bad manners but often bad morals, yet who deserved sympathetic study all the same.

The role of Congress is especially difficult in a time of great and rapid change like the present. For the role of Congress is to make laws and, then, after the event, to find out how they have been applied. As modern society gets more and more complex, the mere text of a law becomes less important. What Napoleon said of war: "A simple art, all is in the application of it," is almost as true of lawmaking. A generation ago the great issues were legislative, issues whose administrative aspects were comparatively simple. Even as late as the Wilson administration, the great measures of the first great presidential term were legislative. Congress and the President worked together to pass measures like the Underwood tariff, the creation of the Federal Reserve System, the establishment of the eight-hour day on the railroads. But once the requisite statutory authority was given, the application of the new powers was fairly simple and comparatively uncontroversial.

But in the modern crisis, administration is nine tenths of the law. This cannot be helped. Rigid definition of every possible case before the event merely paralyzes the administration; it does not add to the authority or prestige of Congress. Indeed, by creating bottle-necks, it may diminish the prestige of Congress, for it is often forgotten, both on Capitol Hill and around the White House, that a loss of prestige by one branch of the government does not necessarily add to the prestige of another branch; it may simply lessen the hold of the whole political process on the imagination of the American people.

The representative and still more the senator is put on a spot. If he insists on hogging the limelight and opposing at length the legislative proposals of the administration, he may be charged, often rightly, with holding up the measures necessary for the promotion of the general welfare. If he agrees to the administration's proposals, he is accused of being a rubber stamp. If he investigates administrative mistakes or follies, he is accused of locking the stable door. If he replies to these criticisms by spontaneous action, by highly publicized vigilance, he gets a bad press. If he goes off on a witch-hunt, he may create the effect of a government in which ballet dancers are investigated by crooners. What is hard, almost impossible, to put across is the fact that most congressmen and senators have to work hard and seriously to keep their jobs, once elected, and that they get elected by giving an impression of being willing to work hard. The American elector, in good times, is not very critical of his representatives. His favor falls on the unjust and on the just alike. But all must be *and seem* "busier than a hound dog with fleas" if they want to please the customer—that is, the voter.

What they are busy about depends both on the senator or representative and on the voters of the state or district. In a state in which politics has, usually for historical reasons, been pretty free from ideological content (for example, Pennsylvania in the good old days), the senators and representatives were mainly busy with the serving of tables. But in more recent years it has been necessary to be busy with other things as well, to be a bit of a Mary as well as a Martha even in Pennsylvania. But although this is an improvement, it must not be forgotten that looking after local interests, local sentiments, local jobs, is a very legitimate concern of the American politician. Not merely will he not get re-elected if he neglects the local chores, but he should not be. One of the things that hold the vast area of the United States together is the belief that the political machinery provides a means whereby local and personal interests and sentiments are really taken into account in Washington. If all decisions of the federal government were handed down from some remote Sinai, the government of the United States might rapidly acquire the appearance—and more than the appearance, the habits—of a remote imperial power; a power more "efficient" perhaps in that it would change its mind less often and make far fewer expensive mistakes. But it would all the time be making the basic mistake of not interesting the average man, three thousand miles away, in his government, if only by showing him that his government is human, fallible, and even feeble. The American may profess to admire efficiency at all costs, but one place where he wants his business suit let out at the seams is politics. If he did not want that, if he did not believe that these adjustments were part of the humanizing side of the democratic process, the American might quite quickly fall a victim to the German passion for leaving it all to the expert—which ends up in leaving it all to the inspiration of the *Führer,* who tells the experts. After all, *somebody* has to tell them.

In America it is the politician. Of course, the politician may tell the expert too much, too often, and in tones that make it certain that experts will prefer to work for anybody rather than the United States. The wiser politicians know this; but not all politicians are wise, and one way of making the headlines is to put on a good show, vaudeville if higher forms of showmanship are beyond you. And members of Congress, like other citizens, now feel more and more that the world is incomprehensible, feel that it is one thing to pursue a possibly Communist dentist, another to deal with the scruples and conduct of a physicist, or even follow the argument. A politician would not be human if he did not dream of, perhaps think possible, a return to a simpler world where there were no questions that an industrious congressman could not master, no secrets beyond the reach of his investigating technique.

Members of Congress are men (and women) of higher than average ability but, like men and women of all kinds with such ability in all countries, they are handicapped by the complexity of modern life, by the increasingly difficult character of its social problems, and by the absence of any generally accepted body of opinion, supported by all experts and intelligible to all reasonably industrious and capable amateurs. It is no wonder, then, that the American politician lends a ready ear to any Mephistopheles who whispers:

> *"Grau, theurer Freund, ist alle Theorie,*
> *Und grün des Lebens goldner Baum."*

So there is a ready welcome for slogans denouncing theorists who have neither (a) "had to meet a payroll," nor (b) "had to get elected to anything." There is something in each of these complaints, for in American society the place of the individual entrepreneur is still great in fact and even greater in fiction. And in a democratic society, having what it takes to get elected is a real quality, not to be assessed too lightly.

Any given elected person may seem to be a proof that "you can fool all of the people some of the time" or "some of the people all of the time," but over any reasonably representative period, the American people get the Congress they want and (I hold) over the same period, better congressmen than they deserve. There is another reason for the distrust of specialists that is humanly understandable though intellectually less defensible. Theory is not what it was a generation or two ago. When Cleveland defended his tariff policy by saying that it was "a condition not a theory that confronts us," Cleveland and his supporters and enemies knew a good deal both about the condition and about the theory. The theory was the theory of Free Trade vs. Protection. Nearly all the theorists (save for a few in the Wharton School of Finance at the University of Pennsylvania) were Free-Traders. The majority of the American people and American politicians were more or less opposed to the theorists. But there was no great mystery about the Free Trade case and only the necessary amount of mystery-mongering about the Protectionist case. And when John Sherman of Ohio insisted, year after year, that "the way to resume is to resume," the case for going back to the international gold standard was fairly clear. So was the question of what sections of the American people would gain (like Sherman's friends) and what sections would lose or thought they would lose, like the supporters of "Silver Dick" Bland, who were to find their prophet in William Jennings Bryan.

But a discussion of tariff or currency questions today is like a discussion of relativity to an old-fashioned physicist or logician: it involves a recasting of the "normal" intellectual order, of the "normal" standard of rationality, of which few people, congressmen or bankers, are capable. The average citizen, in or out of Congress, is puzzled. Those persons who claim to be experts do not all speak with one voice and, confronted with Keynes plans and White plans, with Professor Hansen and Professor Schumpeter, the politician is tempted to despair. And he is still more tempted to conceal his despair, to assume the role of the plain, blunt man, to cry "A plague o' both your houses!" and try something practical—which often turns out to be totally impracticable.

Here, again, Congress suffers from its lack of administrative authority. It has few or no experts of its own. It may hire some from time to time, but it has no permanent substitute for the hired experts of the administration. Nor, even if it had, would its academic studies have the same weight as the reports and decisions of the law-enforcing bodies, of the agents of the Executive departments. As Professor Ralph Barton Perry has pointed out, there is nothing unnatural or discreditable in this human reaction. And if there is any blame on one side or the other, at least as much attaches to the experts, who cannot get their points across, as to the congressmen who seem slow on the uptake. As many of the experts were at one time college teachers, they cannot say that they have no experience in making things plain to non-specialists. After all, they have presumably to do some educational work with their own political chiefs as their English opposite numbers have to do all the time.

But be the causes what they may, the result is unfortunate. It leads to an American version of the great French political heresy that complex social and economic problems can be solved by rhetoric. It is not a case of silly denunciation of rhetoric as a spur to action, as a creator of democratic will, as a builder or sustainer of morale. It is unnecessary to stress the importance of this role in the age of Roosevelt, Churchill, Hitler, Goebbels, de Gaulle, Chiang Kai-shek,[1] and the numerous orators of the Moscow radio. But the place of rhetoric, though great, is limited, and this is too often

[1] I have, of course, no views myself on the oratorical powers of the Generalissimo, but a colleague tells me that his radio speeches in Chinese are admirable, superior to his wife's speeches in English.

forgotten. It is, for instance, often mere rhetoric to denounce a measure, which you dislike anyway and because you dislike it anyway, as "un-American," or, what is an intensive of the same adjective, "unconstitutional."

The worship of the Constitution by the American people and by the American politician is so natural and so valuable, so indispensable an element in national cohesion, that immense tolerance even of the abuse of that worship is necessary. And some politicians who fall back on the Constitution as an answer to all problems, and as a barrier to all change, are perfectly sincere. More or less consciously they are taking the advice that Chesterton gave to a now forgotten English politician:

> *Walter, be wise, avoid the wild and new,*
> *The constitution is the game for you.*

But it can become a monotonous game, and a time-wasting game for the spectator who may wonder how the American nation ever got going and kept going if the job of finding authority for action was as arduous in the early days as it is made to seem today. Of course it was even more arduous, but the ways in which Hamilton, Jefferson, Jackson, Lincoln, Cleveland, Theodore Roosevelt, and Wilson managed to find authority for doing what they wanted to do, and what they believed the nation wanted or needed to have done, are now sanctioned by time and tradition and by the vested interest of great parties.

The division of responsibility between Congress and the President has an important influence on the way in which public opinion is educated, distorted, expressed. Since a congressional speaker normally will not have the responsibility for putting his warmly declaimed principles into action, he can be as hot, dogmatic, and unyielding as he pleases. As debate is rare in the House of Representatives, since nearly all real business is done in the committees, it is natural that such debate as there is should be very oratorical, should be "sounding off," not discussion. And this is one of the reasons why public speaking in America is still so rhetorical, why audiences for example do not often "heckle" a speaker, bombard him with questions, or embarrass him with ironical applause or laughter. It is almost as rare to interrupt a political speech as it is to interrupt a sermon.

In the Senate, things are different. Any senator who can get the floor can talk as long as his wind lasts. He cannot be out of order unless he takes the most extravagant liberties. So Senate debates are often lively, often educational. They are very different from the formal pieces declaimed in the other house, or even printed and sent to the voters without being spoken at all. A senator has to persuade his colleagues, even those of his own party, or he has to intimidate them, and so the Senate has a high representation of public speakers who can discuss as well as declaim. Yet the national tradition is now for declamation. In the old days, joint debates like those between Lincoln and Douglas educated the public and kept the debaters in training. But those old days are past.

The result is that all issues are discussed with oratorical trimmings, reports to the nation are made in tones loud enough to have a chance of being heard over the competing din. Issues are necessarily simplified to fit these conditions; the speaker must know or appear to know all the answers, and he must set them down in a simple oratorical black-and-white. This is especially true if he is a candidate for the presidential nomination (and many are). For he will, if successful, be running for an office in which he will be responsible for all aspects of national policy. He cannot say or imply that his future colleagues will look after this department or that, for he won't have any colleagues, only subordinates.

It is inevitable, therefore, that difficult and complicated

issues should be reduced, in public, to very simple moral issues, with words like "liberty," "constitutional," "states' rights," "the spirit of '76," "the American way," "malefactors of great wealth," "Bolsheviki," "the American home" or "women" or "children" doing duty for argument.

Yet all this is not to be taken too seriously. It does not deceive either the public or the orators. I can remember seeing and talking to a politician then much in the public eye (and still in it though less prominently) after a speech in which he had washed away a number of complicated questions in a flood of adjectives. And the orator, so confident, so simple-minded on the stump, was tired, disillusioned, puzzled, anxious. He had been playing the part assigned to him, but he was much more Hamlet than the simple-minded, quick-acting Othello for which he had been cast by his managers.

But oratory, phrases, the evocative power of verbal symbols must not be despised, for these are and have been one of the chief means of uniting the United States and keeping it united.

4

AMERICA IS PROMISES, but America is words, too. It is built like a church on a rock of dogmatic affirmations. "We hold these truths to be self-evident, that all men are created equal, that they are endowed by their Creator with certain unalienable Rights, that among these are Life, Liberty and the pursuit of Happiness." "We the People of the United States, in order to form a more perfect Union, establish Justice, insure domestic Tranquillity, provide for the common defence, promote the general Welfare, and secure the Blessings of Liberty to ourselves and our Posterity, do ordain and establish this Constitution." These are only two of the most famous assertions of faith in things unseen, of dogmatic articles denied in good faith by many non-Americans but asserted in good faith by millions of Jefferson's countrymen from July 4, 1776 to this day. How absurd an ambition for a people to attempt, by a written constitution, to "establish justice"! It is an ambition to make lawyers laugh and philosophers weep. "To promote the general welfare"; what is this entity, so confidently labeled? What would a Marxian or a Machiavellian make of it? What an overleaping ambition of the Supreme Court to apply not known statute or case law but "the rule of reason"! What complacent courage in the founders of the Massachusetts Bay Company to identify the decision of John Winthrop, Richard Saltonstall, and the rest to transplant themselves to New England with "the greatness of the work in regard of the consequence, God's glory and the churches good"! Nevertheless, Massachusetts was founded, and a Saltonstall is Senator in this year of grace 1956, more than three hundred years later. There have been other consequences, too. What (possibly nonspontaneous) wisdom was shown by Lord Baltimore and the other Catholics of Maryland who in 1649 noted the evils arising from "the inforcing of the conscience in matters of Religion" and so came out for the toleration of all Christians—this in an age when the Inquisition was still going strong, a year after the Peace of Westphalia, the year of the massacre at Drogheda by Cromwell, a generation before the revocation of the Edict of Nantes? With what Hebraic confidence in their mission did the people of Massachusetts in 1780 acknowledge "with grateful hearts the goodness of the great Legislator of the universe, in affording us, in the course of His Providence, an opportunity, deliberately and peaceably, without fraud, violence or surprise, of entering into an original, explicit, and solemn compact with each other; and of forming a new constitution of civil government, for ourselves and posterity; and devoutly imploring His direction in so interesting a design, do agree upon, ordain and establish, the following Declaration of Rights and Frame of Government, as the Constitution of the Commonwealth of Massachusetts." Only a lively conviction of divine interest and direction could have justified so extravagant a hope as that by the mere separation of the legislative, executive, and judicial powers the people of Massachusetts or any people could establish a "government of laws and not of men."

But these aspirations, these hopes, extravagant or meaningless as they may seem to the critical, have been fighting words, hopes and beliefs leading to action. So have been the phrases, the slogans, authentic, apocryphal, half-authentic, with which American history and American memory is filled. This is no country where "what Mr. Gladstone said in 1884" is a comic mystery. These echoes from a heroic if overdramatized past resound still: "Give me liberty or give me death!" "In the name of the Great Jehovah and the Continental Congress!" "First in war, first in peace, first in the hearts of his countrymen." "Don't give up the ship." "We have met the enemy and they are ours." "Our federal union, it must be preserved." "Look at Jackson's men, standing like a stone wall!" "With malice toward none." "Public office is a public trust." "You may fire when ready, Gridley." "Don't cheer, boys! the poor devils are dying." "Make the world safe for democracy." "One third of a nation." The American man-in-the-street may not attribute all these slogans correctly. He may think it was Lawrence of U.S.S. *Chesapeake* who said "Don't give up the ship"; almost uniformly he thinks that it was Washington who warned against "entangling alliances," whereas it was Jefferson. And he *will* mix them up with texts from Scripture. He may have no more knowledge of the historical context than had the badly frightened citizen who, rescued from a lynching bee, protested: "I didn't say I was against the Monroe Doctrine; I love the Monroe Doctrine, I would die for the Monroe Doctrine. I merely said I didn't know what it was." Not all his slogans are reverent. He may, at times, fall back on "Oh, Yeah" or the more adequate "however you slice it, it's still baloney." But he knows too much to despise the power of speech, to think that Bryan was adequately described when he was compared to the Platte River of his native Nebraska: "Five inches deep and five miles wide at the mouth." The power of even bad oratory is still great. The power of good oratory is greater.

So the American suspends his irony when a recognized public figure is speaking, or even when he is merely "sounding off." The American audience listens patiently, even happily, to dogmatic and warm statements in favor of the American Constitution, home, woman, business, farmer. An American college president (from the deep South) has been known to impose a severe strain on the discipline of the undergraduates of an Oxford college by addressing them as "clean-limbed, clear-eyed boys." A pastor has been known to describe casting a ballot as a "political sacrament." Senator Vest's panegyric on the dog is only recently condemned as too lush, and a tribute to Southern womanhood is engraved on the pedestal of a statue to a forgotten statesman in Nashville, Tennessee.

In Chambers of Commerce, at Rotary Club meetings, at college commencements, in legislatures, in Congress, speech is treated seriously, according to the skill and taste of the user. Americans have no fear of boss words or of eloquence, no fear of clichés, no fear of bathos. In short, Americans are like all political peoples except the British. It is the countrymen of Burke and Gladstone and Asquith and Churchill who are the exception. But the difference has now the importance of an acquired characteristic. The British listener—above all, the English listener—is surprised and embarrassed by being asked to applaud statements whose truth he has no reason to doubt, but whose expression seems to him remarkably abstract and adorned with flowers of old-fashioned rhetoric. It is in Congress, not in the House of Commons, that a speaker can safely conclude a speech on the reorganization of the civil service with a parallel between the Crucifixion and what the then incumbent of the White House had to go through. It is in all kinds of American public meetings that speakers can "slate" and "rap" and "score" and "blast"—to the advantage of headline-writers. No words, it seems, can be strong enough to express the passionate feelings involved. It is not quite so bad or good as that; American politicians, American orators, are not so burned up as they seem. But it must not be forgotten that they are often quite annoyed, quite worried, quite angry; that they are taking really quite a dim view, even when all they can find to express their mood, verbally, is an assertion that the American way of life is due to end on the first Tuesday after the first Monday in November every four years. If an American—even a Senator—asks: "Is civilization a failure, or is the Caucasian played out?" it is not necessary to despair. All Americans dislike being beaten at poker and, for the greater gaiety of nations, don't mind saying so.

It is not merely that Americans like slogans, like words. They like absolutes in ethics. They believe that good is good, even if they quarrel over what, in the circumstances, *is* good. It was an American, true, who said: "My country, right or wrong. May she always be right. But, right or wrong, my country!"[1]

But this sentiment is in advance of that of many simple patriots in other lands who cannot conceive that their country could be wrong, who feel no possible risk of moral strain, and who would agree with the British naval officer who thought that even posing the question was improper conduct in an instructor of British naval cadets. To condemn a thing simply as un-American is often foolish, but no more foolish than to condemn a thing merely as un-English. And since the Americans are very articulate about the content of Americanism, while being English is a thing in itself, there is slightly more chance of there being meaning in "un-American" than in "un-English."

This national fondness for oratory, for slogans, has another cause or another result. It was an English Puritan leader on trial for his life who said of the execution of Charles I: "This thing was not done in a corner." It was a very American attitude. What Wilson preached—"open covenants openly arrived at"—is what the American people wants and expects to get. Like Wilson, it exaggerates the degree to which this standard of public negotiation is practicable. It is not always possible to negotiate under the klieg lights of congressional or press publicity. There are some-

---

[1] I have used the popular, not the correct, version of the dictum of Commodore Decatur, U.S.N.

times good reasons not only for secret negotiations but for confidential commitments. But they have to be very good reasons, advanced by leaders, native or foreign, in whom the American people have trust—and that trust will not be unlimited. No American leader, certainly not Washington or Lincoln, not Jackson or Jefferson at the height of their power, was thought to be above criticism or even above a certain degree of legitimate suspicion. Whitman, when he wrote of "the never-ending audacity of elected persons," voiced a general American belief that all leaders bear watching and that they are in duty bound to make frequent reports on the state of the Union, with or without aid of a fireside. The Americans are all, in this connection, from Missouri; they have got to be shown. They have also got to be told, and so has the world. Again, it is a powerful American tradition at work. Every American child used to learn by heart and many still learn by heart a famous plea for telling the world. For the most sacred of all American political scriptures, the Declaration of Independence, opens with a preamble justifying publicity. "When, in the course of human events, it becomes necessary for one people to dissolve the political bands which have connected them with another, and to assume among the Powers of the earth, the separate and equal station to which the Laws of Nature and of Nature's God entitle them, a decent respect to the opinions of mankind requires that they should declare the causes which impel them to the separation."

The Americans expect from their own leaders—and from the leaders of other countries—a regard for the "Laws of Nature and of Nature's God"; they also expect a "decent respect to the opinions of mankind"—publicly manifested in reasons given and discussed with what may seem excessive freedom and candor of comment. It is a view which gives rise to awkwardness and annoyance, but that can't be helped. The ablest modern publicist, native or foreign, is no match for one of the two greatest writers of political prose who have been Presidents of the United States. And, since I have talked so much of the American passion for oratory, for the spoken word, it is worth recalling that Thomas Jefferson, one of the foremost figures in American history, was also easily the worst public speaker of his time, perhaps of any time.

"A decent respect to the opinions of mankind." It is still a phrase to be remembered. It means that the American man-in-the-street expects to get the low-down on all secret conferences, to have international decisions supplied to him before the participants have had time to put their smiles on and pose for the group photograph. If this demand is not forthcoming from official sources, it is provided from unofficial sources. Commentators of varying degrees of knowledge, candor, truthfulness, ingenuity, intelligence, explain and announce. Wildly conflicting guesses are made with equal confidence, and the reader and listener are given a wide range of confidential misinformation—as is their right. The outsider may wonder at the willing suspension of disbelief on which the commentators can count. He may think that Tom Sawyer was a notably representative American in his insistence on romantic possibilities in face of drab and dreary realities. He may wonder whether an eminent law professor has any particular authority for his views on the connection between British policy and Romanian oil. He may wonder whether anybody wanting to keep a secret would tell it to Walter Winchell or even dare to enter the Stork Club. But these doubts are irrelevant. For the dispensers of secrets are catering to a public that has a village horror of the successful privacy of its neighbors. This public could see why Mr. Eisenhower should want to keep his political intentions quiet, any more than Mr. Tommy Manville keeps his matrimonial intentions quiet. Of course, he may *try*, as a football coach keeps his secret plays quiet if the scouts from other colleges let him. But it is the duty of columnists and senators to tell all, as soon as they have discovered it or even before. And no agreement that needs to be kept dark for any length of time has any chance of success in the United States. For the American Republic is much more like the Athenian than like the Venetian Republic. And Americans, though they have a great deal to do, have in common with Saint Paul's Athenian audience a continuous eagerness "to tell or to hear some new thing."

But there is more behind it than this passion for information, for an elaborate version of corner-grocery gossip. The American Republic was founded in the days of the *"secret du roi,"* in the days when Wilkes was, with some difficulty, made a martyr of for revealing the secret of Parliament. A world in which great decisions were made by kings or oligarchies in secret, and the results communicated to docile subjects, this was the world against which the founders of the American Republic revolted. True, great things have been done in secret even in America. The Constitution was made in secret—it could not have been made in public even if the art of eavesdropping had in those days been practiced as expertly as it is now. But it was presented, quickly and in its final form, to the American people, presented to be accepted, or rejected, or amended. Only so could "We the People of the United States" be committed. Only so can they be committed today.

5

THE WORD "SCHOOL" in America covers every type of educational institution. Being "at school" may mean being at a kindergarten or at Harvard. School, too, has kept much of its Greek meaning. It is a system of organization and training for leisure as well as work. And it has become more and more adjusted to its environment, undertaking to do more than it can (which is very American) and doing much more than it seems to do (which is also very American).

The social and political role of American education cannot be understood if it is thought of as being primarily a means of formal instruction. If it is so thought of, it will be overrated and underrated. It will be overrated because the number of college students or high-school pupils will dazzle the visitor used to seeing opportunities for higher education doled out on a combined class-and-intellectual basis. It will be underrated if, at any stage below the highest (that is, below the great universities), the academic standards are compared with those of a good English, French, or pre-Hitler German school. If these millions of boys and girls are to be judged by their academic accomplishments, they will be judged harshly. But they are not to be so judged, for their schools are doing far more than instruct them: they are letting them instruct each other in how to live in America.

Of those millions, a large section will be the children of immigrants to whom English is still largely a foreign tongue. Of these millions, a very large proportion will be the children of migrants from different parts of the United States. Others will be the children of rural-bred parents, forced to adjust themselves to the new urban world. They have to learn a common language, common habits, common tolerances, a common political and national faith. And they do. It is this aim and this success that justify the lavish buildings of the local high school; not merely the classrooms and the laboratories, but the gymnasium, the fieldhouse where basketball can be played in comfort in the depth of the bitter winter, the swimming pools in which the summer heat can be endured.

It is true that the teachers are relatively badly paid and have an inferior social as well as economic standing, insecure tenure and politics making their condition worse. More money spent on men might get better results than more money spent on buildings. But it is easier to get the materials for buildings than the materials for teachers. As long as American society remains individualistic, competitive, confident that the answers to the present are in the future, not in the past, it is going to take more than money to seduce the right men and women in adequate numbers away from the life of action. And, a point too seldom remembered, the necessity for providing teachers for the millions of college students hampers recruiting for high schools. In many cases, the colleges are doing what is really high-school work and it matters comparatively little where the good teachers are, as long as they are teaching.

The political function of the schools is to teach Americanism, meaning not merely political and patriotic dogma, but the habits necessary to American life. This justifies the most extravagant items in the curriculum. Since the ability to play bridge is one of the marks of Americanism in a suburb, it is reasonable that there should be bridge clubs in schools. The main political achievement of the high schools and grammar schools is to bring together the young of all classes and all origins, to provide, artificially, the common background that in an old, rural society is provided by tradition, by the necessary collaboration of village life.

171

The elementary schools—the "grade" schools—do this, too, but as far as an American town is broken up into racial blocs, the Ethan Allen Public School may have mainly Polish pupils, the Zachary Chandler mainly Welsh. Only in the Warren G. Harding High School is a big enough common pool formed in which Americans can be made.

Some of that Americanization is, of course, done deliberately and formally. Mr. Carlton Hayes pointed out long ago that the ritual of flag-worship and oath-taking in an American school is a religious observance. Little boys and girls, in a school from which religion in the old sense is barred, solemnly rising each morning and reciting together the "American's Creed"[1] are performing a religious exercise as truly as if they began the day with "I believe in God the Father Almighty" or asserted that "There is no God but God."

And that these daily rituals are religious has been at last affirmed by the Supreme Court in a series of cases in which the children of a fanatical sect, Jehovah's Witnesses, had been excluded from schools for refusing to give to the flag honors that, so their parents had taught them, were due to God alone. In 1940, all the Court except Chief Justice Stone held that flag-worship was among the things that were Cæsar's. Since that year, however, by a majority they decided that the religious rights of the children were being

---

[1] "I believe in the United States of America as a Government of the people, by the people, for the people; whose just powers are derived from the consent of the governed; a democracy in a republic; a sovereign Nation of many sovereign States; a perfect union, one and inseparable; established upon those principles of freedom, equality, justice, and humanity for which American patriots sacrificed their lives and fortunes. I therefore believe it is my duty to my country to love it; to support its Constitution; to obey its laws; to respect its flag, and to defend it against all enemies." As a result of the current wave of patriotic religion, the phrase "under God" has been inserted into the "American's Creed."

infringed. What is significant in the cases is not the Court's reversal of itself but the reality of the issue presented to it. For to the Court, and to the overwhelming majority of the American people, the objections of the Witnesses were as unintelligible as the objections of the Christians to making a formal sacrifice to the Divine Emperor were to Trajan and Pliny. The school board of Minersville, Pennsylvania, was faced with a real problem when it was asked to admit that children refusing to take part in the most sacred rite of the day should be allowed to associate with the believing children of the formally unestablished national church of the United States. So, too, was the state of Oregon when it found Catholic and Lutheran children refusing to go to the schools it provided. But in both cases the Supreme Court held, finally, that compulsory Americanism was not Americanism at all, that coerced belief was not what the American people needed to stay united. This was not Germany or Russia but the country of Jefferson and Justice Holmes.

The flag-worship of the American school and the American nation was brought home in war time to the British public in an episode that, if funny, was also very revealing. For the London makers of ladies' underwear who adorned their garments with American flags were innocent of any insulting or even frivolous intention. At the same time, a revue chorus in London was attired in Union Jack handkerchiefs and nothing else—to the public indifference. But the flag in America is more than a mere symbol among many others. It is the regimental color of a regiment in which all Americans are enrolled. Its thirteen stripes and forty-eight stars are symbols far better understood than the complicated heraldry of crosses of Saint George, Saint Andrew, and Saint Patrick imposed on each other in a way that only experts understand. It was Lincoln's task to see that the number of stars in the flag was not diminished by eleven during his term of office. It was the discovery that the flag still flew over Fort McHenry, despite the British fleet, that moved Francis Scott Key to write:

Oh, say, can you see by the dawn's early light,
What so proudly we hailed at the twilight's
*   last gleaming;*
Whose broad stripes and bright stars,
*   thro' the perilous fight,*
O'er the ramparts we watched were
*   so gallantly streaming?*

What he wrote in 1814, tens of millions of Americans have since sung or tried to sing. And when Barbara Frietchie in Whittier's poem rebuked Stonewall Jackson with:

"Shoot if you must this old gray head,
But spare your country's flag," she said,

she was speaking for all Americans for whom the Stars and Stripes was still their country's flag as it had been, till recently, that of General Jackson. And the most celebrated ritual moment of the last war was the hoisting of the Stars and Stripes on Iwo Jima, caught, in a happy moment, by a quick-witted San Francisco photographer. The three figures, straining to keep the flag erect, were "the Spirit of '76" in action and symbol.

Thus Americanization by ritual is an important and necessary part of the function of the American school. And because it is best carried out in schools, it matters little that the high-school curriculum has been so widened that it no longer means a great deal that this boy or that girl was graduated from it—if we are looking for proof of academic achievement. But graduation from high school is reasonable proof that a great deal has been learned about American ways of life, that lessons in practical politics, in organization, in social ease have been learned that could not have been learned in factory or office.

And if the high school seems to devote too much time and money to social life, penalizing the poor boy or girl more than a theoretically less democratic educational system might do, it is thus early impressing an awkward truth on the boy or girl who is both mediocre and poor. It also penalizes the really able boy or girl who is not kept in good enough intellectual training. And if the main business of the school is, in fact, the Americanization of the children of newcomers, the parents of "old American stock" have a good reason (to add to less good ones) for not sending their children to learn what they know already, at the cost of diminishing their chance of learning what they do not know. If English is native to your children and to their home, it is not merely "undemocratic" to object to having their progress held up and their accent debased by the tone of a high school largely immigrant in composition.

For the task of an American school in many regions is to teach the American language, to enable it to compete with Spanish, with French, with Yiddish, with Polish, with German, with Swedish. Another task is to give, through the language and the literature of the language, a common vocabulary and a common fund of allusion, fable, and sentiment. With a fluid population this has not been easy. And the countless teachers who have labored, pedantically, formally, with complete and erroneous conviction that there were correct standards, have been heroes as important in the mass as was William McGuffey, whose *Eclectic Readers* sold over one hundred and twenty million copies and helped to make the Union. The teachers were heroes because, although English won against all its rivals, it was itself going through important changes, in vocabulary, in grammar, in sound, becoming the new tongue we are beginning to call

American. The teachers who stuck by the rules, who worshipped at the New England shrines in Concord, were bound to lose, but their struggle was not pure waste. For the common tongue, hammered out by millions of immigrants, by millions of migrants, would have been poor in vocabulary and structure but for the people Mencken called the dominies and who call themselves schoolmen. The creation of general literacy and a common written and spoken tongue, intelligible everywhere except possibly in the deep South, is an achievement as remarkable as the creation of Mandarin Chinese or Low Latin or Hellenistic Greek, and this tongue is certain to be the new *lingua franca* of the world.

The making of American has been mixed-up in English minds with the making of American slang. Slang, as we should know, is one of the great sources of language. French is improved Latin slang. And slang has contributed a good deal to American. It is a generation since Mr. Dooley said that when his countrymen had finished with the English language it would look as if it had been run over by a musical comedy. Since then it has been run over by *Hellzapoppin*. But it is possible, indeed very easy, to overestimate the role of slang. It is more and more the creation of professional artists, "makers." The Hollywood prose masters provide a current and often short-lived jargon; the boys and girls, men and women, who wish to be on the beam or in the groove, may murmur with admiration: "I wish I had said that." And Whistler's classical answer to Wilde is certainly appropriate: "You will, Oscar—you will!" But not for long. Some slang will enter the language; some words will lose their meanings or acquire new ones; syntax will be loosened up. But formal speech as taught in schools will still be very important. The high-school English teacher, for all her pedantry, is as much a maker of the American language as Messrs. Runyon and O'Hara. Two streams of language may run roughly parallel, but in time they will merge; they will provide America with many interesting variations, do for American what its dual Germanic and Latin character does for English. That time has not yet come, but it is on the way. And the future character of this truly national tongue is foreshadowed in the drawing by Mr. Peter Arno in which an indignant citizen tells another: "I consider your conduct unethical and lousy."

Most American parents do not want, or are not able, to send their children to anything but public high schools, and the life in such a school is a training in life for America. It may be and often is a training in life *against* Europe. For Europe is the background from which many of the children are reacting and from which they must be delivered if they are to be Americanized. For nearly all immigrants, America is promotion, and this promotion is more clearly felt by their children. The old people may hanker after the old country, but the children—whatever sentimental feelings for their ancestral homes they may have, especially when provoked—are, above all else, anxious to be Americans.

Necessarily something is lost here. The least-common-denominator Americanism of the schools is not a complete substitute for a native culture. What the first-generation American children learn to despise may include elements in their moral diet that are not replaced. A new American whose pride in that promotion involves mere contempt for the habits, what Americans call the "folkways" or "mores," of his parents is not necessarily a good American. So attempts are made to instill pride in the ancestral cultures of the European lands from which the immigrants come. The University of Pittsburgh, located in one of the main melting pots of America, has a set of rooms illustrating the culture of various European countries. In the case of the Greeks, the room may instill adequate pride; in the case of the Scots (if any such need is felt) a shrine of Robert Burns may serve. But for many of the peasant immigrants, the old country is backward though beloved, while for their children it is merely backward.

Americanization comes not from preservation of Slovak or Italian peasant culture, but from speedy assimilation to "American" culture. And that assimilation may take the form of distinction in anything that the American world obviously values. In the narrow sense of culture, there may even be a temptation to go for those courses that have no immigrant stigma on them. Thus I was told by an eminent Scandinavian-American that it is difficult to get good students of Scandinavian literature and language at the University of Minnesota, though most of the students have fairly recent Scandinavian connections. They will study French but not Swedish, for "French is not a servant's language." Latin, emblem of functionless "culture," plays something of the same role; it is a symbol of liberation. It is said that the only high school in New York where everybody takes Latin is a Negro high school.

Study is not the only way up to Americanization, to acceptation. Sport is another—and one that does the job more dramatically for the newcomers gifted with what it takes to excel in competitive contests, with what is needed to win personal and community and institutional glory.

When Fanny Ellsler, the ballet dancer, came to Boston, her performance was solemnly inspected from the highest motives by Emerson and Margaret Fuller. "The dance began; both sat serenely silent; at last Emerson spoke. 'Margaret,' he said, 'this is poetry.' 'No, Waldo,' replied Margaret; 'it is not poetry, it is religion.' "[2] And the great football games of today are religious ceremonies in this sense. It is significant that the graduating classes in Muncie High School a generation ago took such mottoes as *"Deo duce"*

[2] Barrett Wendell: *A Literary History of America*, p. 301.

and today take mottoes stressing the "Bearcat Spirit," the "Bearcats" being the school basketball team. But a Greek would know where he was at a basketball game uniting boys and girls, parents and civic leaders, in a common passion for competitive achievement. It may be hard on the academic work of the school. It may even slightly annoy a schoolboy who, as Mr. Burton Rascoe did, combines excellence in gymnastic and music, to find that his views on literature are less interesting to the other sex than his prowess at football. But sport, school sport, college sport, does unite the parents, the children, and the community. And sport is rigorously democratic. The sons of Czechs and Poles can score there, can break through the barriers that stand in the way of the children of "Bohunks" and "Polacks." And although Harvard may secretly rejoice when it can put a winning team on to Soldiers' Field whose names suggest the *Mayflower,* it would rather put on a team that can beat Yale, even though it is not a "Yankee" team, than go down to defeat with the descendants of generations of Brahmins. And in the Middle West, sport is a real means of promotion. The Ohio high school that produced the great Negro runner, Jesse Owens, was prouder of him than if he had made Phi Beta Kappa at Ohio State; and Hitler would have made a less serious mistake if he had snubbed a great American scholar whose race he didn't like than he did by sulking at the Olympic Games when the Herrenvolk were beaten by a Negro. It is a frontier tradition; Lincoln's great strength gave him a prestige that helped him as a lawyer and politician. The great athlete performing for the glory of the school, college, state, or nation, is a less egoistic figure than the great scholar pursuing his own studies with an undemocratic concentration. And the Negroes, whose greatest hero is Joe Louis, not Paul Robeson, are not substantially wrong so far. In American society as it is, a Negro heavyweight champion, like a Negro tap-dancer, is a better adjusted figure than a great Negro artist—or America is a less maladjusted society for them. Of course, this will not and should not last. The Irish were rising when their great hero became Governor Al Smith, rather than a successor of John L. Sullivan, the "Boston strong boy." But to get assent to a Negro's *right* to be heavyweight champion is something—as those will agree who remember the frenzied search round 1910 for a "white hope" to save the heavyweight championship from the indignity of being held by Jack Johnson. Great Indian athletes like Jim Thorpe, great Negro football heroes like Paul Robeson in his earlier days, the polyglot teams put on the field by the great Swedish coach Knute Rockne for the "Irish" of Notre Dame—these become "All-American" figures in a wider and deeper sense than that in which the Yale of Walter Camp understood the term. Indeed, when Mr. Camp put Paul Robeson of Rutgers on his All-American team, he was marking, very effectively, the rise of the exceptional Negro. And Negro pioneers in big-league baseball, like Satchel Paige (*monumentum ære perennius*), are more important figures in race history than the universally accepted and admired Willie Mays.

The cheer-leaders, the new *"jongleurs de Notre Dame,"* the "majorettes," shapely young women more or less involved with musical instruments, the massed cheering sections of the students, the massed yelling sections of the alumni—these are the equivalent of the crowds at the great Hellenic festivals in which barbarians were not allowed to compete. The Rose Bowl, the Cotton Bowl, the other intersectional games—these are instruments of national unity, and the provision of such instruments is no mean duty of colleges and universities. It is a religious exercise of a kind a Greek would have understood, however remote it may be from the university as understood by Abelard or Saint Thomas Aquinas or John Harvard.

The university, as these men understood it, exists all the same and exists to play a great national part, for the level of academic learning in America is perhaps the only branch of American life where the promise of rapid progress upward has been consistently kept. It is not as easy to define the nature of that progress as it is to affirm its existence.

Things have changed a great deal since the ideal of American college education was "Mark Hopkins at one end of a log and a student at the other." Then the college existed to provide a common background for lawyers and doctors and divines; it was small and select, not select in a social or financial sense, but select in that only those who accepted the old intellectual order of things were catered for. It was a decisive moment when President Eliot of Harvard (which had long ceased to concentrate on providing for a "learned ministry") introduced the elective system. The college abandoned any idea of imposing a hierarchy of subjects. The student could select what he wanted from the menu provided; *à la carte* had succeeded *table d'hôte*. But in newer, less secure, less rich institutions than Harvard, the change went farther than that, for not only was the student free to choose from what was offered —he was entitled to complain if the college did not offer what he wanted to learn, or even what he wanted to learn in the sense that it was all he could hope to learn. As more and more students came to college with varying school preparation, as life grew more complex and the techniques of life and business more impressive in their results, the unity of college life disappeared. Boys and girls were no longer taken in hand by a successor of Mark Hopkins and given a few general ethical and philosophical ideas suitable to a world still pretty much agreed on fundamentals. They were visitors to an institution that seemed to have more in common with the Mark Hopkins Hotel in San Francisco than with the Williams College of a century ago; and from the glass-walled bar, "The Top of the Mark," they could see the modern world, the bridges and skyscrapers of San Francisco, and across the Bay the lights of Berkeley, where the University of California provides for all tastes from addicts of the Greek theater to the most modern biological and physical techniques.

In this necessary adaptation of the old university ideal to the modern American world, much was lost, or not provided; there was not as yet a common standard of reference for educated men; a mass of information was stored and techniques were imparted in institutes physically associated for historical reasons. But of course the universities and colleges, like the high schools, served other than merely academic ends. *Our Town* illustrates high-school mating which would have taken place anyway. *The Miracle of Morgan's Creek* shows a suitor taking cookery so as to be close to his beloved during her high-school career, but he was bound to be close to her anyway. But the college movie, play (*The Poor Nut*), and novel rightly illustrate the more important phenomenon of exogamous marriage, of bringing together boys and girls who otherwise would not meet at all.

Besides all these activities (formally described as extracurricular) there is, of course, a great deal of first-class academic work done. And in one very important field the American public, if it wills, is given admirable opportunities for learning relevant facts about the modern external world as well as about its own past and present. No charge can be less well founded than that which holds the American school of today up to scorn for its uncritical jingoism. It is no longer true that American history is taught as a simple story of black (George III) vs. white (George Washington). A generation of critical scholarship has borne fruit in an objective and even slightly cynical treatment of the American Revolution and other great crises of American history. If the old simple story is still told and believed, that is not the fault of the schools. And contemporary American life is treated with the same candor. Nothing could be in more striking contrast than the legend of Southern life as it is told and retold by politicians and preachers and the grim, courageous, critical studies of the contemporary South that come from the universities, above all from the University of North Carolina.

It is not only American problems that are studied and analyzed with such learning, acuteness, and candor. World problems are, too. There is no country in the world where discussion of the world's affairs is carried on at such a high level as in the United States. (There are also few countries where it is carried on at such a low level, but that is another story.) Serious discussion, in great newspapers and magazines, in forums and on the air, in universities and institutes, is incessant. And it is discussion by real experts. Unfortunately, it is often discussion for experts, not for the people. For them, as the *Saturday Evening Post* rightly pointed out, the most complicated subjects in international politics are just another "study subject," the theme of accurate and objective but rather chilly debate by those who like that kind of thing.

And the very success of the school system in Americanizing the American young may result in the killing of natural curiosity. For example, the cult of the Constitution leads to the exclusive identification of a political concept like "liberty" with the American constitutional system. This being so, a Latin-American "republic" with a paper constitution like the American is regarded as "free" while Canada is not. For Canada is part of an "empire" with a monarch at the head of it. Some two thirds of the American people, accordingly, quite recently thought that Canada pays taxes to Britain; even in the states bordering on the Dominion, about half the Americans thought this! In the same way, the word "republic" has an almost magical significance for the Americans. Plutarch, as Mr. Wells once suggested, had a good deal to do with this; but, whatever the origins of the belief, it is now part of the American credo that only citizens of a republic can be free. And no matter what romantic interest Americans may display in the human side of monarchy, it should never be forgotten that, politically, they regard it as a childish institution. Mark Twain, a very pro-English American, refused for that very reason to write one of his amusing, critical travel books about England. But he did write two books about England, all the same: *The Prince and the Pauper* and *A Connecticut Yankee at the Court of King Arthur.* How deeply anti-monarchical, anti-clerical, anti-traditional, those books are!

And in *Huckleberry Finn,* the traditional American view of royalty as expensive foolishness is admirably set forth in Huck's remark to Nigger Jim: "Sometimes I wish we could hear of a country that's out of kings."

A great many Americans still think like Huck Finn. And it must be remembered that for Americans the great event of their own and of world history was the destruction of the royal power of George III and the establishment of a Constitution guaranteeing to each state "a republican form of government." It is in that light that the modern world is seen by nearly all Americans.

Nothing is more natural and understandable than the American assumption that all modern historical events are either American or unimportant. The Pole who wrote a book on *The Elephant and the Polish Question* was not merely a typical Pole but a typical human being. There are remote academic subjects that we study, and real, living subjects that concern us. "Listen to my bomb story and I'll listen to yours," as they said in London in 1940. Therefore the American conviction that the First World War really began in 1917, and that the Second one began on December 7, 1941, is simply an American example of a general illusion.

We know that the Chinese were fighting the Japanese long before we were, but we don't *feel* it. We could remember, if we tried, that the Poles were fighting the Germans a little before the British and long before the Russians or the Americans, but we don't feel any urgency to recall it. The Americans who, in March 1944, learned that their countrymen had bombed Berlin for the first time were astonished. The "We" who bombed Berlin in 1943 included Americans psychologically, but the "We" who bombed Tokyo didn't include British either factually or psychologically. This is all part of human nature. The Russians, with little experience of navigating on the high seas, could hardly be expected to appreciate that crossing the English Channel and invading are not quite the same thing as crossing even a wide river. Julius Cæsar's Mediterranean sailors, after all, had to learn that the hard way in 55 B.C. Of course this human attitude can be carried to extravagant lengths. A Frenchman might or might not be amused, but would certainly be surprised, to learn from a handout of the National Geographic Society that it was "Decatur's courage [which] paved the way for colony-minded France to annex most of Barbary to her African empire."[8]

Such an attitude can be very irritating, yet the assumption that world history is part of American history is healthier than any belief that the two are completely separate and that the one is real while the other is merely interesting. It is only when the heads and hearts of the American people are touched that they can be induced to listen to a call from the outer world for leadership. And that leadership will be given only if moral as well as material interests are involved. The only appeal that will be listened to will be the appeal to come over to Macedonia and help.

"It will be no cool process of mere science. . . . The

[8] *New York Times,* February 13, 1944.

feelings with which we face this new age of right and opportunity sweep across our heartstrings like some air out of
God's own presence, where justice and mercy are reconciled
and the judge and the brother are one. . . . Men's hearts wait
upon us; men's lives hang in the balance; men's hopes call
upon us to say what we will do. Who shall live up to the
great trust? Who dare fail to try? I summon all honest men,
all patriotic forward-looking men, to my side. God helping
me, I will not fail them, if they will but counsel and sustain
me."[4] Till that note is struck again, no answer can be expected from the plain people.

But in the meantime millions of young Americans,
serving their country, if not any general cause, were exiled
in a foreign world for which their training in a sense had
unfitted them. Even today, when the necessity of dealing
with the outside world has had more than a decade of habit
to commend it, the American serviceman, exiled in Toul or
Heidelberg, in Cambridge or Wiesbaden, looks more lost,
more conscious of his exile, than do, for example, drunk
members of the Highland Light Infantry, or the Camero-
nians, on a station platform in Hamburg, comfortably convinced that wherever they are, there is forever Glasgow.
The American's training has unfitted him because it was
based on the theory that there is an answer available to every
question; all you have got to do is to find the right authority,
whether the question relates to the technique of football, of
spot-welding, or of love. There is a charming optimism in
this view, an optimism that, in America, is justified most
of the time. It creates a world in which, as a wise American
friend of mine said, there are known Plimsoll lines in most
fields of conduct. It is a world in which formal good manners and comradeship are both happily cultivated between
the sexes. It is true that the hearty camaraderie which is so

---

[4] Woodrow Wilson: *First Inaugural* (1913).

charming at twenty palls a little at thirty and may give superficial justification for the sour remark of a European critic that "what the American woman suffers from is too much poor-quality attention." It may even justify another view—that American men and American women are better company apart than together, and that the men are better company than the women. But these illusions of solutions attained, in politics and in life, are a tribute to the success with which American life has been made attractive to Americans, to the vast majority of Americans who feel at home in America and are consequently swept away from their moorings in a strange world whose standards they cannot understand and from whose apparent moral and political anarchy they long to escape by going home.

Part Three

THE AMERICAN WAY
IN WAR AND PEACE

"I will fight it out on this line if it takes all summer."
—GENERAL GRANT, 1864

"Let us have peace." —PRESIDENT GRANT, 1869

1

FEW CITIES in the world have as many statues of military heroes as has Washington, D.C. There they ride, generals famous and forgotten, from Andrew Jackson on his barely manageable and barely equine steed, to once famous corps commanders of the Union armies. There the men they commanded stream endlessly round the Pension building, memorial of that special feature of American wars, the "donatives," as the Romans put it, that the victorious soldiery have always demanded—and got—at the vote's point. And in every town in the Union, the Washington pattern is repeated. In stone and metal, the embattled heroes stand, from the *Minuteman* of Concord to the straining figures hoisting the flag on Iwo Jima. Sometimes the wars as well as the heroes are forgotten: remote Indian campaigns or the musical-comedy feats of arms of the war with Spain and the reduction to obedience of the rebellious Filipinos.

And it is not merely a matter of the dead, of the heroes commemorated in Indianapolis and Kansas City. There are the titles. As Dickens and others noted, they have been lavished since the earliest days of the Republic. Did not their abundant flowering provoke the greatest of Chief Justices to the only verse epigram any holder of his high office has ever perpetrated:

> *Out in the blue grass country,*
> *A paradox was born.*
> *For the corn was full of kernels*
> *And the kernels were full of corn?*

What was and is the specialty of Kentucky has not been confined to Kentucky. Colonels, majors, generals, have edited papers, run banks, cigar stores, railroads, the Department of State and the Department of the Navy, acted (like Colonel House) as presidential *éminences grises,* become folk heroes like Colonel Cody, "Buffalo Bill."

If one were to go only by the face value of such symbolism, one would be tempted to think of the United States as a military community like Frederick the Great's Prussia or the Paraguay of the younger López. But against such a judgment on America, so many other things fight. The very wideness of the distribution of military honors, of military monuments, makes it plain that there was no military caste. There have been moments in the history of Washington when there have been nearly as many soldiers in bronze as in the flesh available in the capital. The manifestly unmilitary appearance of the White House tells the same story. And so does the fact that an American soldier, however distinguished, elected to a high office—above all, a soldier President—has to put his uniform away in moth-balls. It is in the civilian garb of his time that he must appear. General Jackson and General Grant, Colonel Truman and General Eisenhower have all obeyed this rule.[1]

The Americans, as has been said often enough, are a soldierly but not a military people. They take pride in their feats of arms. They have their legends of victory and even of total annihilation, like Custer at the Little Big Horn and Davy Crockett at the Alamo. They have their dashing legends, of "Sheridan's Ride"; their epic legends like that of General MacAuliffe, descendant of the Danes of Dublin, answering the German call to surrender in short and masculine terms at Bastogne in the dark December of 1944.

[1] It was rumored in 1948 that President Truman would encourage the circulation of photographs of himself in the uniform of a captain of artillery, the rank with which he left the army in 1919. But this was a move designed to underline the fact that his opponent had not served in the Second World War, not a militarist gesture as such.

This dramatic and brilliant military record has too often hidden from the American people, and from their allies, the real character of American military history, the distinguishing mark of the "American way in war." The emphasis on such great masters of maneuver as Robert E. Lee, on such "beaux sabreurs" as J. E. B. Stewart, on such thunderbolts of war as Stonewall Jackson, perhaps *all* the emphasis laid, naturally, on the brilliant and sterile feats of arms of the South in the War between the States, has hidden the real character of the American military genius from the American people, to their surprise and their enemies' discomfiture—but sometimes to their own discomfiture.

It is probably a pity that the Northern opposite number to J. E. B. Stewart, Philip Sheridan, has been kept alive in the popular memory by his famous ride to rally his shattered army, by the legend of his leading his troops up the mountainside at Chattanooga with a whisky bottle in his hand. But what struck that hardheaded and intelligent Bostonian, Colonel Charles Lowell, about the new commander of the Army of the Shenandoah was that he went about his job like a businessman, not like a gay cavalier. And so Sheridan was ready—and on the spot—to hold and drive to surrender the desperate Army of Northern Virginia in April 1865, while "Beauty" Stewart was as fatally absent on the first day of Gettysburg as Drouet d'Erlon at Ligny or Quatre-Bras.

Indeed, from one point of view, the most representative soldier of the Civil War was the slow, fearful, industrious George Brinton McClellan. He was no master of the battlefield, in either the manner of Lee or the very different manner of Grant. But he turned the mob that had fled from Bull Run into the magnificently disciplined Army of the Potomac that survived the brilliant strategy and the occasionally effective tactics of Lee, and possibly, had civilian nerves held out, he would have, in 1862, succeeded in that siege of Richmond which Grant so slowly conducted in 1864–5.

For McClellan with his insistence on supply, on logistics, on accumulating overwhelming resources, on taking the long way round, was representative of the American way in war as Lee was not. Lee demanded of his troops as "toilsome they wandered Virginia's woods," success in maneuvers that Napoleon in 1806 or Moltke in 1866 could not have demanded of their armies. Sometimes he got the results; sometimes he failed. But brief and brilliant victories could no more wear down the North than Cannæ could break the power of Rome. And all successful American soldiers who have been successful in the long run have been McClellans. No doubt McClellans with more resolution, with a clearer grasp of the truth that "the battle is the pay off," but Mc-Clellans, not Stewarts, Jacksons, or even Lees. It was by his care for supply, for the accumulation of force in overwhelming superiority, that Washington survived disasters and lived to see General O'Hara surrender a British army at Yorktown as his bands played *The World Turned Upside Down*. It was the same spirit that made General Eisenhower refuse the various recipes for complete and speedy victory offered him in 1944 until the Third Reich was breached, the dike broken so that no desperate energy could stop the flood. Perhaps it was a pity. The political results of a Western victory in the autumn of 1944 were so desirable, and remain so tantalizingly desirable, that we may regret the decision. But General Eisenhower may have remembered what he had certainly been taught at West Point, of what had happened when the cry: "On to Richmond!" had replaced serious thought about how the South could be conquered.

That General Eisenhower should have thought and acted this way was not merely a result of a military doctrine taught at the Military Academy. It was a result of a tradition imposed on the Americans by their oldest experience. We all know that Keats was wrong when he made stout Cortés see the Pacific "silent, upon a peak in Darien." But Cortés did see the Pacific all the same, and the contrast between Cortés and Coronado and the more prudent English leaders, advancing a few miles in each generation, is to be noted. So is the contrast between the English and the French. Marquette and La Salle represent another tradition from that of Captain John Smith or Miles Standish. But the bases occupied and used by the English settlers were never lost; there was no ebb in the tide. In each generation the "Anglo-Saxon" settlers could have quoted Dr. Donne, not on islands, but on the great strength that made the thirteen colonies and so the United States. "No winter shall abate this Spring's increase."

For the great enemy that the early American settlers had to conquer was space. The Spaniards landed on a narrower part of the North American continent. The French were tempted by the dangerously easy route to the heart of the continent offered by the St. Lawrence. Geography, and the fact that behind the English settlers was not the expansive imperial tradition of the Spanish "Reconquista" or the imperial designs of Richelieu or of the Society of Jesus, kept the ambitions of the settlers healthily modest. And fortunately for them, they had not to face a first-rate native military power. There was no Aztec military empire; no Indian Sparta like the Iroquois Confederacy. King Philip's

[2] It is perhaps significant that the English in New York were able to use the Iroquois at the height of their power, not fight them. Governor Frontenac in Quebec may well have cursed his fellow Catholic, Governor Thomas Dongan in New York, that great, neglected, first Irish-American politician, overthrown by the "Glorious Revolution" of 1688. There was to be no other Catholic governor of New York for two hundred and thirty years, until the election of Alfred E. Smith in 1918. But Dongan had done his job and when, during the Revolutionary War, General John Sullivan finally broke the power of the Iroquois, it was more a matter of a military

War, serious ordeal as it was for New England, was a storm, not a hurricane like that which beat on New France. No frontier of New England or the Carolinas knew an ordeal like that inflicted for generations on New Mexico by Navajo and Comanche.[2]

The effective leaders in the centuries-long war with space were pathfinders like Conrad Weiser and Kit Carson, surveyors like young George Washington, tamers of rivers like Colonel Robert E Lee. They were organizers of great wagon trains like Brigham Young; builders of railways like Captain McClelland and James J. Hill. The picture of the pioneer dashing into the wilderness was far from the truth. People who dashed off like that, who started too late or too early, who had no clear idea of where they were going, who took short cuts like the hand-cart migration that was Brigham Young's great failure (he, prudently, took no part in it himself), ended in all kinds of disasters, culminating in the cannibalism of the Donner party on their way to golden California.[3] After all, it was starvation that forced the young George Washington to surrender on his first campaign, a lesson that he took to heart.

And not all those who effectually planned to conquer the wilderness found it necessary to undergo the hardships of the campaign against the wilderness. From the very beginning of the American conquest of America, there were chair-borne warriors (John Jacob Astor is perhaps the most

parade than a real war such as that which crippled and perhaps permanently stunted the growth of New France.

[3] "With no other guide but the starry heavens, and, it may be, a pocket compass, the party embarked upon the arid plains which extended far and wide before them to the Cimarron River." In this cool and not very sympathetic fashion Josiah Gregg recounts the misfortunes of the Becknell party. Evidently they had it coming to them! Josiah Gregg: *Commerce of the Prairies,* edited by Max L. Moorhead, p. 14.

famous) whose services were not the less real for being unromantic and, possibly, overpaid. Heroic follies like the Alamo provided themes for ballads, but even Texas was conquered by prudent and, in the case of Stephen Austin, evasive and unheroic men.

But the result is there. Texas has remained American or at least Texan. Austin and Houston, Dallas and Fort Worth commemorate very different men, only one of whom could make the grade on television or the movies today. Huntington and Stanford, Mark Hopkins and Crocker (not Crockett) are great, constructive names in California, but where is Sutter and where Frémont, New Helvetia, and Mariposa? Gone with the wind.[4]

To the light-minded, American history, realistically studied, may be depressing. The rewards went to the wrong people; the wrong side won at Appomattox. It is right that we should, at some time in our lives, be for the romantic lost causes, for Bonnie Prince Charlie or Charles I, for Lee against Grant, for Hector against Agamemnon. But it is also right that we should, later, learn that great states are not built only or mainly on high, heroic deeds, but on prudence, cautious courage, enlightened selfishness.

To amend Holy Writ. If only heroes keep the city, the watchman watcheth but in vain. And one great lesson of American history is that its greatest figure knew that prudence is the greatest of political virtues and it was the prudent, the astute, the adroit Lincoln who was the real hero of the Civil War, not the Bayard Lee or the would-be Bayard, Jefferson Davis.

And the American people in canonizing Lincoln showed great good sense as well as a sense of piety, a deep religious

---

[4] A descendant of one of the big four of the Great Bonanza told me that his prudent ancestor did not go to the mines. He ran a bar on Market Street in San Francisco and listened to the confidences of his inebriated customers, back from the diggings.

feeling that the murder of Lincoln was a divine punishment for the sins set out in the Second Inaugural. But the lesson of the Civil War was also that war, above all, was a national enterprise that Americans could turn to at any time they had to—and with great and rapid success. There *had* to be professional soldiers like Grant and Sherman to command the great citizen masses, but a few of them went a very long way. No army had as many admired heroes as had the American army after the Civil War. No victorious army has been more neglected as a fighting force, as the deplorable record of the Spanish War showed. For the average American still thought that the professional soldier, if he was a ranker, was not a gentleman ranker, but a very inferior type of citizen (often he was not a citizen at all) and, if an officer, an odd type who had contracted out of real life. This was a view held not only by civilian and pacific characters, but often by the volunteer soldiers like Colonel Roosevelt, who attributed to West Point blindness and selfishness and incompetence the refusal to see in the charge of the Rough Riders at San Juan Hill[5] a feat of arms equivalent to the Charge of the Light Brigade or of Pickett's division at Gettysburg (with the important difference that it succeeded). Roosevelt was representative. The American people did not take its army—above all, its officers—nearly seriously enough in peace time.

---

[5] They charged on foot.

2

IN THE DISILLUSIONED AFTERMATH of the First World War, H. L. Mencken noted one legacy it had left to the American people. He contrasted General Grant, on his way to receive Lee's surrender, distinguished from a private soldier only by the badges sewn on to his shoulder "to indicate to the army who I was," with a major that Mencken had just spotted from his window. "Like General Grant, he employs shoulder straps to indicate to the army who he is. But there is something more. On the left breast of this officer, apparently a major, there blazes so brilliant a mass of color, that, as the sun strikes it and the flash bangs my eyes, I wink, catch my breath and sneeze."[1] The same contrast used to be seen in the Army and Navy Club portraits in Washington; the veterans of the Civil War, in full uniform, with formidable epaulets are provided with a single medal, while quite junior officers of the recent World War are entitled to so much "fruit salad" that they recall Oliver Gogarty's Dublin drinker:

> *And not Alcmena's chesty son*
> *Find room to put your ribbons on.*

No doubt, as Dr. Mencken suggested, the army was influenced by the rash of decorations provided by the Nobles of the Mystic Shrine, the Elks, and the other organizations destined to bring the court of King Arthur to Connecticut and other Yankees.[2] The same democratic movement that led the once aristocratic polity of England to add the Order

[1] *The Vintage Mencken,* gathered by Alistair Cooke, pp. 106–7.
[2] Of the great fraternal orders, only the Knights of Columbus (as far as I know) were founded in Connecticut.

of the British Empire to the Garter, that in France reinforced the Legion of Honor with "Knights of Agricultural Merit," was at work in America and perhaps the downtrodden American male was anxious to have something to offset the pearls and rubies, the diamonds and emeralds with which, traditionally, he was forced to cover his womenfolk. But that was not the only importance of the change from the republican austerity of the Civil War.

The army, once neglected if not despised, was becoming a more and more important political and economic force. In the past it had had, of course, prestige at moments of danger. When West Point gave the only good technical education in the United States, nomination to the Academy was prized. Some of the pride, pomp, and circumstance of glorious war was reflected over into peace time, especially in the backward South.[3]

But the army, less than 100,000 strong in 1914, stationed for the most part in remote Western posts, relics of the Indian wars, or in still more remote garrisons in the Philippines, Hawaii, the Canal Zone, was remote, mysterious, thought of by most Americans as a mere necessity and by some as not even that. A pious Christian pacifistic family like the Eisenhowers of Abilene, Kansas, were only moderately gratified when their son Dwight was nominated by the local Congressman "to the Point." Some of the rising generals of this neglected force, like Funston and Leonard Wood, had come in by the back door (by the Spanish War and the Philippine insurrection). Wood had been a doctor before he turned combatant. Something of a hereditary

[3] Outside the South, an indigenous anti-militarism was also powerful. Thus General Grant tells us that when he first donned his uniform, thinking that he would be observed of all observers, he was hailed by an urchin who called out: "Soldier! Will you work? No sir-ee; I'll sell my shirt first." The future commander-in-chief took the lesson. This gave him "a distaste for military uniform that I never recovered from" (*Personal Memoirs* [London, 1895], p. 30).

military caste was growing up, personified in young George Patton and young Douglas MacArthur. There were army families as there were academic families. The militia, the National Guard, was politically useful and attracted men who had taken up military service as a hobby, as others had bird-watching, horseshoe-pitching, and the like. But the army was on the edge of national life. Except possibly in the South, it was not a normal career for anyone. It had no financial and little social prestige. The navy was even more eccentric to the national life. But it had had the *beau role* in the Spanish War, and in a country in love with machines, the men who ran such big machines as battleships were to be taken seriously.[4] But the Philadelphian who shot a postman in mistake for a Confederate soldier merely exaggerated a national attitude. He might never have seen a soldier dressed in the gray drab that had replaced in the federal army the traditional blue of the War between the States. Even in places less remote from the pulsing tide of national affairs than Philadelphia then was, the army was a strange and probably obsolescent institution.

The First World War changed that. The army was immensely expanded and the ignored regular officers not only got their own back (outsiders like Wood and Funston got no overseas commands). They showed a high degree of competence in managing the vastly extended forces and many a snooty businessman or sportsman, even college professor, noted that there was a lot to say for the army way of doing things, even if the main advantage of the regular officer was his knowledge of army forms and formulas.

[4] It is usually and probably truthfully asserted that the navy had more social prestige than the army. It was "smarter." But a friend of mine told me that even between the two World Wars her mother never invited any naval officers from the base and schools at Newport to any of her really smart parties.

Yet how soon the prestige of the army faded! No political careers were made by the generals of that war. General Pershing slumbered in his office in the old State, War, and Navy Department or in his club, not in the White House or the Senate. The army was starved again, and if the navy was not starved as badly (anybody could understand that ships became obsolete as well as cars), its demands were not fully met, were often attributed to the ingenious lobbying of the "Merchants of Death," the munition-makers, and the interest taken by President F. D. Roosevelt in the fleet was attributed to an overhang of his yachting hobby or to the need to prime the pump by a type of spending that could not possibly be thought to compete with business or be any form of "creeping socialism." In 1939 the United States was spiritually as hostile or indifferent to the claims of the armed forces as to the claims of the fine arts.

The experience of the Second World War was formally like the First. Again the regulars got all the good commands.[5] Again the peace-time training of the regulars stood them and their country in good stead. Indeed, there could be no greater compliment to the sense of duty of young, peace-time officers like Major Eisenhower, than the zeal with which they went to army school after army school, acquiring masses of knowledge and preparing themselves for a war that few can have seriously thought would come

---

[5] Not all of the regular officers were West Pointers. General George Marshall, a Democrat in a Republican district, could not get a nomination to West Point and so went to the Virginia Military Institute. General Bedell Smith entered from the Indiana National Guard. But neither of these generals owed his rise to politics. Even under a Democratic administration, no one thought that General Marshall's political origins accounted for his success. He was not a Leonard Wood. And in the Indiana in which General Bedell Smith began to rise in the armed services, the National Guard was no aid to political success as compared with the American Legion.

in their time of service. They were like conscientious musical amateurs dutifully conning their scores, suddenly called on to conduct a full orchestra. And it is one thing to be a happy warrior

> *who when brought*
> *Among the tasks of real life, hath wrought*
> *Upon the plan that pleased his boyish thought.*

It is something else again to respond to the call and use effectually skills laboriously acquired, with little hope of their being used, in middle age. The result showed that the American military schools, not only West Point but the specialist schools, even the Cavalry School, had deserved well of the country. And again, the hundreds of thousands of amateur officers had often enough to note that the professionals did know their business, and that a difficult, complicated, and supremely important business. The lesson had been taught twice in a generation. War *was* important and it had, at all but the highest level, to be left to the generals who repaid the confidence put in them. Never in any other American war was there less suspicion of political interference at the top or more harmonious relations between the civilian commander-in-chief and the service leaders. There was no martyr like Leonard Wood, no political exhibitionism like that of Theodore Roosevelt in the First World War. True, the commanders at Pearl Harbor may have been made scapegoats for faults not peculiarly theirs, but Messrs. Short and Kimmel were no more political victims than were Generals Auchinleck and Ritchie, though all may have been victims of rough justice.[6] Even General MacArthur, whose political ambitions were not in the least disguised, was not

[6] I am aware that there are persons who believe or affect to believe that the fleet at Pearl Harbor was deliberately exposed to trick the Japanese into attacking. "The bleating of the lamb excites the tiger." But this legend

hampered in his exercise of his command or controlled in the exuberant and self-centered accounts of his achievements that flowed from his headquarters. A division of labor between the professional military leaders and the professional politicians seemed to have been achieved. And with the extraordinary triumphs of American arms on land, sea, and in the air, unparalleled in their geographical extent and in their technical power in the history of the world, again the professional military class might well claim to have deserved well of the country. Yet it might well have feared that, with the return of peace, its claims would be honored, by decorations, by formal honors, by ranks enabling generals and admirals (and their wives) to keep their ends up with British field-marshals and admirals of the fleet, but that the American people would again turn away to the pursuit of happiness in civilian terms and leave the soldiers and sailors in their quiet and decorous Capuas in San Antonio and San Diego.

For there can be no doubt that the attitude of the American people at the time of VJ-day in 1945 was profoundly pacific. It is possible that had F.D.R. survived, he might have been better able than a new and unknown President was to slow down the pace of demobilization, to suggest that military victory did not solve all problems and that the newly launched United Nations would have more to do than keeping a benevolent eye on a world that had learned its lesson that war and force do not pay. But no leader, however bold, adroit, and farseeing, could have swum successfully against the tide that washed over the United States that summer. Emotionally, the American people began demobilizing at once. Administrative decisions like the

is part of the pathology of American life, and of its most vocal exponents one may charitably say:

Non ragionam di lor ma guarda e passa.

immediate suspension of Lend-Lease were made in the innocent assumption that the road back to what Warren Harding called "normalcy" was open and easy.[7]

All over the world the American fighting men began to flow home. No army (it was and is a great tribute to the United States) had so few men in it who had no desire to return to their own country. No American policy, in Europe or Asia, that called for the use of sizable American forces was politically possible. Only the blindness bred by hindsight makes it plausible to suggest otherwise in 1956. It was 1919 all over again. And the same results might have followed for the services, if the Russians had shown more tact, less eagerness to pick up quick tricks, had waited till the American euphoria had become a way of life and it had again been possible to assume that the United States could live "the world forgetting, by the world forgot."

In such an atmosphere, the claims of the services were sure to be neglected. It is possible that, even then, some of this sense of security came from what was thought to be the monopoly of the atomic bomb. War and victory could be bought cheap. (No one knew, outside a very small circle, what the bomb cost, even in terms of money.) But it is more probable that the confident assumption that "the world is weary of the past" owed nothing to the knowledge of the bomb if only because so little knowledge of the bomb was in the public domain. America had won by her own valor, by her immense stores of know-how, by the skill of her military leaders, who could be thanked and sent about their

[7] I returned from the United States late that summer in the *Queen Mary,* still stripped for service as a troop ship. The food was very bad. I was told that the cuisine was made deliberately meager to impress on the numerous American officials on board that Britain couldn't afford to feed them any better, now that Lend-Lease was cut off. Even Spam was expensive.

now unimportant business.[8]

What saved the American services and what presented the American political and social system with a problem for which it had no theory and no practice was the cold war. It is difficult to say when the man in the street began to realize that the gallant Russian allies of the war had been no more allies than are strangers who climb on to the same raft in a great storm. The storm had abated and the allies of the storm ceased to be fellow passengers and showed that they had never been fellow travelers. Possibly the dismissal of Mr. Henry Wallace by Mr. Truman in 1946, at, it was believed, the instigation of the then Secretary of State, Mr. Byrnes, was the turning point, for Mr. Truman was a very representative American and Mr. Wallace a symbol of that common zeal for the common man which, it had been innocently assumed, warmed the heart of Stalin as it did that of Mr. Wallace. Be that as it may, by the spring of 1947 the love affair was over. It would have been relevant to quote:

> *Plaisir d'amour ne dure qu'un instant,*
> *Chagrin d'amour dure toute la vie.*

(It would also have been wrong, for in America *"chagrin d'amour"* doesn't last for all of life. There is, in more than marriage, always Reno and another day.)

---

[8] It is and was commonly said that reflection on American atomic superiority explained the moderation of American policy. This may have been so at a very high level. But at a lower level, there was at the beginning a great sense of guilt and of alarm and regret that the bomb had been used at all. Three days after President Truman's brief announcement that the bomb had been dropped on Hiroshima, I was a guest at a lunch in New York of a representative group. Only one other person present approved of dropping the bomb. Nor was its unique character generally appreciated. I can well remember a distinguished soldier saying on the night of the news of Hiroshima: "They always think they can abolish the infantry."

The continuation of the cold war, or rather the intensification of its coldness, prevented that complete demobilization of the American mind and of American life which had followed the peace of 1919. There was now no formal peace, but a war waged all over the world, in some areas by arms, in some by "political warfare." Yet what is surprising is the failure of the American people and government to see the world as it really was. Peace, real peace, was just around the corner, and the Democratic administration of Mr. Truman was, like the Republican administration of Mr. Hoover in the depression years, always a little bit behind the timetable, was continually patching up leaks after they had occurred, was being continually taken by surprise, continually refusing to see what the enemy was up to—and continually overestimating the strength of the allies and near-allies that the United States had to rely on.[9]

But the diplomatic position of the United States was inextricably mixed up with and was profoundly affected by the military weakness of the American armed forces. That weakness was unsuspected by the American people, who, indeed, wanted a cheaper and less burdensome defense force but had no notion that a cheap defense force in the postwar world was a dangerously bad bargain. There were good arguments for the unification of the three services under one Department of Defense, but the argument that appealed most to the voter and the politician was economy. Whether, if James Forrestal had been a more zealous and hopeful Democrat in 1948, he would have been retained by Mr. Truman as Secretary of Defense is still an open question. Whether if he had been, he would have successfully

[9] Thus, I am convinced that, unrealistic as were the conditions of the British loan, the American negotiators were convinced that the terms, if not soft, were equitable and reasonable. One would, of course, in making any such assessment of the American negotiators, have to allow for an unknown, the real aims and the real power of Harry Dexter White.

resisted the policy of putting not merely the fleet but all the defense installations of the United States into mothballs, is also an open question. But there was no doubt that the policy of Mr. Louis Johnson, former National Commander of the American Legion, was to reduce all defense expenditure—that is, all expenditure that was directly connected with present military efficiency and future possibilities of combat. Other economies were necessary, too. Probably only in America would it have been thought, and have been rightly thought, that a general of the eminence of Omar Bradley was usefully employed at the head of the Veterans' Administration. And for part of his term of office as head of the Joint Chiefs of Staff, General Eisenhower must have thought he was back in the days when he and other ambitious young officers played "war games" at various army schools, moved paper armies, and mobilized mythical armament plants.

The disarmament of the United States did not go so far as it had after the Civil War, when, within twenty years, the United States might have been beaten by Chile, or as it did after the First World War when, within a few years, the American army would not have been a match for the armies of Poland or Finland. But when the North Koreans crossed the border in July 1950, the United States was little better prepared for the role that President Truman bravely committed it to than it had been to maintain the balance of Atlantic and Pacific power, singlehanded, in the dreadful summer of 1940.

These sad truths, naturally, could not be published to the world though they were well known to the enemy. In America, as elsewhere, official information succeeded in confusing its own without deceiving the other side. A nation confident that it was safe, powerful, feared, could not easily accept the news that came from Korea. That news merely reflected the fact that the United States, with possibly misguided good faith, had made it certain that South Korea could not successfully attack the North—and equally could not defend itself against a progressive and enlightened government that acted on the old Western maxim:

Thrice armed is he that hath his quarrel just,
But six times armed that gets his punch in fust.

Nor was the United States, at that moment, in any condition to punish the insolence of the North Koreans. There were few combatant troops in Japan and the neighboring islands, and in more islands than Okinawa was too much time devoted to the contemplation of the August Moon.[1]

Since it was inconceivable that American troops could be beaten by Koreans by any fair methods, it was necessary to invent flattering explanations, and that became even more necessary when the victors were Communist Chinese. It was, indeed, ominous that the first white troops over which Chinese troops gained a brilliant victory were Americans (a fact widely noted in Asia). That had to be explained or explained away. So, too, had the fact that the defeated general had acquired (with his own warm support) the reputation of being the American who best knew the realities of the Orient and who had just redeemed the first disasters of the Korean War by the landing at Inchon, a brilliant contrast, it might be pointed out, with such operations of the late World War as Anzio and Arnhem.

An explanation was provided. It was the story of the "living sea" tactics of the Chinese, of their total indifference to losses. Such tactics, it was suggested, were unsporting. American troops had not enough of the killer spirit; human life (their own and their enemies') was too precious to

---

[1] Many a soldier, induced to enlist by advertising that suggested that his sole duties would be receiving lessons in the tea ceremony and so on from geishas, might have sued for misrepresentation or at any rate lodged a complaint with a Better Business Bureau.

them. Yet Germans, faced with overwhelming masses of Russian troops, as careless of losses as the Chinese, had managed to win great victories and so had American troops faced with equally fanatical Japanese. The simpler truth, that there had not been enough American troops and that General MacArthur had committed all the textbook mistakes in his advance to the Yalu, were not tolerable explanations. Only treason could explain the disasters of November 1950. If General MacArthur had been thought of as a very competent soldier who, underestimating his potential enemy, had acted more like Pope or Hooker than like Grant or Lee, there would not have been such moral and mental disarray.

3

THE LESSON of American history is that no nation more cheerfully turns swords into plowshares or puts them in the deep freeze (where weapons, unlike meat, do not retain their pristine freshness). The other side of the lesson is that no nation turns plowshares into swords with such speed or has so many plows to turn. The country that was using wooden model weapons on maneuvers in 1940 and 1941 was a great military power by the end of 1942 and a very great military power by the spring of 1944. It was a lesson that the Germans had been taught in the First World War, but had to be taught all over again in the Second.

But there were differences in the American experience of conversion in the Second War, differences that all postwar developments have accentuated. By the time the United States entered the first war in 1917, it was nearly three years old, and one of the chief combatants, Russia, was about to drop out. No serious body of American troops was engaged for over a year after American intervention, and the American major military effort was made in a few, tense, and overwritten months. The American economy had been geared by British and French orders to produce shells and other military equipment, but by the end of the war the American army had still not produced an effective American field gun; it used the French "75." And even if the Springfield was an admirable rifle, it was more convenient to use the British Lee-Enfield. The American economy had not devoted much thought or the best efforts of its designers to military matters, except possibly in the naval field, and the American navy played a very small part in the First World War.[1]

The Second World War was very different. America was a belligerent for much more than half of the time and a major belligerent for most of that time. The United States found itself, in one theater, fully engaged from the morning of December 7, 1941. The American navy began its wartime career reeling under the shock of a great disaster, and its recovery from that disaster was as surprising as the recovery of a boxer knocked down and nearly out in the first round. The speed of the recovery was a tribute to the training and character of the American naval officer, even if the great and, in the defensive sense, decisive American victory of Midway owed much to Japanese vanity. The United States was desperately engaged on land, too, with Corregidor and Bataan as Forts Donelson and Henry, in reverse. Within a year of becoming an active belligerent, the invasion of North Africa made her a major belligerent in the "European theater." There was no time to wait or waste. If there was an exchange of techniques, America was far more a leader in the field of armament than in the First War and such characteristic American contributions as the jeep and the bulldozer were probably as important as British radar. American industrial conversion had to be more rapid, more profound than it had needed to be in 1917–18. It was—and the whole world learned to know, to admire, and to fear that magical power of transformation, in itself a result of that increasing predominance of the American economy in most fields of mechanical industry and technology.

But the greatest American achievement illustrates the character of the American contribution to war and power.

[1] It is therefore impossible to judge its technical preparedness. But no other big navy copied the American basket masts, or so firmly ignored the qualities of the battle cruiser.

For the atom bomb, in its origin, was not an American type of weapon. It was not only that Einstein, Fermi, Fuchs were not Americans. Even their American colleagues were not typical Americans. They were not slightly more sophisticated Edisons or Fords any more than the Cavendish Laboratory in Cambridge (England), where the foundations of the atomic revolution had been laid, was like Menlo Park or Dearborn. What the American way of life specifically contributed was immense material and technological resources (including the power of the "socialistic" Tennessee Valley Authority and the silver bought to pacify the senators of the Rocky Mountain states). What it contributed was the unprecedented surplus that the American economy produced, even at the height of its war effort, a surplus that went into many things other than atom bombs (nylon stockings, for instance) and which enabled the United States, alone of all the belligerents, to go "all out" in conventional weapons while making the most terrible of unconventional weapons.

This accumulation of a surplus in wartime was not new. During the Civil War while the South was being stripped of all capital resources by its excessive war effort, the North was not only overwhelming the South with comparative ease, but building new railways, expanding its manufacturing resources, raising even bigger crops. The war effort of 1917–18 was only an eddy in the tide of American economic expansion. But the application of the surplus to the making of the bomb *was* new; for the scale that the bomb called for was new and it called, in addition, for two un-American activities. The putting of the government into economic production on a colossal scale and of a type that could not be abandoned to private enterprise or to rust, as had happened to the installations at Muscle Shoals after the First War, was un-American. So was the undertaking of a kind of economic activity not reducible to normal American categories, not easily manageable by any reasonably competent American with "git-up and git," whether he was a soldier (of the type that built the Panama Canal) or a civilian (of the type that built General Motors). It was necessary to employ "scientists" who were not just long-haired specimens of that well-known American type, the inventor. It was necessary to deal with "idea men," and "idea men" not of the type familiar on Madison Avenue.

The problem was a new one. Until the problem of the atom bomb was dumped in the lap of the American constitutional and economic system, the men that the system called on to deal with the recurrent military crisis were admirably equipped for the job, whether they were soldiers, sailors, businessmen, lawyers, or mere politicians.[2] The professional soldiers and sailors were trained to deal with these types. Businessmen had to be dealt with as contractors; lawyers were indispensable as part of the army system (some eminent soldiers became members of the bar); and politicians had the power of life or death—that is, of money—over the services. The army, at least, had, in the Bureau of Army Engineers, one of the finest schools of lobbying in Washington.

Then, an oddity of the administration of the American armed services (an oddity since it was not the English way of doing things) meant that a large number of senior officers had had, in spells of duty in Washington bureaus, to carry out very important and quasi-political administrative duties, duties of the type that in England were carried out by senior and civilian civil servants.

Thus whatever the limitations of the curriculum at the Military Academy or at the Naval Academy, the professional soldier or sailor who rose to the rank of colonel or captain

---

[2] The three most successful war administrators in American history, Stanton, Baker, Stimson, were all very eminent lawyers.

had some chance—indeed, some necessity—of acquiring political know-how. He had it for personal as well as official reasons, since his chance of promotion depended on senatorial approval. Nor was the curriculum at the academies, whatever its limitations, the only political education the cadet got. For his nomination to the academy had, in nearly every case, been a minor piece of political patronage, and class politics (or so it is asserted) were not unknown at West Point and Annapolis.

As the result showed, the cadets received an excellent technical education not only in the sense that they were trained to command men and ships in action, but that they could design ships and guns, deal with the chemistry of explosives, apply their mathematics to the solution of logistical problems or to the mysteries of army accounting.

But the atomic bomb, perhaps even such lesser innovations as radar and guided and unguided missiles, presented a problem that the traditional military or naval education could not meet. A cadet got an education justifying the grant of a degree of B.Sc. But he did not get an education that would have justified the granting of a degree of Ph.D. in the now decisive field of physics. More than that, while it was not unlikely that there would be good run-of-the-mill engineers, naval architects, even metallurgists among the teachers and taught, it was more than unlikely that any potential Nobel prizemen in physics were to be found at West Point and Annapolis.

Suddenly the officer was forced to deal with a new type. His education had been rigorous in more senses than one. In the classroom, as on the football field, he was one subject to authority. There were, there *had* to be, answers to the problems daily posed, to the "lesson." Knowledge had to be cut up into neat segments to which known answers had to be and could be provided. For training officers, this was an essential. "A soldier who thinks will run away," was an old

German saying, and a certain type of suspension of judgment, legitimate in a professor, is intolerable and dangerous in a soldier.

But now both services had to deal with physicists or highly refined and sophisticated types of engineers and chemists, men to whom the whole concept of "the lesson" was nonsense and men who, even if given military or naval rank, even if proud of it, remained incurably civilian. They were the type of men that the regular officer would have had little or nothing to do with if they could have been done without. For one thing, a distressingly large number of them were foreigners or Jews or both. They had odd hobbies, Sanskrit and Bach; were often indifferent to college football, even to golf. Their minds were dangerously open to political ideas not set out in "the lesson." Their dress, morals, manners marked them off. How could you tell whether a man who was indifferent to football, baseball, old-time religion, and poker was a traitor or not? How— and this was far more serious—could you understand his conversation, his ideas and ideals, the things that made him happy, the things that disturbed him while they did not disturb the regular American?

Alas, few really good physicists were regular Americans or, if you like, few regular Americans were good physicists. Science for the regular American was technology, was know-how. American education was more and more practical, less and less ready to ask any fundamental questions of any kind. The "grind" was not a hero in any high school, and it was undemocratic to cater to the very exceptional boy, even if you could coax into the average high school the exceptional teacher with exceptional qualifications to teach him. To some extent, the weakness of the school system was a reflection of a strength, of a social strength. The millions admitted to the colleges drained away the teachers who, in other countries, would have been found in high schools, and the democratic gain of equal opportunity for all had to be paid for in the lowering of the content of the opportunity. The mother of West Point, the École Polytechnique in Paris, trained soldiers and civilians together, and a French officer might well have a future Nobel prizeman among his fellows and was certain to have one or two among his teachers. But not all or perhaps not many of the cadets at West Point or Annapolis could have gained admission to "Polytechnique." American education had made its choice, it obeyed the orders given by the American way of life. Again,

> *Grau, theurer Freund, ist alle Theorie,*
> *Und grün des Lebens goldner Baum.*

Unfortunately, golden as were the apples on the American tree of life, they were not the apples that were now wanted, the apples of the knowledge of good and evil. It was too late to wish away "all that the brigand apple brought." In Chicago, at Los Alamos, the American Adam had succumbed to the new Eve.

It was natural that the armed services should wish to control the new weapon; it was necessary that they should not. But the weapon itself presented problems that no ordinary system of control could meet; civilian or military control was faced with novel problems. Nor could control be left to the scientists themselves, if only for the good reason that they might decide not to go on down the alphabet, decide not to run the gamut from A to H, but, like a film star, stick to B. Nor would scientists, trained to regard publicity as the utilitarian necessity and the moral imperative of the health of their craft, take easily to secrecy, to denying information to their colleagues in other countries or in America kept outside the magic circle of esoteric knowledge. There could be no "master of them that know," in the not very long run, except their consciences. What did average men, the average soldier, or congressman, or voter, know of the consciences of these strange creatures?

The average voter? The average voter had taken a beating in his pride and self-confidence. He had been involved in a war of unprecedented magnitude over issues and countries that he knew little of and whose complexities had been simplified for him by a simplifier of genius. He had gained, in his capacity as a citizen of the United States, a complete victory over the forces of evil and he had then to learn that he must not relax. He had thought that, at any rate, he had the monopoly of the atomic bomb and, confident in his own pacific intentions, saw in that monopoly a guarantee of world peace. He learned that he had lost the monopoly and he learned, or thought he had learned, that he lost it through treachery.

It was not all that he learned or thought that he learned. He learned that the United States had "lost China." He was not told that he had never "had China." A great revolution, affecting a fourth or fifth of the human race, had been represented to him in simple terms as a continuation of the work of George Washington. It was only a few decades since American Protestantism had seriously thought it possible to convert China to Christianity if not quite certain what kind of Christianity China was to adopt. China had been the main mission field, white for the harvest; now what was in American eyes an eleventh-hour harvester and robber had stepped in and reaped where American Christians had sown. Or, to change the metaphor, Americans, like Saint Monica contemplating the sinful life of her son, Augustine, asked could the child of so much love be lost? That American Protestantism by importing Western ideas and techniques had been one of the forces destroying the old China was true. By abandoning, for the most part, the old view that they had come to save China by preaching the true faith, by concentrating on works, listening to Mrs. Buck rather than to Dr. Graham Machen, the great Protestant missions had entered into competition with a rival doctrine, held more firmly and preached more confidently than the missions now preached Christianity and competing in works by offering the Chinese masses, worn down by a generation of civil and foreign war, an end to the war and an answer to the problems left by the war and by the unfinished business of the Chinese revolution.

Inevitably, the United States was a partisan of Chiang Kai-shek and of the once revolutionary and now satisfied party of the Kuomintang. It is possible that, if there had been a truce, the healing effects of time and peace might have won back the loyalty of the Chinese masses to the Kuomintang. It is possible, though unlikely, that the adoption of a wiser military policy by Chiang might have ended in a Communist defeat. But the Generalissimo (whom the American public had been taught to regard as a George Washington) was rather like General Halleck, who sat out the Civil War in Washington, rubbing his elbows and issuing orders to remote armies, claiming credit for victory and disclaiming responsibility for defeat. Even Grant would have found it hard to win under Chiang's remote and jealous control. "If he's a generalissimo, why doesn't he generalize?" asked Senator Connally with Texan sense and candor. But it was necessary to explain that Chiang was not Washington, his wife not Joan of Arc or even Mollie Pitcher, and too many people had told the other tale, too long, to bear to unravel the story now.

It is formally possible that if the American people, in 1945, had been willing to continue a serious if secondary war in China, keep much more than the Marines there, and support the American government in giving orders, not advice, to Chiang, China, in that sense, could have been "saved," the withdrawal of the "mandate of Heaven" from the old order (so recently so new!) postponed. But the physical and moral demobilization of 1945 made such a policy beyond the power of any administration.

There was nothing, on the face of it, surprising in the fact that the Chinese revolution should take forms displeasing to the American people and government. There were five Chinese for every two Americans. There was nothing surprising in the fact that Russia was able to aid its friends more effectually than were the Americans. Russian public opinion had not to be conciliated as had American opinion. There was no ill-disciplined "China lobby" in Moscow. And the Marxian missionary schools in Moscow were more effective in training loyal disciples than was Yale-in-China. Above all, Russia was close at hand; was an Asiatic power; had managed to get dissociated in the Asiatic mind from the curse of being "white." (It was only on a colored race that the A-bomb had been dropped by America, as all Asia was reminded.)

But these truths were hidden from the average American. Was it not due to the folly of Roosevelt, to the treason of his entourage, that Russia had become a Pacific power? (Russia was a Pacific power before the United States existed.) Was it not because of treason that the secret of the atom bomb had fallen into Russian hands?

The American public was well prepared to find in treason the explanation of its troubles. It was an old American belief that treason explained most disasters. There was reason for this belief. Benedict Arnold was a traitor on the heroic scale; Wilkinson was a traitor on the non-heroic scale. No one was quite sure what Aaron Burr was. To many good Republicans, the Democratic cabinet on the eve of the Civil War was full of traitors, and the frenzy of Henry Cabot Lodge's denunciation of Woodrow Wilson during the First World War forced Henry Adams to remind the Senator that he did not allow treason to be talked at his table. Pearl

Harbor, for many, was an example of a double treason, for Roosevelt betrayed the United States and Japan. It was a *"bellissimo inganno"* worthy of the admiration of Cæsar Borgia or Machiavelli.

And now what could explain the bitterness of the fruits of victory but treason? This view was helped by the widespread distribution of what may be called "the illusion of American omnipotence." If the American people wanted something and didn't get it, the fault must lie not in their stars, but in the malignant ill will of the agents of the people of the United States. There must be treason.

Then, the American people was especially ready to believe in this because it had an innocent belief that all the knowledge and skill that really mattered was American. The schools, the movies—above all, advertising—had taught the Americans that they led the world in everything that really mattered. Not one American in a thousand, for instance, reflected that the most important modern invention, the internal-combustion engine, had been invented in Germany and perfected in France, that the American contribution was belated and secondary. There was nothing strange in the Russians being able to make the atom bomb; it was certain that sooner or later they would do so.

Sooner or later; there was the rub. For it was now known that it had been sooner, because of treason, treason by one of the mysterious, ill-disciplined, irregular physicists, Klaus Fuchs. The average American thought that the treason of Fuchs was sinister and symptomatic. He was right. He thought that British complacency was dangerous. He was right. He thought that there were more men of double loyalty—or perhaps only of single loyalty and that not to their own country—at work in important jobs. He was right. He had none of the naïveté and unworldly credulity that a British ex-Lord Chancellor had managed to preserve after a life at the bar. There *was* something rotten in the state of Denmark.

And when the much abused House Committee on un-American Activities flushed Alger Hiss, the white-headed boy of so many eminent, liberal Americans, suspicions that had deep roots suddenly flowered. The United States and the world were faced with Senator McCarthy. He was more important as a symptom than as a person. That was agreed. But what was he a symptom of?

He was, obviously, a symptom of the uneasiness with which the average American watched a world get out of hand and dangerous to a degree that the human race had never known. It was possible now, he feared, to destroy ". . . the great globe itself And all that it inherit." He was naturally alarmed. And his suspicions turned to that strange, semi-foreign, "undemocratic" world of the Eastern universities, of strange arts and strange morals, of the combination of Picasso, homosexuality, incomprehensible sciences, un-American political views. The old isolationism, the old village intolerance, the spirit of the not very long dead Ku Klux Klan, awoke. It was probably fortunate that the leader in this crusade against anything that the average man could not understand was an Irish-American Catholic. Senator McCarthy would have been far more formidable if he had been a Baptist or Methodist, able to appeal to the great Protestant heart of rural America. For he would have been appealing to a tradition of rural radicalism, not very long dead, which, in many of its elements, including its faintly concealed anti-Semitism, was sympathetic to McCarthyism. A "dry," evangelical McCarthy would have had more effect and lasted longer. But the rural masses that feared and hated everything foreign ranked the Pope high among the dangerous foreign elements. And ingenious Communist agents had successfully played on this deep instinct and helped to keep many a loyal American eye vigilantly on the Vatican when it ought to have been on the Kremlin.

It is not extraordinary that so many millions of Americans felt this way. It was rather a wonder that more of them didn't. And fewer of them would have felt this way if the eminent and deceived liberals had been quicker to admit their own errors of judgment, of issues, and of men.

4

THE EXPERIENCE of the past ten years has both modified and confirmed the general American way of waging war and securing peace. Technical know-how, the provision of military "hardware," are more important than ever. A small, poor, non-industrial country cannot fight a "real" war any longer. What the late World War proved for small countries, the development of military technique has suggested as true of reasonably large and wealthy countries. A bomber, even a fighter today, costs as much as a respectable warship used to cost and makes as great demands on technical resources. The burden of armaments is intolerable for all but very rich states, and even formally great powers have to attempt, feebly, to conceal their weakness. Everything has apparently combined to make the United States automatically the greatest military power in the world, and since the alert given by the Korean War, there has been no disbanding of American armed forces in the old, confident way.

But the Korean War taught another and less comforting lesson. It showed that there were wars where the old, poverty-line methods could still be used, where the very wealth that resulted in the abundance of hardware could be a handicap. Armies that were trained only to fight with the latest, most expensive, most elaborate equipment were not necessarily fit to fight in country where the equipment could not be used or where it tied its users to few and bad roads while the poorer enemy was free to take to the open country. And a society where it was the greatest testimony to the merits of a cigarette that men would walk a mile to get it does not naturally produce good infantry. It was an old theory that Yankee mechanical ingenuity was the product of Yankee laziness, and in Korea, in more ways than one, the United States was revealed as a country of sprinters not marathon runners. Part of the disillusionment of the American public came from its failure to realize that, in 1950, it was not prepared for *any* war of *any* kind, except atomic war. The retreat (or the advance in another direction) of the Marines in Korea, one of the most magnificent feats of war in the history of the corps—that is, in the history of war —showed what a *corps d'élite* could do. But the American army did not run to *corps d'élite*. The tradition of remote, hot, cold, dirty, dangerous foreign service, only too familiar to the British and French armies, was novel in America. The regular soldiers, the "thirty-year men" of *From Here to Eternity,* were more isolated from the national life than were the British soldiers Kipling knew in Lahore. There was no more un-American sentiment than Rupert Brooke's "corner of a foreign field that is forever England." Even ignoring the interest of the morticians in the return of the American dead, there was a genuine sense of pollution in the wasting of American blood on non-American soil, and on wasting it again so soon. A French scholar asked in anguish, in 1940, the Virgilian question why:

> *Nec fuit indignum superis, bis sanguine nostro*
> *Emathiam et latos Hæmi pinguescere campos?*

The Korean War, its occurrence, the revelation that the threat to use American force was not in itself adequately intimidating, the inability to win a decisive victory, the revelation of Chinese military power, that it was as rash to lead with your chin, in face of it, as it would have been to do the same in face of the Army of Northern Virginia, all these discoveries sobered the American public (if, what is doubtful, it really needed sobering). To explain the unsatisfactory character of the war, legend had to be called on. It was the fault of allies who would neither send adequate forces themselves nor permit the full use of American power. There was some justice in the first complaint. The nations of the United Nations who condemned North Korea, then Communist China, without doing anything in particular about it, were blameworthy; they gave every kind of aid except help, as a wit put it in a slightly different connection. It was an old story; in 1939, how unanimous was the opinion of the free world in condemnation of Hitler, how unanimous, too, the resolution to let Britain and France do the job! "Include me out" was a very human reaction. The American people were just discovering part of the cost of being an imperial power, what it cost to "spare the weak and war down the proud." It had, willy-nilly, to accept the imperial task, but it did not like it. Nothing could have been more of a fairy tale than the European left-wing legend of an American people and government "rarin' to go," to rule the world in the high Roman fashion. The world might have been a safer place if the picture had been a true one. It was ludicrously false. The American people were still not reconciled to the job that history had given them; the American way of life was to be shown and, of course, to be admired and copied, but not imposed in the bad old way by arms.

Nor was the American people, as yet, fully ready to accept the fact that allies are necessary and that there are never, never any really satisfactory allies. Indeed, in their attitude to the unsatisfactory allies fate had given them, many Americans were only too ready to imitate the high Roman fashion with the "allies" of the Senate and the Roman people. But Britain, France, Belgium—even, it was soon discovered, Dr. Syngman Rhee—were not yet ready to accept the role of Attalus or of Herod the Great. They had wills, interests, sentiments, fears of their own.

Especially fears. These fears may have been unworthy, but they were not unnatural. They were human, all too human. To many excessively fearful Europeans, the loud noises coming from the United States, the stern threats from rear-gunner McCarthy for instance, recalled the once celebrated anecdote of the great and infamous Irish landlord who wrote to his tenants from his London club: "If you think that you can intimidate me by shooting my bailiff, you are very much mistaken." The Europeans thought that they were cast as bailiff.

They thought, too, that they observed a certain lack of realism in the common American complaint that General MacArthur had to fight with one hand tied behind his back. So had the other side (self-tied no doubt, but tied all the same). For if, as was vociferously declared, the real enemy was Russia, General MacArthur, drawing his troops and supplies across the Pacific, in face of a land-based power that, even in the primitive days of 1904–5, had kept a great army in Korea and Manchuria, was lucky. No Russian submarines emerged from Vladivostok, no bombers from Sakhalin; no Russian volunteers followed the Chinese volunteers into Korea or created a diversion elsewhere much more serious than the Berlin blockade that had alarmed Europe in 1948.

But, and this is a point too much ignored in Europe, General MacArthur was not given a free hand. The atom bomb was not used. The hotheaded suggestions went off as hot air. American policy was prudent, accepted necessary limitations, did not accept the slogan that only complete victory would do. The pacific temper of the people was shown in 1952 when, if there was any one explanation of the election of General Eisenhower, it was his promise to end the Korean War.

It is, of course, one of the drawbacks of the American temper and the American system that discussions are carried on vehemently, noisily, that it is only too easy to speak up loud, in meeting. But in America it is not true that "a noisy man is always right" or even always listened to, and so it has proved.

For what can be more indisputably proved than the teachability of the American people? As late as 1939 they clung to isolation, to the belief that they could shut out the world. Their government, with a straight face, forbade hostilities inside an arbitrarily defined area, nicknamed at once "the chastity belt." The idea was as irrelevant to the modern world as the device to modern matrimony. Within a dozen years of that comic gesture, American troops were scattered round the world. England, Germany, "ultima Thule," and the Americans could say with Æneas:

"Quæ regio in terris nostri non plena laboris."

And the burden was real, resented, accepted.

So was the financial burden. Year after year, billions of dollars were poured out to allies, ex-enemies, tepid friends. In a sense this was an old policy. England had long fought wars with guineas, what the indignant French called "the cavalry of St. George," which the English, in turn, countered with the "cavalry of St. Louis" (or of St. Denis). Subsidies to buy allies, to keep armies in the field, were an old story. But subsidies in peace time, gifts to feed the hungry and clothe the naked, to introduce spades into Afghanistan and good stock into India, were new. The Americans, a simple people, expected gratitude, forgetting both that "do a man a good turn and he will never forgive you" and that American generosity was enlightened self-interest. (How scarce and desirable a political commodity today!) This generosity was denounced by Communists and party-lining politicians as an attempt to buy countries which they, as far as it was in their power, had already sold.

But not only Communists and party-liners sneered and criticized without going to the absurd lengths of refusing. Plenty of sound conservatives resented the need for the gifts and blamed the giver. American wealth was resented; it had been in some way stolen from England and France. How? It did not matter. "Why," Napoleon was asked, "do your brothers and sisters, whom you have made kings and princesses, criticize you so much?" "Because they think I have cheated them of their share in the inheritance of our father, the late king." So every lavish demonstration of American generosity abroad or extravagance at home was pointed to as proof of the barbaric greed of the Americans. The Shamrock Hotel was less resented than Marshall aid. The Americans were not fit to have money and we were doing them a favor by taking it off them.

It is a tribute to the political maturity of the American people that the bad manners, the imbecile bad manners of so many Europeans, the complacent moral superiority of so many Asiatics, have not sickened them with their new historical role. Their faults of taste and judgment have been numerous. An unpunished pathological murder in Mississippi can do—and should do—damage that months of propaganda by "The Voice of America" or of sermons by Dr. Billy Graham cannot undo. The resentful, suspicious, politically illiterate millions who followed McCarthy (who would, in countries like France or Italy, be largely Communist) are a handicap. But the mass of the American people and the elected leaders of the American people have, at each challenge, risen to it, as they have had to rise to so many challenges in the past.

In the world in which the Americans have to live, the "American way of life" in its simple, naïve, confident form is not exportable. In many regions it is a way of life that will be, in any foreseeable time, beyond human means. In others it will be, it is to be hoped, not universally welcomed even if it is materially within grasp.

There is ground for the alarm that European intellectuals express at the invasion of their life by the products of mass culture. But here the Americans are telling Europe something about themselves, not about America. When Georges Duhamel pessimistically wrote his "scenes from a future life," he cannot have foreseen how soon France, the French people, would turn to "Americanism," which is simply the life of the new industrial societies that England (not the United States) created. This is the most democratic of cultures. It has to be banned, harassed, distorted, to prevent its sweeping even over and through the Iron Curtain. "What will come of it all, knows God," as was said in another connection. But in a world prating of democracy, it is worth noting that it is this culture that, given a choice, the masses want. Even criticisms of the United States reveal this truth. For it is the burden of complaint that the United States puts up barriers at its doors, betrays the promise of the verses on the Statue of Liberty, that the McCarran-Walters Act is a denial of the promise of American life. It is, but what a change from a society that devotes far more energy to keeping people in than the United States does to keeping them out!

For the new world in which we have to live, no nation is morally or intellectually fit. Our world is changing at a racing speed that threatens to throw us off. And it is not only our world, for who knows?—we may have to deal with other worlds. And he would be a wise Martian, male or female, who if offered a choice between Russian or American liberators, chose Americans. And as for Venus, it is not necessary to ask the question.

Even that intellectual defect, the dislike of theory, which irritates the European observer and is often a great practical defect, may be, will be in the unprecedented events and unpredictable problems that face us, an asset. A journey into space, a landing on brave new worlds, will be safer, for both sides, if the landing party is equipped with a vague, ambiguous document like the Declaration of Independence, instead of a detailed blueprint drawn up after consulting the sacred texts and deciding, out of the *Anti-Dühring* or *The State and Revolution,* that this is how to court Miranda. If we have to chose between two guides, let us choose Ariel rather than Caliban.

A note about this book

The text is set in Granjon,
a Linotype face named for Robert Granjon of Lyons,
the famous 16th Century French designer of italic letters.
Granjon combines qualities of Garamond,
a French type of the 16th Century, and Caslon,
which is 18th Century English.

The cover was designed by Leo Lionni.

The text was composed by
The Atlantic Linotype Co., Inc., Brooklyn, New York,
and printed by J. W. Clement Co.,
Buffalo, New York.
The cover was printed by Livermore and Knight Co.,
Providence, Rhode Island.
The paper is by The Mead Corporation, Dayton, Ohio;
cover material by The Plastic Coating Corp., Holyoke, Mass.